D0900332

FLORIDA STATE
UNIVERSITY LIBRARIES

MAY 7 1996

TALLAHASSEE, FLORIDA

RESTRAINED TRADE

RESTRAINED TRADE

Cartels in Japan's Basic Materials Industries

MARK TILTON

Cornell University Press

Ithaca and London

HD
2907
T545
1996

The costs of publishing this book have been defrayed in part by the 1993 Hiromi
Arisawa Memorial Award from the Books on Japan Fund with respect to *Rivals beyond
Trade: America versus Japan in Global Competition*, by Dennis J. Encarnation,
published by Cornell University Press. The award is financed by the Japan Foundation
from generous donations contributed by Japanese individuals and companies.

Copyright © 1996 by Cornell University

All rights reserved. Except for brief quotations in a review, this book, or parts
thereof, must not be reproduced in any form without permission in writing
from the publisher. For information, address Cornell University Press,
Sage House, 512 East State Street, Ithaca, New York 14850.

First published 1996 by Cornell University Press.

Printed in the United States of America

Library of Congress Cataloging-in-Publication Data
Tilton, Mark, 1956–
    Restrained trade : cartels in Japan's basic materials industries / Mark Tilton.
        p.   cm.
    Includes bibliographical references.
    ISBN 0-8014-3099-2 (cloth)
    1. Cartels—Japan. 2. Industrial policy—Japan. 3. Japan—Commerce. I. Title.
HD2907.T545   1995
338.8'7—dc20   95–35447

∞ The paper in this book meets the minimum requirements
of the American National Standard for Information Sciences—
Permanence of Paper for Printed Library Materials, ANSI Z39.48-1984.

To Pat

Contents

Acknowledgments

Many friends and colleagues, both in Japan and in the United States, have contributed to this book. I am particularly indebted to Chalmers Johnson for his advice, both practical and theoretical. His encouragement has kept me going at many rough spots in the process of completing the manuscript.

I cannot to begin to thank individually all the people in Tokyo who helped me. I am especially grateful to Itoh Motoshige, Kudō Akira, Shibagaki Kazuo, Yamazaki Hiroaki, and Horiuchi Akiyoshi of the University of Tokyo, and Yūi Tsunehiko of Meiji University, for their support and assistance. I am indebted to many librarians who went to great efforts to help me find sources. In particular I thank Takano Masao, Satō Shōhachi, Hōjō Tadasu, Wada Takako, and Nishiyama Tsunekiyo. I also owe a great debt to many friends and neighbors who helped my family and me enjoy life during our stays in Tokyo. I am grateful to Watanabe Naho and Taeko Lee, who supported and encouraged me in my early Japanese language study.

John Campbell, Berenice Carroll, Mark Elder, Karl Fields, Thomas Gold, Eleanor Hadley, Ward Hanson, Roger Haydon, Ellis Krauss, Leonard Lynn, Jim Mahon, Margaret McKean, Deborah Milly, Elizabeth Norville, Ōyama Kōsuke, T. J. Pempel, Dawn Potter, Frank Schwartz, Koji Taira, and Daniel Unger read all or parts of the manuscript and offered valuable suggestions and criticisms.

I am grateful to the Fulbright Program, the Social Science Research Council, the Association for Asian Studies, the Japan Foundation, the University of California, the University of Chicago, the University of Michigan, and Purdue University for supporting the research. Portions of the material in chapters 4 and 5 appear in an earlier version in my article, "Informal Market Governance in Japan's Basic Materials Industries," *International Organization* 48 (Autumn 1994), pp. 663–85, published by MIT Press.

Finally, I would not have finished this book without the unflagging support of my wife, Pat Boling, and the versatility and good cheer of my children, Ellen, Clio, and Andy.

M. T.

A Note on Japanese Usage and Pronunciation

Personal names in text and notes appear in the order the individual concerned normally uses. Japanese authors use surname-first order for Japanese-language publications, but in their English-language publications their names usually appear surname-last, with no diacritics. Where possible I have used Japanese companies' English names, which usually include no diacritics.

Japanese consonants are pronounced approximately as in English. The "r" is similar to a single "r" in Spanish or southern German, though with something of an "l" quality. The five vowels are similar to those in Spanish. The macron (ō, or ū) indicates that the same quality vowel is held out twice as long (like the two "o's" in "co-owner" in rapid American speech). "Ei" or "aa" also indicates simply an "e" or "a" held out for two beats of time. The combination "ai" is pronounced as it would be in Spanish, roughly like "eye" in English (but without a dipthong glide). Japanese has no stress accent.

Acronyms

DIL	Depressed Industries Law
DSP	Democratic Socialist party
FTC	Fair Trade Commission
JAF	Japan Aluminum Federation
JETRO	Japan External Trade Organization
JIS	Japanese Industrial Standards
JSP	Japan Socialist party
LDP	Liberal Democratic party
MHI	Mitsubishi Heavy Industries
MITI	Ministry of International Trade and Industry
MOF	Ministry of Finance
MOT	Ministry of Transportation
NICs	Asian newly industrialized countries
OECF	Overseas Economic Cooperation Fund
PARC	Policy Affairs Research Council
PVC	polyvinyl chloride
SCAP	Supreme Commander for the Allied Powers
SCFL	Structural Conversion Facilitation Law
SDIL	Structurally Depressed Industries Law

Informal Governance and State Strategic Goals

Economists and political scientists have long debated whether economic or political factors are more critical to Japan's postwar economic success. One group emphasizes private economic factors, such as the nation's alleged conformity to neoclassical principles or the success of long-term relational contracts in nurturing Japanese industry. Others argue that the state played a key role in guiding Japan's economy into sunrise industries and out of sunset ones. Despite their disagreements, both groups have generally agreed that the country is good at getting out of declining industries. The private initiative school argues that competitive pricing and market mechanisms forced change and explains any tendencies to buffer market trends through the effects of private-sector ties between firms. Those who emphasize the state see the Ministry of International Trade and Industry (MITI) as responsible for shepherding declining industries to their graves (often with subsidies but usually with a positive pro-market push). Japan, from both perspectives, is not particularly sensitive to pressures from interest groups demanding government subsidies. Indeed, some observers believe that part of the nation's overall economic success is the result of its ability to resist such counterproductive, anti-market bailouts. Both schools point to Japan's almost complete shutdown of its aluminum refining industry and to a considerable transfer overseas of productive capacity in apparel, electronics, and autos as evidence of its penchant for structural adjustment.

These arguments imply that Japan is more open to trade competition than American policymakers tend to believe, and thus, by extension, U.S. concerns over the bilateral trade balance with Japan may be misplaced if not absurd. Although Japan might be scolded for trying to grab rising industries with strategic trade policies, it is willing to give up industries in which it is losing comparative advantage. And when the country appears closed to imports, often the problem is a "spontaneous" resist-

1

ance to imports produced by long-term ties between buyers and suppliers rather than moves intended specifically to exclude imports.

Most of these arguments, however, miss important points about Japan's political economy. First, trade associations and cartels are critical intermediaries between the state (principally MITI) and the market (or individual firms). How strong they are and how they act typically determine how quickly and easily Japan moves out of declining industries—a movement that is by no means automatic.

Although firm-to-firm (or dyadic) relational contracts are important in stabilizing the Japanese economy, they are often supported by relational contracts between trade associations under which entire industries commit themselves to support one another in times of adversity. Trade associations are fundamentally private, but the rules they establish, either independently or in cooperation with related trade associations, provide important governance for Japanese markets. In this role, trade associations often act as instruments of government policy.

The Japanese government, MITI in particular, is not so positive about international market forces that it loses sight of the importance (in its view) of maintaining domestic or Japanese-owned overseas sources of strategic materials. MITI has joined forces with the trade associations and cartels to support domestic production, even when it is economically inefficient by international standards. In cases where interindustry relational contracts do not provide satisfactory support, links between trade associations and the Liberal Denocratic Party (LDP) have moved Japanese bureaucrats toward greater subsidies than they might otherwise have been inclined to provide. The importance of government-supported, interindustry relational contracts is that they can block access to Japanese markets. These relational contracts explain the lack of significant import penetration in Japan's basic materials industries even though those industries lack international competitiveness.

MARKET AND STATE IN THE JAPANESE ECONOMY

Those contending that the state has successfully boosted Japan's economic growth argue that it has done so by implementing industrial policy to direct the economy toward high growth sectors. The principal way industrial policy functions here is by allocating resources to favored sectors. It can do so through policies that directly provide resources to industry, such as tax breaks, loans, subsidies, and import protection. More important, however, have been policies to reduce competition among firms.[1] To the degree that these policies raise prices, they channel

[1] Ryutaro Komiya, *The Japanese Economy: Trade, Industry, and Government* (Tokyo: University of Tokyo Press, 1990), p. 289.

resources from consumers toward targeted industries, though such policies may also increase productivity through such cooperative ventures as pooling expenses for transportation or research and development. Industrial policy may also support industry by providing or helping to circulate information about market or technological opportunities.

The principal argument as to why industry policy is beneficial is that it expands the economy, either by correcting market failures or advancing strategic trade policy. A market fails when it doesn't give firms the necessary signals to maximize overall welfare. One instance of market failure is hesitation by firms in a backward country to invest in an industry with large setup costs for fear of the short-term losses from competition with lower-cost foreign producers.[2] The Japanese government dealt with this problem by providing import protection, subsidies, preferential financing, and assistance in cartel formation to encourage investment in heavy industry in the 1950s and 1960s. After a period of support from the state, most of these industries became able to compete, at least for a while, in world markets on their own.[3]

Another example of market failure cited in Japan is excessive competition, described as a condition of great excess supply, prices below costs, and producers in danger of being pushed out of business.[4] Proponents of the concept argue that excess competition results from high sunk costs, which make firms reluctant to abandon production, and say intervention may be justified to avoid the excessive monopoly rents that the remaining firms would exact after weak competitors had been pushed out.[5]

A second form of industrial policy, strategic trade policy, seeks to appropriate the benefits of strategic industrial sectors by promoting them at home and helping them gain a larger share of world markets. Paul Krugman points to two reasons why industries can be strategic. First, some industrial sectors may offer large returns because of high barriers to entry, either because capital requirements are high or because technology is sophisticated. These industries enjoy a kind of monopoly rent, and by targeting them a country may increase its share of these rents.[6] A second

[2] Alexander Gerschenkron, *Economic Backwardness in Historical Perspective* (Cambridge: Belknap Press of Harvard University Press, 1962).

[3] Itoh Motoshige, Kiyono Kazuharu, Okuno Masahiro, and Suzumura Kōtarō, "Sangyō ikusei to bōeki" (Infant industries and trade), in Komiya Ryūtarō, Okuno, and Suzumura, eds., *Nihon no sangyō seisaku* (Japan's industrial policy), (Tokyo: Tokyo University Press, 1984), pp. 231–54.

[4] Hiroshi Iyori and Akinori Uesugi, *The Antimonopoly Laws of Japan* (New York: Federal Legal Publications, 1983), p. 114.

[5] Itoh Motoshige, Kiyono Kazuharu, Okuno Masahiro, and Suzumura Kōtarō, "Shijō no shippai to hoseiteki sangyō seisaku" (Market failure and compensatory industrial policy), in *Nihon no sangyō seisaku*, pp. 225–28.

[6] Paul Krugman, "Strategic Sectors and International Competition," in Robert Stern, ed., *U.S. Trade Policies in a Changing World Economy* (Cambridge: MIT Press, 1987), pp. 209–20.

reason is that their new technology may spill over into other industries, increasing productivity outside the industry as well.[7]

Many have concluded that industrial policy was indeed effective in Japan and that a strong, cohesive state was key to its formulation.[8] According to these scholars, the state was able to make effective policy because it was protected from meddling in day-to-day policy by the support of the conservative LDP. It was able to implement its policies flexibly and effectively through use of administrative guidance—that is, ordering industry to comply with policies not clearly based on any specific law.[9]

Some scholars, however, have emphasized that, while industrial policy may have been effective, the state did not impose it unilaterally but cooperated with business in formulating and implementing it. Richard Samuels, for example, writes that state intervention in the economy, while important, "has depended upon the cooperation and preferences of private actors."[10] He recognizes the importance of state policy but emphasizes the influence business has over policy formation through constant negotiations with the state.

Other scholars have contended that stable, long-term relations between state and business facilitate cooperation in planning and support government leadership.[11] Such scholars share with analyses of European corporatism an emphasis on direct, close, and ongoing negotiations between the state and interest groups that have a monopoly on the representation of their constituencies, bypassing elected representatives.[12]

[7] Ibid., pp. 221–25.

[8] Ira C. Magaziner and Thomas M. Hout, *Japanese Industrial Policy*, Policy Papers in International Affairs, Institute of International Studies (Berkeley: University of California, 1981); Takafusa Nakamura, *The Postwar Japanese Economy: Its Development and Structure* (Tokyo: University of Tokyo, Press, 1981); Chalmers Johnson, Laura D'Andrea Tyson, and John Zysman, eds., *Politics and Productivity: How Japan's Development Strategy Works* (New York: Harper Business, 1989); Marie Anchordoguy, *Computers, Inc.: Japan's Challenge to IBM* (Cambridge: Harvard University Press, 1989); Chalmers Johnson, *MITI and the Japanese Miracle: The Growth of Industrial Policy, 1925–1975* (Stanford: Stanford University Press, 1982); T. J. Pempel, *Policy and Politics in Japan* (Philadelphia: Temple University Press, 1982); Richard J. Samuels, *"Rich Nation, Strong Army": National Security and the Technological Transformation of Japan* (Ithaca: Cornell University Press, 1994); Chalmers Johnson, *Japan: Who Governs? The Rise of the Developmental State* (New York: Norton, 1995).

[9] Frank K. Upham, *Law and Social Change in Postwar Japan* (Cambridge: Harvard University Press, 1987).

[10] Richard J. Samuels, *The Business of the Japanese State* (Ithaca: Cornell University Press, 1987), p. 2.

[11] Daniel Okimoto, *Between MITI and the Market* (Stanford: Stanford University Press, 1989); William G. Ouchi, *The M-Form Society* (Reading, Mass.: Addison-Wesley, 1984); Ezra Vogel, *Comeback: Case by Case: Building the Resurgence of American Business* (New York: Simon and Schuster, 1985).

[12] Philippe Schmitter, "Still the Century of Corporatism?" in Fredrick Pike and Thomas Stritch, eds., *The New Corporatism* (Notre Dame: University of Notre Dame Press, 1974).

T. J. Pempel and K. Tsunekawa have pointed out that this corporatism in Japan lacks the representation of peak labor organizations that made possible, at least at one time, pacts to ensure stable wages and employment.[13] Japanese corporatism without labor, however, seems increasingly to fit the European pattern as labor's power has eroded in Europe with the decline of old-line manufacturing and the replacement of peak associations' macro-level corporatism with the meso-level corporatism of negotiations between state and business groups at the sectoral level.[14]

In contrast to scholars who argue that the state played an important role in boosting economic growth, others take the view that the state had little positive influence and that market forces alone explain Japan's rapid economic growth. Neoclassical economists focus on the importance of macroeconomic forces in explaining Japanese success.[15] Many students of microeconomic policy note that firms often refused to cooperate with government policy, cheated on cartels sponsored by MITI, and improved productivity by doing so.[16] Kent Calder contends that Japan's most successful industries succeeded by rebelling against MITI guidance. John Haley advances the idea that this cheating on cartels shows the weakness of informal administrative guidance compared to legally based formal policies.[17]

Another approach that underscores the importance of private initiative in economic growth is the emphasis on relational contracting in the Japanese economy.[18] Here, firms commit themselves to dealing with one another over the long term, even when price changes make the relation-

[13] T. J. Pempel and K. Tsunekawa, "Corporatism without Labor? The Japanese Anomaly," in P. C. Schmitter and G. Lembruch, eds., *Trends toward Corporatist Intermediation* (Beverly Hills, Calif.: Sage, 1979).

[14] Alan Cawson, "Varieties of Corporatism: The Importance of the Meso-Level of Interest Intermediation," in Cawson, ed., *Organized Interests and the State* (London: Sage, 1985), p. 11; Philippe C. Schmitter, "Corporatism Is Dead? Long Live Corporatism?" *Government and Opposition* 24 (Winter 1989): 54–73.

[15] David Friedman, *The Misunderstood Miracle: Industrial Development and Political Change in Japan* (Ithaca: Cornell University Press, 1988).

[16] Miwa Yoshirō, *Nihon no kigyō to sangyō soshiki* (Japanese firms and industrial organization) (Tokyo: Tokyo Daigaku Shuppan Kai, 1990), p. 311; Gregory W. Noble, "The Industrial Policy Debate," in Stephen Haggard and Chung- in Moon, eds., *Pacific Dynamics: The International Politics of Industrial Change* (Boulder, Colo.: Westview Press, 1989), pp. 53–96; Brian Ike, "The Japanese Textile Industry: Structural Adjustment and Government Policy," *Asian Survey* 20 (May 1980): 532–51.

[17] Kent E. Calder, *Strategic Capitalism* (Princeton: Princeton University Press, 1993); John Haley, "Administrative Guidance versus Formal Regulation: Resolving the Paradox of Industrial Policy," in Gary Saxonhouse and Kozo Yamamura, eds., *Law and Trade Issues of the Japanese Economy: American and Japanese Perspectives* (Seattle: University of Washington Press, 1986), pp. 107–28.

[18] Ronald Dore, *Flexible Rigidities: Industrial Policy and Structural Adjustment in the Japanese Economy, 1970–1980* (London: Athlone, 1986).

ship temporarily disadvantageous for one party. Proponents of its importance claim that relational contracting has boosted Japanese growth by giving firms the security to make bold, long-term investments.[19] Relational contracting with a customer who promises to buy over the long term or with a bank or stock purchaser who promises to support the firm over the long term gives firms the confidence to make larger investments or invest in a particular quality of dedicated productive capacity. Firms can increase productivity by investing in assets that will be highly productive if dedicated to a particular transaction partner, although less valuable in producing for other partners available through the open market. A good example is Japanese petrochemical companies that build plants next to one another and connect them by pipeline. Each can buy or sell on the open market, but they will economize on transport costs if they deal with one another. Other forms of asset specificity include investment in other physical assets, such as equipment, or in personnel or skills training for employees that are more valuable in transactions with a particular firm than with other firms.[20] With the exception of sites, such asset specificity results from some kind of difference in technology between producers. Thus, for instance, a car-parts manufacturer produces a sophisticated part for a particular model manufactured by a specific car maker. In doing so, the parts maker may invest in machinery, dies, and employee training that are specifically oriented to manufacture of that part. The part company can switch to manufacturing a different part for another company, but only at the sacrifice of at least a portion of the value of its investment. The parts and the car manufacturer thus both have an incentive to stick to their relationship rather than shop around constantly for a better price. In contrast, an aluminum refiner that produces a standard 99 percent pure ingot has made no investment that commits it to producing for a specific firm.

Another form of asset specificity involves investment in information about a particular transaction partner. A firm may invest in gathering information about the product quality, reliability, or creditworthiness of a particular transaction partner and then economize by sticking with that partner, thus avoiding the expense of gathering information about alternatives and the risk that the information might be faulty.[21]

There is convincing evidence that relational contracts have promoted investment by providing security for Japanese firms and helping them

[19] See Michael L. Gerlach, *Alliance Capitalism: The Social Organization of Japanese Business* (Berkeley: University of California Press, 1992), pp. 9–14, for a concise discussion of the literature on this topic.

[20] Oliver Williamson, *The Economic Institutions of Capitalism: Firms, Markets, Relational Contracting* (New York: Free Press, 1985), p. 55.

[21] Motoshige Itoh, "Organisational Transactions and Access to the Japanese Import Market," in Paul Sheard, ed., *International Adjustment and the Japanese Firm* (St. Leonards, N.S.W.: Allen and Unwin 1992), pp. 50–71.

economize on transaction costs. As we shall see, however, trade associ-ation and state governance is crucial for backing up relational contracts and making them work.

Both those who emphasize the role of a strong, forward-looking state and those who emphasize the role of market forces have argued that Japan is good at abandoning declining sectors and shifting resources into new ones. Because they consider its industrial policy goals to be shifts into sectors with new technologies and high returns, many assessments of the country's declining industries policies have concluded they are more forward-looking than those of most countries, and oriented to moving out of industries where Japan is losing comparative advantage.[22] The principal evidence in support of this explanation is Japan's use of cartels to cut back capacity in declining basic materials industries without any formal restrictions on imports.[23] These measures include the Depressed Industries Law (DIL) of 1978, the Structurally Depressed Industries Law (SDIL) of 1983, and the Structural Conversion Facilitation Law (SCFL) of 1987. The last of these laws formally abolished cartels but appears to have continued them in a weaker guise as plans worked out between individual firms and MITI.

Praising these laws, Michèle Schmiegelow described them as con-cessions in international negotiations about excess capacity, although they appear, in fact, to have been unilateral policies.[24] Everyone acknowl-edges that certain important industries (such as agriculture, lumber, and textiles) with large numbers of workers located in the politically overrepresented rural areas of Japan have been protected to varying degrees.[25] But many believe the policy bias of the economic planning

[22] Gary Saxonhouse, "Industrial Restructuring in Japan," *Journal of Japanese Studies,* 5 (Summer 1979): 273–320; Douglas Anderson, "Managing Retreat: Disinvestment Policy," in Thomas McCraw, ed., *America versus Japan* (Boston: Harvard Business School Press, 1986), pp. 337–72; James C. Abegglen and George Stalk, Jr., *Kaisha: The Japanese Corporation* (New York: Basic Books, 1985), pp. 22–28.

[23] Jimmy Wheeler, Merit E. Janow, and Thomas Pepper, *Japanese Industrial Develop-ment Policies in the 1980s* (Croton-on-Hudson, N.Y.: Hudson Institute, 1982), p. 187; Merton J. Peck, Richard C. Levin, and Akira Goto, "Picking Losers: Public Policy toward Declining Industries in Japan," *Journal of Japanese Studies* 13 (Spring 1987): 79–123; Haruo Shimada, "Japanese Capitalism: The Irony of Success," *Economic Eye* 13 (Autumn 1992): 30; Ippei Yamazawa, *Economic Development and International Trade: The Japanese Model* (Honolulu: East-West Center, 1990); Tsuneyoshi Tatsuoka, "Government Policy toward Declining Industries in Japan and the U.S." U.S.-Japan Program Occasional Paper, 89-01, Harvard University, 1989.

[24] Michèle Schmiegelow, "Cutting across Doctrines: Positive Adjustment in Japan," *International Organization* 39 (Spring 1985). Michèle Schmiegelow and Henrik Schmiegelow also argue in *Strategic Pragmatism: Japanese Lessons in the Use of Economic Theory* (New York: Praeger, 1989) that the 1978 and 1983 laws did "not aim at the maintenance of capacities that are not viable" (p. 97).

[25] Kent E. Calder, *Crisis and Compensation: Public Policy and Political Stability in Japan* (Princeton: Princeton University Press, 1988).

bureaucracy favors shifts out of declining and uncompetitive sectors, which contrasts with nations that take a more static view of national power or whose economic policy-making processes are more easily affected by lobbyists from declining industries.

Some scholars have criticized the DIL and SDIL for preventing industry from taking drastic measures to increase efficiency while forcing consumers to pay higher prices. Nevertheless, these scholars have not explored the implications of such policies for preventing Japan from ceding market share to countries with more efficient producers.[26] Others have emphasized the role of private institutions in producing smooth transitions out of declining industries, particularly through relational contracts. They argue that both capital providers and downstream buyers give private support to firms in declining industries, obviating the need for the heavy-handed protection provided in the U.S. and Western Europe.[27] Paul Sheard has argued that such insurance-oriented private relationships are more helpful to troubled firms than government assistance and has criticized emphasis on the state's role in helping industry adjust to economic change.[28]

Ronald Dore believes that firms in a long-term relationship have a moral obligation, as well as self-interested motives, not to abandon one another when changes in market prices make the relationship disadvantageous to one of the parties. He argues that this commitment gives Japan a "natural immunity to imports" and thus cushions it from the jolts of price changes.[29] Nevertheless, he thinks this protection is usually temporary. Eventually buyers will switch to new, cheaper supplies, enabling the Japanese economy to change and grow without suffering the shocks that plague economies based on colder, more strictly market-based relationships.

Although most of the literature on Japanese declining industries disagrees, Japan has not done well at responding to market signals and moving out of declining industries. The DIL, SDIL, and SCFL targeted

[26] Kozo Yamamura, "Success That Soured: Administrative Guidance and Cartels in Japan," in Yamamura, ed., *Policy and Trade Issues of the Japanese Economy: American and Japanese Perspectives* (Seattle: University of Washington Press, 1982); Mark Ramseyer, "Letting Obsolete Firms Die: Trade Adjustment Assistance in the United States and Japan," *Harvard International Law Journal* 22(Fall 1981): 595–619; Itami Hiroyuki, *Nihon no kagaku sangyō, naze sekai ni tachiokureta no ka* (Japan's chemical industry: why is it behind the rest of the world?) (Tokyo: NTT Shuppan, 1990).

[27] Iwao Nakatani, "The Economic Role of the Financial Corporate Grouping," in Masahiko Aoki, ed., *The Economic Analysis of the Japanese Firm* (North Holland: Elsevier 1984), pp. 227–58.

[28] Paul Sheard, "Corporate Organisation and Industrial Adjustment in the Japanese Aluminum Industry," in Sheard, ed. *International Adjustment*, pp. 125–39.

[29] Dore, *Flexible Rigidities*, p. 84.

basic materials industries, which MITI defines as "industries positioned in between end-product manufacturing industries and natural resource industries, and which refine and process raw materials to provide intermediate goods to other industries."[30] According to MITI, basic materials industries include five main branches: steel, nonferrous metals, kiln industries (ceramics, glass, and cement), chemicals, and petroleum and coal products. This last category was not addressed under the 1978, 1983, or 1987 laws but was protected under the 1962 Petroleum Industry Law.[31] The three later laws targeted the core production of industrial basic materials, the largest of which included one industry in each of the four nonenergy categories: cement, petrochemicals, blast furnace steel, and primary aluminum smelting. These industries suffered from high energy costs due to the oil shocks of 1973–74 and 1979–80; from stagnant demand, as the economy became more sophisticated and less reliant on basic materials for economic growth; and from competition from newly industrializing countries.

Japan's basic materials were affected by internationally high costs. With the exception of aluminum, the industries have been able to maintain high domestic prices without seeing any significant increase in net imports. Three of the four core industries covered under cartels have commanded high prices for standardized goods, ranging from an average of 60 percent above import prices for petrochemicals (1982–92), to 48 percent for most blast-furnace steel plate (1981–91), to 57 percent for cement (1984–92).[32] Aluminum, which only commanded a 13 percent premium from buyers over the import price (1980–92), went out of business and was replaced by imports. Nevertheless, imports caused very little industrial adjustment in either basic materials or other sectors (see table 1–1).

Japan's overall trade balance in manufactured goods relative to domestic manufacturing production dropped by 2 percentage points from 1980 to 1992, despite an increase in the overall trade surplus. Japan was spending a large amount of foreign exchange on petroleum imports in 1980. With the decline in the price of petroleum, the proportion of spending on manufactured goods imports increased from 23 percent in 1980 to 50 percent by 1992.[33] All the industry groups showed at least a slight decline in net exports as a proportion of production from 1980–92.

As a group, the low-wage, nonmachine, consumer goods sector ex-

[30] Ministry of International Trade and Industry, Sankōhō no kaisetsu (Commentary on the Structurally Depressed Industries Law), 1983.
[31] See Samuels, Business of the Japanese State, for a full discussion of the energy sector.
[32] See tables in chapters 3–6 for sources and explanations of these prices.
[33] MITI, communicated by telephone, 1994.

Table 1–1. Change in Japan's net sectoral trade: 1980–92. Manufactured goods trade/ domestic production of manufactured goods

	Net trade/ production 1980	Net trade production 1992	Change in net trade/ production (million yen)
Industrial basic materials	3.1%	0.7%	−2.4%
Chemicals	0.7%	0.9%	0.2%
Petroleum and coal products	−7.3%	−7.4%	−0.1%
Cement, glass, and ceramics	4.0%	2.1%	−1.9%
Iron and steel	18.5%	7.3%	−11.2%
Nonferrous metals	−7.2%	−8.3%	−1.1%
Core industrial basic materials			
Petrochemicals	1.7%	3.0%	1.2%
Cement	9.1%	5.9%	−3.3%
Ordinary-grade steel (by vol.)	26.9%	10.0%	−16.9%
Primary aluminum	−47.6%	−1464.8%	−1417.2%
Processed and consumer materials	1.9%	1.5%	−0.3%
Lumber and wood products	−4.3%	−9.1%	−4.7%
Pulp, paper, paper products	−1.7%	1.4%	3.1%
Rubber products	13.7%	10.4%	−3.3%
Metal products	4.6%	2.3%	−2.3%
Machines	20.8%	19.0%	−1.9%
General machinery	18.6%	23.2%	4.6%
Electrical machinery	16.3%	14.6%	−1.7%
Transportation machinery	29.2%	19.7%	−9.4%
Shipbuilding	45.3%	137.3%	92.0%
Precision instruments	1.5%	31.3%	29.9%
Nonmachine consumer goods	3.3%	−3.9%	−7.1%
Textiles (not including clothing)	10.0%	4.8%	−5.2%
Clothing	−8.1%	−27.7%	−19.6%
Furniture	5.0%	−3.9%	−8.9%
Publishing and printing	−0.2%	−0.1%	0.1%
All manufacturing	10.4%	8.4%	−2.0%

Source: MITI, *Kōgyō tōkei hyō, sangyō hen* (Census of manufactures, report by industries), 1980, 1992; Nihon Kanzei Kyōkai (Japan tariff association), *Gaikoku bōeki gaikyō* (Foreign trade conditions), 1980, 1992. Cement and aluminum figures are from the *Semento nenkan*, various issues, and the Japan Aluminum Federation, respectively. Steel volume figures come from *Tekkō tōkei yōran* (Steel statistical abstract), published by the Tekkō Tōkei Iinkai (Steel Statistics Committee), 1980, 1992.

Notes: This table compares nearly all of Japan's manufacturing sectors with trade figures for the same manufactured goods. Two domestic industrial sectors were excluded because of the absense of corresponding trade statistics: processed food and leather goods.

Trade figures were chosen that most closely corresponded to industrial sectors, but in a few cases they are not precise matches. Thus, net trade/production is a rather rough figure. "Cement, glass, ceramics" is compared with imports of nonmetallic mineral manufactures minus diamonds and precious stones. The import category of refined petroleum products was compared with the domestic category of refined petroleum and coal products. This imprecision does not greatly distort the net trade figures in either case and does not distort the direction or scale of change because the same categories were used for both 1980 and 1992. It was difficult to think of meaningfully separate steel trade figures to compare with blast-furnace steel production (a method of production rather than an industry producing a particular product; the electric-furnace industry also produces many of the same products), but volume figures for ordinary-grade steel were put in to round out the table. Because this steel statistic is based on volume, it was not possible to calculate totals for core industrial basic materials.

perienced the most change, with a drop in net exports equivalent to 7.1 percent of overall production. It was the only manufacturing sector in which Japan was a net importer. Within it, the low-wage apparel industry experienced the most change, dropping to a net trade deficit of 27.7 percent of production. The machine sector experienced a small drop in net trade over production, although the transportation machinery sector, while remaining a strong exporter, experienced a large drop from net exports of 29.2 percent in 1980 to 19.7 percent in 1992. The shipbuilding industry export figures in table 1–1 exceed 100 percent because of the lumpiness and cyclical sensitivity of ship sales. While shipbuilding remained export-dependent and resistant to imports, its overall sales declined dramatically.

Japan remained a net exporter of processed and consumer materials and experienced negligible change in net trade. The low-wage lumber and wood products sector was an exception, with its trade deficit growing from 4.3 percent to 9.1 percent of domestic production. The country also remained an overall net exporter in industrial basic materials, although its trade surplus here dropped from 3.1 percent to 0.7 percent. Two sectors did run net trade deficits: petroleum and coal products and nonferrous metals. Japan's net imports of refined petroleum products did not increase over the period. In nonferrous metals, the nation moved from imports of 47.6 percent of primary refined aluminum in 1980 to 97 percent by 1992. As Edward Lincoln has pointed out, however, Japan does not import *fabricated* aluminum products in significant quantities. Therefore, it was able to keep its trade deficit in nonferrous metals fairly steady at 8.3 percent of domestic production.[34]

My case studies have examined the core industrial basic materials sectors and have revealed that Japan still runs significant surpluses in steel, cement, and petrochemicals. Statistics cited earlier in this chapter for exports and imports in these sectors were in volume terms and show larger surpluses than are reflected in these value statistics: as we have seen, Japanese domestic prices are high compared to the prices of its exports and imports. Nevertheless, the overall value statistics for the large chemical, kiln products, and iron and steel industries, as well as for the subsectors of cement and petrochemicals, show that while Japan's surpluses have shrunk, the country remains a net exporter. In none of these high-cost and high-price sectors (except primary aluminum) did a shift to net imports force Japan to cut back its domestic production.

Trade forced structural change in four sectors of industry. That is, Japan experienced a significant drop in its net trade balance in four sectors where it ended up a net importer: low-wage, labor-intensive

[34] Edward Lincoln, *Japan's Unequal Trade* (Washington, D.C.: The Brookings Institution, 1990).

clothing, furniture, and lumber; and nonferrous metals. Essentially, then, net imports have not forced structural change on Japan's uncompetitive industries. Although the Japanese talked about hollowing out as domestic production was replaced by imports, that event only happened in aluminum smelting, apparel, and, to a very limited degree, lumber and furniture.

PRIVATE INTEREST GOVERNANCE BY TRADE ASSOCIATIONS

Clearly, long-term relations are important in the Japanese economy, especially for purchases of intermediate goods, a category that includes the basic materials that have been the focus of Japan's declining industries policies. One study of large firms found that 60.7 percent bought almost all their intermediate goods from firms with whom they had maintained a relationship for at least five years, while another 37.1 percent bought most of their intermediate goods from such firms. The most important reasons firms gave for these stable ties were price, quality, security of supply, established financial relationships, and mutual trust; a much smaller number of firms listed *keiretsu* ties.[35] Firms often also prefer domestic rather than foreign suppliers because they believe them more dependable. For instance, a Fair Trade Commission (FTC) survey found that paper users were willing to pay 10 to 15 percent more for domestic than imported paper in part because of concerns about security of supply.[36]

Long-term ties between firms are important to the success and stability of the Japanese economy. Nevertheless, the fact that relational contracting buffers the economy from the shocks of sectoral decline does not in itself support the free-market argument that spontaneous market relationships are more important than the government in explaining Japan's success and stability. In fact, interfirm relational contracts are supported by trade association actions (see figure 1–1). I noted earlier that individual firms may prefer domestic sources of supply. But how can firms that buy expensive domestic supplies compete with those that buy cheaper imported supplies? Because many basic materials are completely standardized products, one would expect buyers to face exactly this dilemma.

In insurance-oriented relational contracting, individual firms ordinarily commit themselves to a long-term relationship in order to buffer one

[35] Komine Takao, "Wagakuni kigyō no keizokuteki torihiki no jittai" (The reality of long-term relations between firms in our country), *Kōsei torihiki* 438 (April 1987): 29.

[36] Kōsei Torihiki Iinkai Jimukyoku (FTC), ed., "Shijō akusesu no kaizen to kyōsō seisaku" (Improving market access and competitive policy), *Dokusen kinshi konwa kai shiryō shū* (Anti-monopoly discussion group materials) 10 (1984–87), published 1988.

Figure 1–1. Factors supporting interindustry relational contracting

Necessary factor:	One of these two factors necessary:	Helpful but not necessary factors:
Industry concentration in upstream industry	Technological hook: either production differentialtion or link to differentiated product	Product standardization
	Downstream cartel or import protection	Price of upstream good is small part of production cost of downstream good

another from the shocks of changing market conditions. Logically, however, relational contracting can also be done on a suprafirm basis between trade associations. A trade association representing a downstream industry buying intermediate materials and one representing an upstream industry selling the materials can agree to commit themselves to one another regardless of whether the relationship might prove disadvantageous to one party in the short term. Such an agreement ensures that *all* buyer firms commit themselves to paying a premium for the domestic good and compete on an equal footing. It may be necessary at times to use sanctions to make sure all the firms within the trade association abide by the agreement. The cement and construction industries have agreed to use such sanctions and the steel industry threatens its users with them.

How can we predict whether trade association relational contracting will be successful? There appear to be certain variable factors that are necessary for private-interest governance based on relational contracting to work. These factors are derived inductively from a large number of cases, which I will review in Chapter 7.

First, industry concentration is always necessary in the upstream industry that wants to organize a cartel and control its market. Only a small number of firms will be capable of coordinating a cartel. With MITI assistance and FTC indulgence, even somewhat fragmented industries, in which firms bemoan excessive competition, can often coordinate effective cartels. Cement, with twenty-one firms, and petrochemicals, with eleven, have done quite well. Textiles, however, with hundreds of firms, has not been able to use cartels effectively.

Second, the upstream industry must have a technological hook to secure buyer loyalty, or the downstream industry must be protected from competition by either a cartel of its own or trade barriers to foreign imports. I use the term ·*technological hook* because downstream firms may be motivated by a genuine desire for the technological differentiation of the product or may feel they should buy some undifferentiated product from their long-term suppliers so that the suppliers can continue to supply a different, more sophisticated product. The supplier may use some element of coercion: for example, steel firms may suggest they won't supply high-grade steel if shipbuilding firms don't buy ordinary-grade steel from them.[37]

Many downstream industrial users of basic materials appear to benefit from protection from competition. Construction, which uses all of Japan's cement and half its steel, has enjoyed cozy bid-rigging arrangements for government procurement that have enabled it to absorb the high cost of domestic materials.[38] Electronics, while experiencing considerable competition in overseas markets, benefits from a continued paucity of discount stores, which prevents discount sales from taking more than 10 percent of the domestic market.[39] Capital goods and auto-parts makers benefit from restraints on competition that have permitted prices that are 17 percent and 108 percent higher than U.S. prices, respectively.[40]

There are other factors that broadly characterize Japan as a system and thus are not specific to particular industries. One is a nationalist orientation toward securing supplies domestically, which was made clear in my interviews with electronics, shipbuilding, and auto-industry purchasers of steel and chemicals. This broad-based orientation is difficult to explain in terms of individual firms' rational self-interest. As I have shown, this nationalist impulse is not enough to ensure loyalty and must be reinforced by other technical hooks. Nevertheless, it is a necessary background factor that makes interindustry relational contracting possible.

A second characteristic is a state that is willing to support informal price cartels and import protection.[41] As I will detail later in the chapter, the state has a special interest in basic materials and new technology sectors and less interest in low-wage, low-skill, labor-intensive sectors. State support, however, is broadly available for any capital or skill-

[37] *Nikkei sangyō shinbun*, 6 April 1987.

[38] Jun Mamiya, "The Iron Triangle and Corruption in the Construction Industry," *Tokyo Business Today* 61 (November 1993): 10–13.

[39] Interview with executive of large electronics firm, Tokyo, 1994. This book draws on my forty-five interviews with business and government officials in Tokyo in 1986–88, 1992, and 1994, and nine in Seoul in 1988. In addition I conducted six interviews with journalists during the same period and benefited from numerous discussions with academics. I conducted all the interviews in person with the exception of a few telephone interviews, which are noted. I am not using the names of interviewees because of the sensitive nature of the topic of cartels and trade. Interview locations are in Tokyo, unless otherwise noted.

[40] United States Commerce Department and Japanese Ministry of International Trade and Industry, "U.S.-Japan Price Survey 1991" (May 1991).

[41] J. Rogers Hollingsworth and Marc Schneiberg, "The Governance of the American Economy: The Role of Markets, Clans, Hierarchies, and Associative Behavior," in Wolfgang Streeck and Philippe C. Schmitter, eds., *Private Interest Government: Beyond Market and State* (Beverly Hills, Calif.: Sage, 1985), pp. 221–54.

intensive sector able to successfully organize market-governance structures.

Other factors support private-interest governance based on interindustry relational contracts but are not decisive—for example, price. Buyers ran aluminum refiners out of business by refusing to pay more than a 13-percent premium above import prices; but cement, petrochemical, and steelmakers got margins of 48 to 60 percent and have lost little market share to imports.

The share of costs that materials account for might seem important in determining whether buyers can afford to stick with domestic suppliers. The aluminum industry believed that the market was vulnerable to imports because aluminum rollers could not afford high-priced aluminum, which accounted for 60 percent of their costs. Other industries, however, such as plastics and cement, also have intermediate processors with high materials costs, but end users support domestic materials. A fairly large chunk of Japanese industries' costs are composed of basic materials purchases—from 10 to 15 percent for the machine sectors and 29 percent for construction (table 1–2). Nevertheless, construction, which pays the highest sum proportionately for what are mostly standardized basic materials, has also been a fairly loyal customer. In more market-driven economies, price might be a more decisive factor. Here, it does not appear to be helpful in explaining which industries succeed at informal market governance.

Another supporting factor is product standardization, which makes it easier to negotiate limits on volumes of production and price levels that can be uniform for a given product. For instance, while the petrochemical

Table 1–2. Basic materials cost as a percent of end value produced by machinery and construction sectors, 1985

	General machinery	Electrical machinery	Transport equipment	Precision instruments	Construction
Pulp, paper, lumber	0.2	0.9	0.2	0.7	5.4
Chemicals	0.6	1.8	1.2	0.8	0.5
Petroleum and coal products	0.3	0.4	0.4	0.2	1.1
Cement, glass, ceramics	0.6	1.2	0.7	1.6	7.9
Steel	9.0	2.2	4.9	1.6	3.3
Nonferrous metals	1.5	3.8	1.8	3.6	0.9
Metal products	3.0	2.1	1.0	1.6	9.8
Total basic materials	15.2	12.3	10.2	10.1	29.0

Source: Japan Statistical Yearbook (Tokyo: Sōrifu, Tōkeikyoku [Prime Minister's Office, Statistical Bureau], 1991), p. 574.

Note: This source listed no separate figures for rubber products, another basic material, which would probably add two or three percentage points to the materials cost for transport equipment.

industry may be able to come up with a single price for ethylene, a completely standardized good, it is impossible to come up with a single price for derivatives that have numerous fine gradations in quality. Thus, while product differentiation strengthens interfirm relational contract, product standardization strengthens intertrade association relational contracting.

One might conclude that groups of industries in which relational contracting is desirable because of product differentiation would mutually exclude those in which it is enforceable with cartels because of product standardization. Certain tensions are inevitable in interindustry relational contracting because either product differentiation or standardization must be weak. Nevertheless, desire for security of supply can motivate such contracting even when there is no product differentiation, as in cement markets; and setting prices for standardized intermediate products on an industry-wide basis can stabilize prices for differentiated derivative products, as in the case of petrochemicals.

A final supporting factor is a history of cooperation between government and business, among competing producers, and between upstream and downstream industries.[42] Ironically, these patterns may be best developed in industries that have suffered from past barriers to easy monopoly and have had to work hard to overcome them. Japan's aluminum refining industry enjoyed high prices and profits in the 1960s as a result of the North American–dominated international aluminum cartel but did not develop a resilient domestic cartel or ties of mutual obligation with its downstream industry, which resented what it saw as its exploitation by the refiners and MITI.[43] In contrast, the petrochemical industry developed a system of cartels that tended to break down during boom times but could be depended on during busts.[44]

Private-interest Governance as Public Policy

Concerted, private action by trade associations to back up dyadic relational contracts is public in two senses. First, it serves as a form of private-interest government, defined by Wolfgang Streeck and Philippe Schmitter as "associative, self-interested collective action [that] contribute[s] to the achievement of public policy objectives."[45] Streeck and Schmitter apply the term to the way European countries entrust interest associations with regulating markets such as dairy, pharmaceu-

---

[42] See Ouchi, *M-Form Society.*

[43] Interview with aluminum rolling official, 1987.

[44] Kagaku Keizai Kenkyū Jo, *Sekiyu kagaku kōgyō no kōzō kaizen to sekiyu kagaku seihin kakō ryūtsūgyōno arikata* (Structural improvement in the petrochemical industry and the nature of the petrochemicals processing and distribution industries) (Tokyo: Kagaku Keizai Kenkyū Jo, 1984).

[45] Streeck and Schmitter, *Private Interest Government,* p. 17.

ticals, and advertising. Their definition also fits informal cartels in Japanese basic materials, although the Japanese cartels differ in being illegal. Nevertheless, they are tools of public policy because they are tolerated by the government and share with formal cartels the goals of supporting prices and maintaining domestic production.

Although emphasis on state guidance of the economy has overlooked state ties to private-interest governance, the state has indeed played a major role in helping trade associations organize official cartels and in supporting and placing limits on informal cartels. My study confirms the finding of many observers: the state does not usually impose its will unilaterally on business but works with business to solve common industry problems in ways that serve national industrial policy goals. MITI has typically provided the initiative for the capacity cartels that firms want but are unable to coordinate on their own. Margaret McKean describes this contribution as skill rather than strength.[46]

Chalmers Johnson has noted that the balance between state and business participation ranges from self-control by business to state control and joint public-private cooperation. Self-control means that business runs cartels on its own with state authorization, as was done under the Important Industries Control Law of 1931 and the public sales system for steel from 1958 to 1965. State-control was the model favored by bureaucrats from the late 1930s through the early 1950s. Johnson argues that Japan largely moved to the third type, public-private cooperation, by the high-growth period of the 1950s and 1960s.[47]

By the early 1970s nearly one thousand cartels were formally authorized by the government, but the many illegal cartels that operated under administrative guidance also fit the public-private cooperation model.[48] As we shall see, major government-directed informal cartels in the petrochemical industry continued through the late 1980s, and at least one was still in effect by 1992. Other important price cartels are also run independently by business with tacit state support. If we take these illegal cartels into account, Japan's swing from self-control to public-private cooperation may not have gone as far as Johnson concluded.

Private-interest governance has several advantages: the state does not bear the costs of governance, such governance is more effective in certain ways, and it provides a semisecret form of trade protection. The administering trade association, which is composed of the firms it oversees, knows them better than the government can. It can apply rules in a less

[46] Margaret McKean, "State Strength and the Public Interest," in Gary D. Allinson and Yasunori Sone, eds., *Political Dynamics in Contemporary Japan* (Ithaca: Cornell University Press, 1993), pp. 73–105.
[47] Johnson, *MITI*, pp. 310–11.
[48] Yamamura, "Success That Soured," p. 82.

formal way to fit different situations.[49] Industry generally prefers self-regulation to state participation because it can orient cartels more directly to increasing prices and fattening profits.[50] Despite informal cartels' greedy preoccupation with price hikes, the state believes they extend the scope of governance beyond the limits set by the FTC and Japan's foreign trading partners.

Direct state involvement in managing official cartels helps balance industry greed and orient them toward state goals.[51] The FTC has placed limits on legal cartels, and both MITI and the FTC have pushed industry to use them for productivity gains as well as raising prices. At the same time, state participation often offers member companies legitimacy, freedom from prosecution, and bureaucratic leadership and authority. Although the state does not play a direct role in administering illegal cartels, the FTC is often able to restrict them enough to keep their prices within the range warranted by policy goals. While public opinion and the FTC have tolerated cartels that help uncompetitive industries cover their costs, they have frowned on cartels producing large profits.

Informal cartels among uncompetitive basic materials industries are not completely outside the main corporatist relationship between business and the state. Rather, they represent a portion of governance that is tacitly delegated to trade associations. Alfred Stepan offers a useful model for understanding this delegation of power. In his discussion of the Velasco regime in Peru in the early 1970s, he argues that the state attempted to control society indirectly by giving corporatist bodies autonomous control over sectors of society in return for their allegiance to the state.[52] Similarly, the Japanese state delegates governance to private-interest government to help stabilize markets in key industries. MITI delegates this power in part because it cannot control markets so tightly on its own but also because direct state controls would make cartels too strong and distort the market excessively.

In addition to providing public-interest governance, the informal cartels build directly on public policies, extend its goals, and are sometimes supported by the state. Sueo Sekiguchi has argued that, although official policy has not directly protected the domestic market, government sup-

[49] Streeck and Schmitter, *Private Interest Government*, p. 20.

[50] Ōyama Kōsuke, "Gendai Nihon ni okeru gyōsei shidō no seiji kōzō—Shin sangyō taisei ron to tokushin hōan ni shōten wo atete" (The political structure of administrative guidance in contemporary Japan: The new industrial system thesis and the Special Measures Law for the Promotion of Designated Industries), *Shakai kagaku kenkyū* 4 (1989): 86–102.

[51] Johnson, *MITI*, p. 310.

[52] Alfred Stepan, *The State and Society: Peru in Comparative Perspective* (Princeton: Princeton University Press, 1978).

port for industry collusion may support actions by private business that have the effect of excluding imports.[53] I believe that official cartels have indeed supported informal cartels and that both have been intended to maintain uncompetitive domestic industry and prevent their markets from being taken away by imports from countries with lower production costs. The state has directly supported informal cement cartels by setting up informal trade barriers—something it failed to do with aluminum. In the case of petrochemicals the state offered less assistance but did organize an informal joint-sales company to supplement official sales companies.

The State's Goals

If Japan's official cartel policies have not been intended to ease companies out of inefficient, declining industries, what interest does the state have in encouraging production in such industries? One possible answer is that pressure groups have forced the state to support them. It is certainly true that banks, dismayed at the financial difficulties of some of their largest debtors, and troubled firms themselves, have supported the depressed industries laws. When it comes time to implement the laws, however, firms in designated industries have had to be prodded by MITI to overcome their mutual distrust and form capacity-cutting cartels and joint-sales corporations.

Another possible motive for preserving basic materials industries is to prepare for the possibility of war. According to Paul Seabury, such preparedness requires a country to have not only end-product defense industries, but also an industrial base that permits rapid, large-scale mobilization in time of war.[54] Certainly, production of basic industrial materials seems necessary for such mobilization; but not all materials for war need to be available domestically. The most important ones are technologically sophisticated goods such as computer chips, not standardized basic materials. A close information exchange goes into incorporating sophisticated goods into weapons production, and the fact that they are specialized and produced by few suppliers makes the purchasing country vulnerable to political boycotts.[55] Although Ishihara Shintarō has argued that Japan's control of key technologies has given it de facto

[53] Sueo Sekiguchi, "Japan: A Plethora of Programs," in Hugh Patrick, ed., *Pacific Basin Industries in Distress: Structural Adjustment and Trade Policy in the Nine Industrialized Economies*, Studies of the East Asian Institute (New York: Columbia University Press, 1991).

[54] Paul Seabury, "Industrial Policy and National Defense," in Chalmers Johnson, ed., *The Industrial Policy Debate* (San Francisco: Institute for Contemporary Studies, 1984), p. 204.

[55] Martin C. Libicki, "What Makes Industries Strategic," McNair Papers, No. 5 (Washington, D.C.: Institute for National Strategic Studies, 1989).

military power, Japanese industrial policy gives little attention to military needs when compared to American industrial policy.[56]

In his study of armaments production, Richard Samuels finds that Japanese planners do not make sharp distinctions between military and nonmilitary technologies but see national technological autonomy as important for both military and broader economic security. In their general discussions of basic materials industries, Japanese industrial policymakers largely ignore direct military concerns; but they have expressed strong concern about security of supplies for broad economic purposes. The country has experienced frightening losses of foreign supplies a number of times: when the U.S. cut off oil in 1941 and food supplies in the final years of World War II, and when Arabs cut off oil in 1973. It was also threatened by the loss of key supplies when Nixon clumsily announced a ban on soybean exports in 1971 to reduce American food prices. These experiences have given Japan a sense of vulnerability to outside suppliers.

MITI stated that its goal for the SDIL was structural improvement, which did not mean doing away with the faltering basic materials industries to make way for new industry. Rather, it meant strengthening them because of their importance to the overall health, dynamism, and security of the economy. In *Commentary on the SDIL*, MITI listed five important roles played by basic materials in the national economy. First, basic materials contribute to "the development of related manufacturing industries and the raising of national standards of living."[57] That is, although their direct contribution to national standards of living may be minor, they provide the materials for sophisticated industries that do raise the standard of living. Second, basic materials play an important role in "technical innovation in new materials." This view is directly opposed to the neoclassical economic view that the nation should specialize in industries in which it excels and allow other nations to take over industries in which it has lost competitiveness. Third, basic materials industries permit "a flexible national economic response to international changes."[58] This implies that secure domestic supplies of basic materials prepare the nation to better survive external shocks. Fourth, basic materials industries promote "the stability of regional economies and small and medium-sized firms." After this nod to the needs of labor, the list returns to industrial structural goals, saying that basic materials industries are important "for the building of a balanced industrial structure."

[56] Ishihara Shintarō, "Gendai nihonjin no ishiki kaikaku koso ga hitsuyō da" (What has to be changed is the consciousness of the contemporary Japanese), in Shintarō and Akio, eds., *"No" to ieru nihon* (The Japan that can say no) (Tokyo: Kōbunsha, 1989), p. 20.
[57] MITI, *Sankōhō no Kaisetsu*, p. 7.
[58] Ibid.

This final point sums up the first three and presents a distinctly non-neoclassical prescription: the economy must not simply rely on its comparative advantages but maintain a balance of vital sectors.

One MITI official I interviewed pointed out that the *Commentary*'s mention of new technologies is a stock defense made for all policies and should not be taken seriously. Indeed, whatever the original intent of the SDIL, old-line basic materials firms have been unsuccessful at applying their skills to diversification into new areas. On the other hand, my informant suggested that MITI's concern over security of supply was genuine.[59]

While MITI was interested in security of supply, it provided little money to shore it up. The principal strategy for channeling resources to beleaguered basic materials industries was to use cartels to help domestic firms get the highest prices they could from domestic buyers. The political discipline that prevented large government subsidies was provided by the Ministry of Finance early during the discussion of measures to help the aluminum refining industry. Although MITI, at industry's behest, asked for large subsidies, the Ministry of Finance firmly refused them.[60] The decline of the aluminum refining industry shows that the Japanese government was unwilling to make major sacrifices to maintain domestic production of this vital metal. At the same time, the industry's dramatic decline brought out a great deal of discussion about the importance of security of supply and produced policies to encourage the establishment of Japanese equity investment overseas. The aluminum case shows that MITI had a significant, although limited, interest in security of supply. This is not to say that the Japanese government is more interested in security of supply than is the U.S., which keeps large reserves of petroleum to guard against embargoes. What makes Japan different from the U.S. is that the toolbox of policies available to pursue security of supply includes a combination of formal and informal cartel policies.

The government's industrial policies were intended to make the economy more efficient, to correct the market failure of excess competition, and to achieve the strategic goal of preserving the externalities from basic materials production for the domestic economy. The cartels do not appear to have produced efficiencies; more than a decade after they began, the cement and petrochemical industries are unable to produce at internationally competitive prices. The policies have, however, achieved MITI's goal of preserving security of supply by maintaining domestic production.

[59] Interview, 1992.
[60] *Kinzoku tokuhō*, 11 November 1978; *Nihon keizai shinbun*, 18 September 1981.

Trade Associations and Japanese Antimonopoly Law

This chapter will explore the institutions of cartel policy: trade associations, which, sometimes with MITI help, make the cartels; the laws that govern them; and the Fair Trade Commission (FTC), the agency that regulates them.

The institutions that carry out the cartels are usually trade associations, organizations of firms for the purpose of furthering the members' collective interests. They may be either industry-specific or peak associations, combining businesses from many industries. While peak associations, like the Keidanren (Federation of Economic Organizations) and the Nikkeiren (Japan Federation of Employers' Associations), play an active role in broad economic policy-making, the industry-specific associations carry out governance of individual markets. Trade associations representing concentrated industries provide the best examples of strong governance. Many of the most concentrated industries are in basic materials, where economic efficiency dictates large factories and therefore a relatively small number of firms.

Many of the most powerful trade associations are in the basic materials industries. In 1986 the FTC surveyed the 163 most powerful trade associations in manufacturing industries, of which eighty-eight were in the four nonenergy basic materials sectors.[1] Chemicals and the kiln-based industries (principally cement and glass) are noteworthy for the large number of powerful trade associations they have created, each accounting for thirty-eight.

One measure of trade association power is staff size. Although association employees do not act as the principal negotiators or decision makers, they serve as information gatherers and support staff for the

---

[1] Kōsei Torihiki Iinkai (FTC), *Kōsei torihiki iinkai nenji hōkoku* (FTC annual report), 1989, pp. 80–81.

decision-making committees, which are made up of executives from the member companies. The Japan Cement Association and the Japan Iron and Steel Federation had 117 and 131 employees respectively in 1993, making them unusually large; even this select group of powerful associations averages only seventeen employees each. The Japan Petrochemical Industry Association and the Japan Aluminum Federation had smaller staffs—thirty-six and thirteen respectively. Reflecting varying degrees of success at fending off foreign competition, the Cement Association's staff grew by 60 percent from 1980–93, while the Aluminum Federation lost half its staff, and the other two associations' staffs shrank slightly.[2] Most trade associations' budgets are funded largely by membership dues, although 17 percent also receive government subsidies, an indication of the quasipublic status these associations enjoy.

One of the principal functions of trade associations is to collect information about management, technology, production, sales, and prices. Officially, the FTC regards exchange of specific information about the individual transactions of members (such as buyers' names, prices, rebates, and exact production and sales figures) with suspicion because sharing information may be combined with understandings on price or production levels.[3] According to an FTC survey, 88 percent of powerful manufacturing trade associations did surveys of the domestic market; and 70 percent did surveys of import and export markets. Seventy-nine percent collected data from their members; and of these, 83 percent released production volumes or prices on a monthly basis.[4]

While part of this information helps firms reduce competition, trade associations also gather information more broadly. Yūi Tsunehiko notes that U.S. and Japanese trade associations have very similar organization goals on paper. While U.S. trade associations are largely staffed by lawyers and lobbyists, however, the core of the Japanese trade association is its research section (*chōsabu*). Research sections are staffed by bright graduates from the best universities who not only study foreign and domestic markets but follow what foreign companies are doing and the technologies they are developing. They have large libraries and are the principal information source for MITI, the Japan External Trade Organization (JETRO), and individual member firms.[5]

Michael Atkinson and William Coleman have noted that reliance on

[2] *Kakushu dantai meikan* (Directory of associations), 1980, 1993.

[3] Wada Tateo, "Jigyōsha dantai no kinō" (The functions of trade associations), *Jurisuto*, 15 February 1990, p. 59.

[4] Kōsei Torihiki Iinkai (FTC), "Shijō akusesu no kaizen to kyōsō seisaku" (Improving market access and competitive policy), *Dokusen kinshi konwa kaiwa shiryō shū* 10 (1984–1987), published 1988.

[5] Personal communication from Yūi Tsunehiko.

trade associations for information restricts bureaucracies' autonomy.[6] But power related to information gathering goes both ways. One former president of a large chemical firm (also an ex-MITI official) argued that MITI plays an important role in the trade associations' information gathering. He noted that while companies need good information and the trade association is a neutral institution that can collect it, companies are reluctant to divulge sensitive information such as investment plans. The bureaucracy is strong enough, even without any formal law, to use administrative guidance to get the information for the trade association.[7]

Another function the association can play is to set product standards. According to the FTC survey, 74 percent of powerful manufacturing trade associations are involved in disseminating industry standards.[8] The establishment of product standards may spur competition by making products more closely interchangeable in the market and thus permitting comparison shopping. Nevertheless, product standards may also be used to close competitors out of a market and thus may have anticompetitive effects. In addition, trade associations engage in joint manufacture, sales, purchasing, storage, shipping, and R & D. Because all these areas are part of the production process, cooperation efforts increase the danger of monopolization.[9] That trade associations do manage to use their powers not simply to enhance the competitiveness of the market but to reduce competition is evidenced by the fact that trade associations were named in over half the findings of violation of the Antimonopoly Law from 1947 to 1988.[10]

Establishing long-term ties of personal trust between members is an important way in which trade associations promote cooperation among firms. William Ouchi argues that many Japanese trade associations act as clans—that is, as organizations with which members are associated over a long time and where they expect cooperation to be mutually reward-ing.[11] To develop long-term personal ties between firms, trade associations provide opportunities for employees of member firms to get to know each other over the entire span of their careers, by both working together in committees and socializing. According to the FTC survey, over 90 percent of major trade associations in manufacturing industries

---

[6] Michael M. Atkinson and William D. Coleman, "Corporatism and Industrial Policy," in Cawson, ed., *Organized Interests and the State: Studies in Meso-corporatism* (Beverly Hills, Calif.: Sage Publications, 1985), p. 30.

[7] Interview, 1992.

[8] FTC, "Shijō akusesu," 1988.

[9] Wada, "Jigyōsha dantai no kinō," p. 59–61.

[10] There were fifty-two violations of the Trade Association Law from 1947 to 1952, and 364 violations of section 8 of the Antimonopoly Law from 1953 to 1988. FTC, *Nenji hōkoku*, 1989.

[11] Ouchi, William G., *The M-Form Society* (Reading, Mass.: Addison-Wesley, 1984).

sponsored interfirm social activities.[12] Atsuya Jōji has contrasted trade associations in Europe and the U.S., which rely on contractlike relationships between firms, and the more sociable (*tsukiai-teki*) Japanese associations.[13]

Frank Upham illustrates the importance of developing personal relations for interfirm cooperation in his account of the process of hammering out a capacity-cutting cartel in the petrochemical industry. When the industry was stalled in negotiations over capacity cuts, MITI sent the company presidents off to Europe, ostensibly to study the petrochemical industry there but in fact to get to know each other. The returning presidents claimed to have developed mutual trust, and the capacity-cutting agreements went ahead.[14]

Rogers Hollingsworth and Leon Lindberg compare the clanlike organization that characterizes the American dairy industry to the absence of clans in mature, heavy industrial sectors in the United States. They argue that cultural homogeneity among producers, government involvement in supporting prices, and the exemption of many agricultural cooperatives from antitrust legislation (as called for in the Capper-Volsted Act) foster such ties in the dairy industry. In contrast, firms in heavy industrial sectors tend to keep each other at arms length, primarily because of concerns about antitrust law.[15] In a small sample of major U.S. trade associations, Leonard Lynn and Timothy McKeown found that association rules emphasize that lawyers must be present at all trade association discussions or at least approve the minutes from such meetings in order to guard against antitrust violations. This concern with legal restrictions suggests the difficulty of establishing the informal clanlike atmosphere in U.S. manufacturing industries that is fostered in Japanese trade associations and the U.S. dairy industry.[16] The fact that the government not only permits but actively supports market governing activities is an important reason for the sociable atmosphere of Japanese trade associations in heavy industry. Since the 1991 strengthening of the Anti-

[12] FTC, "Shijō akusesu," 1988, p. 316.

[13] Atsuya Jōji and Ueno Hiroya, "Jigyōsha dantai bunseki no wakugumi" (An analytical framework for trade associations), *Keizai seminā* (Economics seminar), Special Issue: "Shūdan to soshiki no seiji keizai gaku" (The political economics of groups and organizations) 265 (February 1977): 23.

[14] Frank K. Upham, *Law and Social Change in Postwar Japan* (Cambridge: Harvard University Press, 1987), p. 196.

[15] Rogers Hollingsworth and Leon Lindberg, "The Governance of the American Economy: The Role of Markets, Clans, Hierarchies, and Associative Behaviour," in Wolfgang Streeck and Philippe C. Schmitter, eds., *Private Interest Government: Beyond Market and State*, Sage Series in Neocorporatism (Beverly Hills, Calif.: Sage, 1985), pp. 221–52.

[16] Leonard H. Lynn and Timothy J. McKeown, *Organizing Business: Trade Associations in America and Japan* (Washington, D.C.: American Enterprise Institute for Public Policy Research, 1988), pp. 48–49.

Monopoly Law and the FTC's new emphasis on publishing guidelines about it, business has become more aware of the law and has worked at compiling manuals to disseminate information about it. Nevertheless, Japanese business still appears less wary of violating competition law than U.S. firms do.

The only activity that surpasses social activities in the FTC survey of manufacturing industry trade associations is "communication with the government," engaged in by 98 percent of the trade associations.[17] It is important to note that the survey does not use the term *lobbying*, which is not how Japanese trade associations usually participate in policy-making. When asked if his trade association ever lobbied the government, one official said, "No, the only lobbying Japanese trade associations do is in Washington."[18] In other words, Japanese trade associations do not simply petition the government for changes in government rule over industry, but discuss policy with the bureaucracy as partners in joint state-trade association administration of industry.

Japanese trade associations do lobby the Diet in certain situations—for instance, when they want Diet approval of disbursement of funds to subsidize industry, as we shall see in the case of the aluminum industry. Generally, however, because MITI policy toward large firms has been aimed at helping industry financially through cartel arrangements, few government expenditures are necessary and trade associations have not needed to lobby the Diet.[19]

Trade association leaders do, of course, emphasize industry interests in their communication with the bureaucracy and pursue company interests through their cartel activities. Nevertheless, associations are called "corporations for the public benefit" (*kōeki hōjin*) and are considered to represent the public in promoting their industries. Ueno Hiroya suggests the term is used "because MITI considers their growth to be in the public interest."[20] According to MITI, strong trade associations are in the public interest in part because they promote economic development along with private gain. One petrochemical company executive revealed the degree to which industry sees trade associations as quasipublic. He said the trade association was so important that, "if it didn't exist we'd have to

[17] FTC, "Shijō akusesu," 1988, p. 316.
[18] Interview, 1988.
[19] Small firms do lobby the Diet heavily for aid. Kent E. Calder, *Crisis and Compensation: Public Policy and Political Stability in Japan* (Princeton: Princeton University Press, 1988).
[20] Atsuya Jōji and Ueno Hiroya, "Jigyōsha dantai bunseki no wakugumi" (An analytical framework for trade associations), *Keizei Seminaa* (Economics seminar), Special Issue: Shūdan to soshiki no seiji keizai gaku (The political economics of groups and organizations) 265 (1977): 25. For a discussion of Japanese concepts of public and private see Patricia Boling, "Private Interest and the Public Good in Japan," *The Pacific Review* 3 (1990), 138–50.

create a voluntary organization to take its place."[21] Although this seems a bizarre statement if viewed from an American perspective, Japanese don't see trade associations as true voluntary associations because they are required to be licensed by the government. Trade associations are also considered quasipublic because they provide important services for the bureaucracy, services that are often handled directly by the U.S. government. First, the Japanese government relies on trade associations' extensive information-gathering activities for its own information about industry. Second, the trade association acts as a government communications channel to individual firms. Typically bureaucracies communicate policy to the trade association and rely on it to relay the information to individual firms. Third, trade associations play an important role in helping government implement its policies. Ueno remarked in 1977, "Presently in Japan, administrative functions depend heavily on trade associations. If the trade associations were restricted as closely as they are in the U.S., they wouldn't be able to do anything and administrative guidance would also lose effectiveness."[22] Trade associations are able to help implement MITI's policies by informally coordinating activities among themselves and thus are crucial to effective industrial policy. Because firms see trade associations as providing public functions, they often see membership as a way of supporting the bureaucracy and join the association to enhance their relationships with the bureaucracy.[23]

HISTORY OF JAPANESE CARTELS AND TRADE ASSOCIATIONS

More than one scholar of Japanese antimonopoly policy has noted that cartels have considerable political legitimacy in Japan because they are seen as responsible for the development of capitalism rather than as a corruption of it.[24] The Japanese government has a long history of actively encouraging and administering cartels. According to Yūi Tsunehiko, Japan destroyed its traditional guilds more quickly and thoroughly than Europe did. But in the 1880s the commerce and agriculture ministries decided to establish trade associations (dōgyō kumiai) to regulate quality control and protect firms from excessive competition.[25] Two of these

[21] Interview, 1992.
[22] Atsuya and Ueno, "Jigyōsha dantai no bunseki."
[23] Ibid., p. 23.
[24] Heiwa Keizai Keikaku Kaigi (The Conference on Planning for a Peace Economy). *Kokumin no dokusen hakusho: Dokkin seisaku no tenkai to dokkin hō kaisei mondai* (The people's monopoly white paper: Problems regarding the development of antimonopoly policy and antimonopoly law reform) (Tokyo: Ochanomizu Shobō, 1977), p. 121. Also, Misonō Hitoshi, *Nihon no dokusen kinshi seisaku to sangyō soshiki* (Japan's antimonopoly policy and industrial organization) (Tokyo: Kawade Shobō, 1987).
[25] This discussion of dōgyō kumiai is drawn from Yūi Tsunehiko, "Senzen nihon ni okeru kyōsō to dokusen naishi tōsei ni tsuite" (Competition, monopoly, and control in prewar Japan) (in three parts), *Kōsei torihiki* 395 (September 1983): 9–13; 396 (October 1983): 33–37; 397 (November 1983): 22–25.

early trade associations were established explicitly as cartels: the paper manufacturers' cartel of 1880 and the spinners' association of 1882. In the 1890s the government became more optimistic about economic growth and less concerned about excessive competition and therefore formally barred trade associations from cartel activities. In fact, however, most trade associations engaged in cartels that the government actively helped set up, including, for example, those in flour milling, sugar refining, and fertilizers. The only truly independent cartels were in spinning, paper, and cement. The ease and willingness with which Japanese business worked with government contrasts with the resistance of European business to government participation in cartels.[26]

The early development of cartels took place in industries dominated by small and medium-sized firms. Highly oligopolistic heavy industry did not develop true cartel organizations until the 1920s. Although the state played a major role in setting up heavy industries by establishing factories and selling them to private entrepreneurs, it did not initially create cartel organizations for these industries. There was no need; because the same handful of *zaibatsu* dominated most of the oligopolistically structured industries, they were able to coordinate price collusion without formal agreements.[27]

During the World War I economic boom, cartels in light industrial sectors fell apart; but they came back in full force in the 1920s in response to a series of sharp price drops during the postwar recession and the financial crisis of 1927.[28] With the Important Industries Law of 1925, government took a stronger role in cartel supervision and established them in oligopolistic industries. The law gave industry associations the right to set prices and production quotas and to force outsiders to join cartels.[29] As the effects of the Great Depression hit Japan in 1930, the government took an even stronger role, mandating cartel formation in some sectors and supervising their implementation.[30]

By 1932, virtually all heavy industry was organized into cartels. Until 1937 the cartels were not actually government-dominated but were run by the trade associations with government backing. Cartels were not always effective, but government backing allowed the trade associations to run more effective cartels than would have been possible if the government had been indifferent or hostile to them.

Although neoclassical economic theory holds that cartels make an

---

[26] Johannes Hirschmeier and Tsunehiko Yui, *The Development of Japanese Business, 1600–1973* (London: Allen and Unwin, 1975).

[27] Ibid., p. 177; Eleanor M. Hadley, *Antitrust in Japan* (Princeton: Princeton University Press, 1970), pp. 358, 362.

[28] Eleanor M. Hadley, *Antitrust in Japan* (Princeton: Princeton University Press, 1970).

[29] Yūi, "Senzen nihon," 1983, p. 37.

[30] Hirschmeier and Yūi, *Development of Japanese Business.*

economy less efficient by distorting prices, in a late-industrializing country the state can use price distortions to promote industries that would not develop through the market.[31] Japan successfully used cartels to raise and stabilize prices for goods produced by heavy industry, thus encouraging investment and helping firms survive depressions.

Kikkawa Takeo argues that cartels in the pre-war and wartime period were able to promote economic development because state restrictions and market pressures maintained some competition.[32] Cartels were generally only successful during depressions, in part because of import pressures in industries like iron and steel, electrical equipment, and copper and because many downstream industries were also oligopolistic and able to resist price hikes by cartels in upstream industries. While the government supported cartels when they served the purpose of stabilizing prices, it regulated them when business tried to raise prices too much, especially in the 1930s.[33] Thus, while cartels supported prices during depressions, they were not allowed to become so strong as to excessively dampen consumption.

During depressions, cartels enabled marginal firms to survive, preserving heavier competition during growth periods than would otherwise have been the case. This use of cartels enabled firms to adopt a long-term, growth-oriented strategy and avoid layoffs, thus shortening depressions for the nation as a whole. Over the long term, cartels enabled Japanese firms to increase productivity and become more internationally competitive.[34] Japan repeated this pattern in its postwar use of cartels to help firms survive periods of depression.

As part of its effort to democratize Japan, the Supreme Commander for the Allied Powers (SCAP) attacked monopoly power in the economy by dismantling the zaibatsu, establishing the Antimonopoly Law and the Trade Association Law, and creating the FTC to enforce the laws. Many SCAP officials were idealistic and wanted to establish an antitrust law even stronger than the law in the United States, but SCAP did not effectively institutionalize the law and created no real base of political support for it. Both business and labor were opposed to the law, in part because they considered the U.S. to have imposed such a strict law in order to weaken Japan.[35]

[31] See Alice Amsden, *Asia's Next Giant: South Korea and Late Industrialization* (New York: Oxford University Press, 1989), p. 8.

[32] Takeo Kikkawa, "Functions of Japanese Trade Associations before World War II: The Case of Cartel Organizations," in Hiroaki Yamazaki and Matao Miyamoto, eds., *Trade Associations in Business History*, International Conference on Business History, Vol. 14, Proceedings of the Fuji Conference (Tokyo: University of Tokyo Press, 1988), pp. 53–83.

[33] Ibid., pp. 73, 85–86.

[34] Ibid., pp. 76–85.

[35] Heiwa Keizai Keikaku Kaigi, *Kokumin no dokusen hakusho*, p. 120.

Conservative and moderate political opinion in immediate postwar Japan was generally positive towards cartels, which were considered to have played an important role in the nation's development. Their quasipublic aura was another factor behind the support they enjoyed. People didn't support the Antimonopoly Law in part because they were unaccustomed to the American distinction between government controls and cartels.[36] Nor was the working class interested in supporting the law, although for different reasons. Because Marxist working-class leaders in the late 1940s criticized capitalism in general, there was no enthusiasm on the left for reforming capitalism by imposing limits on capitalist monopoly. Sōhyō, the powerful radical organization of trade unions, considered monopoly a necessary product of capitalism and therefore impossible to eliminate through the legal system. Moreover, Sōhyō, the Japan Socialist party, and others on the left criticized the law as a state attempt to cover up capitalist monopoly.[37]

Because there was no tradition of strong antimonopoly law in Japan, the FTC lacked a pool of knowledgeable people from which to draw staff. The only person on the original commission who knew anything about antimonopoly law was a former Japanese consul who had served in Chicago.[38] Therefore, during the early period of the U.S. occupation, SCAP relied on its own antitrust division to handle most antimonopoly enforcement. Even later in the occupation, antitrust findings often did not go through proper FTC procedures.[39]

The Japanese antimonopoly system differs from the U.S. system in that all antimonopoly law is embodied in one law. While enforcement in the U.S. is shared by the antitrust division of the Justice Department and the Federal Trade Commission, in Japan it is concentrated in an independent FTC. This independence and complete authority might have made the FTC very powerful; but once SCAP's protection was lost at the end of the occupation, the centralization of authority made it easy for opponents of the law to limit enforcement by simply controlling a single institution.[40] In addition, it is still very difficult for a private party to bring an antitrust suit. Therefore, the FTC always acts as both judge and prosecutor. According to Fujiwara Ichirō, a former MITI official, this dual role is a problem because the Japanese are uncomfortable with the litigiousness of the Antimonopoly Law. The FTC therefore avoids spending excessive time and expense on cases in favor of discussion and compro-

---

[36] Misonō, *Nihon no dokusen kinshi seisaku*, p. 32.
[37] Ibid., p. 27.
[38] Ibid., p. 30.
[39] Heiwa Keizai Keikaku Kaigi, *Kokumin no dokusen hakusho*, pp. 121–22.
[40] Misonō, *Nihon no dokusen kinshi seisaku*, pp. 21–22.

mise.[41] Nevertheless, such a cultural argument is unnecessary for explaining the FTC's weakness. Its lack of political support is due to the historical association of cartels with development and the considerable obstacles to bringing suit within the legal system.[42]

The end of the U.S. occupation invited strong attacks on SCAP's antimonopoly system. One casualty of these attacks was the Trade Association Law, which SCAP had enacted to prevent the reestablishment of the wartime control associations. The law provided clear, strict prohibitions on eighteen trade associations activities: "control of production and distribution, concerted activities, unreasonable restraint of trade, price control, limiting the number of entrepreneurs, boycott[s], supervising business activities of constituent members, limiting the function[s] of constituent members," various forms of direct business activities, financing, "acting as [an] agent for transactions, collecting accounts for entrepreneurs, arbitration of commercial matters, unduly influencing legislation, and regulating [rigging] bids."[43] These detailed restraints were much criticized by business and were abolished promptly after the occupation ended. Some of the Trade Association Law's provisions were added to the 1953 amended version of the Antimonopoly Law, although in a much weaker form.

In its amended form, the Antimonopoly Law, like the Trade Association Law, states that trade associations are able to violate the law independent of its members. It eliminates, however, virtually all the specific prohibitions of the Trade Association Law in favor of a few more general prohibitions.[44] The overall provisions prohibit firms from engaging in private monopoly, unfair trading restrictions, and unfair trading practices. Section 8, which directly addresses trade associations, generally prohibits them from regulating or controlling members in such a way that market competition is avoided or affected (section 8–1, 2, 4) and placing restrictions on association outsiders (section 8–3, 5).[45]

[41] Fujiwara Ichirō, "Samazamana kyōsō shijō" (Various kinds of competitive markets), *Kōsei Torihiki* 441 (July 1987): 28.

[42] J. Mark Ramseyer, "The Costs of the Consensual Myth: Antitrust Enforcement and Institutional Barriers to Litigation in Japan," *Yale Law Journal* 94 (January 1985): 604–45.

[43] Hiroshi Iyori and Akinori Uesugi, *The Antimonopoly Laws of Japan* (New York: Federal Legal Publications, 1983), p. 13.

[44] Specifically, section 8 prohibits trade associations from "(i) substantially restricting competition in any particularly field, (ii) entering into an international agreement [that constitutes an unfair restriction on trade], (iii) limiting the present or future number of entrepreneurs in any particular field of business, (iv) unduly restricting the functions or activities of the constituent entrepreneurs, and (v) causing entrepreneurs to do such acts as constitute unfair business practices." Iyori and Uesugi, *Antimonopoly Laws*, p. 220.

[45] Wada, "Jigyōsha dantai no kinō," p. 58.

The Antimonopoly Law of 1953 was weakened by its provisions for depression cartels. These cartels may control prices, production, or sales and can be used to help industries facing either short- or long-term depressions. Their purpose is to support prices and prevent firms from going out of business in industries suffering from low prices and depressed demand. The Antimonopoly Law permits depression cartels in industries affected by what is considered "excess competition," which is defined by the following conditions:

(a) "there exists an extreme disequilibrium of supply and demand for a particular commodity;

(b) "the price of said commodity is below the average cost of the product; [and]

(c) "a considerable number of the entrepreneurs in the trade concerned may eventually be forced to discontinue production."[46]

Many Japanese believe that excessive competition is caused by lower-than-expected growth in a sector combined with resistance of both firms and labor to withdrawing from an industry. Growth can be slowed by such external factors as shifts in demand to other products (such as from coal to oil) or changes in the international environment, such as the increasing competitiveness of other countries' products (whether due to changes in relative productivity, wage levels, or exchange-rate fluctuations), the raising of trade barriers overseas, or the lifting of domestic trade barriers.[47]

Neoclassical theory holds that, as prices drop below production costs, firms either leave the industry in search of profits or less efficient producers go bankrupt, reducing supply and allowing prices to rise. In Japan, however, firms often ride out a period of low prices for a long time because of various reasons that enable and impel them to pursue long-term strategies. Managers are able to ignore pressure from stockholders to produce short-term profits because most stocks are held by firms committed to long-term ownership.[48] Managers are not only relatively free to maintain production in the face of low prices, but also have a strong incentive to maintain production because of a commitment to avoid laying off the large segment of the work force considered lifetime employees.

A former MITI official suggests that another reason for excess compe-

[46] Iyori and Uesugi, *Antimonopoly Laws*, p. 114.

[47] Tsuruta Toshimasa, "Kōdo seichōki" (The high growth period), in Komiya Ryūtarō, Okuno Masahiro, and Suzumura Kōtarō, eds., *Nihon no sangyō seisaku* (Japan's industrial policy) (Tokyo: Tokyo University Press, 1984), pp. 59, 84.

[48] Ulrike Schaede, "Understanding Corporate Governance in Japan: Do Classical Concepts Apply?" *Industrial and Corporate Change* 3 (1994).

tition is firms' expectation that the state will bail them out of trouble. While the lack of an interventionist state forces American firms to look after their own interests by forming private cartels, Japanese firms are less likely to form informal cartels and more prone to engage in reckless competition with the knowledge the state will help them in times of difficulty.[49] I believe that the expectation of state assistance does not so much encourage firms to compete more aggressively as to stay in the game rather than leave an ailing industry. As we shall see, the aluminum refining industry is an example of aggressively continuing to invest in an industry with poor prospects while beginning to appeal to the state for aid.

Although the revised Antimonopoly Law of 1953 established criteria for approving depression cartels, the FTC was so weak in the early 1950s that trade associations did not bother to go through commission procedures to form cartels but simply formed their own illegally or participated in MITI-led recommended cutbacks. The initial impulse for cartels was the drop in U.S. military procurements at the end of the Korean War, which left Japanese firms with overcapacity, especially in such industries as cotton and wool spinning, synthetic fibers, tires, fertilizer, steel, and petroleum refining. To cope with overcapacity during the recession, most firms engaged in illegal cartels, which the FTC was aware of but powerless to stop.[50] The FTC also tacitly condoned the resumption of government-guided cartels in the form of *kankoku sōtan*, or government-recommended cutbacks in which MITI led the formation of cartels and pressured individual firms to participate. The cutbacks were useful in industries where large numbers of firms made it difficult to arrange an informal private cartel and were also a good way to get the government to put restrictions on outsiders. Thus, the recommended cutbacks were the first MITI-sponsored cartels in the postwar period. Their success was due in part to the fact that both government and the trade associations had learned to manage cartels before and during the war.[51] One of the factors that facilitated the establishment of cartels in the 1950s was the institutional legacy of wartime control associations. The Japan Spinners' Association (Nihon Bōseki Kyōkai), for instance, which participated in the first recommended cutback, was essentially the same organization as the wartime Japan Spinners' Federation (Nihon Bōseki Rengō Kai). The same companies belonged to both organizations and the same personnel (below the representative director (*senmu riji*) level) staffed both the wartime and postwar organizations.[52]

[49] Fujiwara, "Samazamana kyōsō shijō," p. 27.
[50] Heiwa Keizai Keikaku Kaigi, *Kokumin no dokusen hakusho*, p. 122.
[51] Misonō, *Nihon no dokusen kinshi seisaku*, p. 60.
[52] Ibid., p. 24.

The recommended cutbacks started after the Korean War in cotton spinning, chemical fibers, and tires and spread to cement, chemicals, steel, coal, and other industries. In 1957 a worsening balance of payments led to scarce financing, which prompted the extension of recommended cutbacks to nonferrous metals, paper pulp, textiles, and other industries. In March 1958, fifteen industries were under recommended cutbacks; and by March 1960, there were twenty-eight industries. At the same time, cutbacks expanded to include freezing of stocks and equipment, buying up of stocks, and open pricing.[53] Although MITI had a great deal of power to enforce such cartels because of its control over foreign currency and other matters, industry cooperated with MITI voluntarily to a considerable degree.[54]

Numerous other laws were passed in the early 1950s to facilitate cartels, especially in weak industries. The Small and Medium-sized Business Stabilization Law made it easier to get cartels approved for small firms. The Import-Export Trade Law facilitated the development of export cartels. Laws such as the Textile Equipment Temporary Measures Law, the Ammonium Sulphate Rationalization Law, the Coal Mining Industry Rationalization Law, and the Fertilizer Price Stabilization Temporary Measures Law facilitated cartels in other depressed industries.[55]

In 1957 MITI and big business pushed a new bill that would have largely done away with the Antimonopoly Law. The bill was killed, however, because its introduction coincided with strident opposition-party criticism of the Police Duties Law, which Prime Minister Kishi was trying to pass.[56] Although the Antimonopoly Law survived this challenge, enforcement continued to be extremely weak. For example, in 1959 the FTC searched the offices of leading newspapers to investigate why they had all raised their prices simultaneously. Although the commission found evidence that the newspapers had colluded to raise prices, it ruled that because there was no evidence that the newspaper companies had established penalties for failing to comply with the cartel, "no binding agreement" had taken place. In effect the FTC was saying that it would not rule against gentlemen's agreements. Even in cases where it did crack down, penalties were light, and violating companies were generally not forced to lower their prices significantly.[57]

In the 1960s, both competition among firms and FTC strength in-

[53] Heiwa Keizai Keikaku Kaigi, *Kokumin no dokusen hakusho*, p. 128.

[54] Misonō, *Nihon no dokusen kinshi seisaku*, p. 62.

[55] FTC, 1989, pp. 226–27; Heiwa Keizai Keikaku Kaigi, *Kokumin no dokusen hakusho*, p. 224.

[56] Chalmers Johnson, *MITI and the Japanese Miracle: The Growth of Industrial Policy, 1925–1975* (Stanford: Stanford University Press, 1982), p. 226.

[57] Heiwa Keizai Keikaku Kaigi, *Kokumin no dokusen hakusho*, pp. 130–31, 163.

creased. Competition increased because Japan loosened its foreign-exchange controls to become an article 8 nation at the IMF, and it opened its markets to more imports. In addition, the "full set strategy," the attempt by each individual financial group to establish a presence in all industries, increased the number of firms in many oligopolistic industries. At the same time, the FTC became stricter with cartels, in part because of concern about inflation. The commission increasingly recommended that firms desist from antimonopoly violations, jumping from just two recommendations per year in 1958–61 to twenty-six per year in 1962–65.[58]

As part of the government's anti-inflation campaign, the cabinet abolished the use of recommend cutbacks in 1964. They were abolished, however, with the understanding that the FTC would allow MITI's recommended cutbacks to continue as depression cartels; and the FTC was quite free in permitting them. As can be seen in table 2–1, the number of depression cartels greatly increased from 1965 on. The FTC approved eighteen depression cartels in 1965, more than twice the total number that had been used up to that point. The peak period for depression cartels was in 1965 and the early 1970s before the enactment of the DIL in 1978, although large numbers of depression cartels continued to be used through the early 1980s. As shown in table 2–2, most of these cartels limited production, one-third limited the use of equipment, and smaller numbers controlled sales volume and prices.

The FTC was so lenient in granting depression cartels in the period leading up to the first oil shock that it renewed depression cartels in the steel industry even when the economy was overheating under Tanaka Kakuei's plan to restructure the Japanese archipelago in 1972. Not only was it easy for industries to receive permission for legal cartels, the atmosphere of permissiveness invited illegal cartels as well. Such widespread cartel activity was perceived as being partly responsible for the rampant inflation that preceded and was then exacerbated by the 1973 oil shock.[59]

In 1973 the FTC did finally crack down on illegal cartels, recommending that sixty-seven industries involving thirty-three trade associations desist from monopolistic activities.[60] In addition, for the first time, the commission filed criminal charges against firms involved in illegal cartel activities. The oil companies that were charged did not dispute that they had conspired to fix prices and restrict output, but they argued that in doing so they were obeying MITI's administrative guidance and therefore were not guilty of violating the law.

The Petroleum Industry Law of 1962 gave MITI authority to monitor

[58] FTC, *Nenji hōkoku*, 1989, p. 186.
[59] Misonō, *Nihon no dokusen kinshi seisaku*, pp. 223–24.
[60] FTC, 1989, p. 189.

Table 2–1. Depression cartels, 1958–88

Recession period	Number of cartels
1958	6
1962	2
1965	18
1971	13
1975	21
1981	11
1987	2
1992	0

Source: Kōsei Torihiki Iinkai, Kōsei Torihiki Iinkai nenji hōkoku (FTC annual report), 1989, 1993.

Table 2–2. Recession cartels, 1958–88, by type

Type	Number
Production	53
Equipment	25
Sales volume	11
Price	5
Total number of cartel restrictions	94
Total number of industry cartels	72
(some had more than one type of restriction)	

Source: Hiroshi Iyori and Akinori Uesugi, The Antimonopoly Laws of Japan (New York: Federal Legal Publications, 1983); Kōsei Torihiki Iinkai, Kōsei Torihiki Iinkai nenji hōkoku (FTC annual report), 1989, 1993.
Note: An equipment-restricting cartel is one that restricts members' use of their capital equipment by shortening workdays and sealing off machines and tools.

the petroleum industry, decide whether to approve capacity expansion, advise firms to restrict output, and propose resale price guidelines for petroleum products. The law is ambiguous, however, about MITI's actual authority to carry out the law. The Tokyo High Court ruled in 1980 that the lack of explicit authority means that MITI's use of administrative guidance does not legitimate the cartels that such guidance might produce.[61] The court's decision left some ambiguity: in some cases a statute could legitimate anticompetitive actions if such actions were necessary to the implementation of the law and if the administering

[61] Lawrence Repeta, "The Limits of Administrative Authority in Japan: The Oil Cartel Criminal Cases and the Reaction of MITI and the FTC," Law in Japan: An Annual 14, no. 24 (1982): 24–45.

bureaucracy approved. But the court left it unclear whether MITI's own judgment sufficed to make anticompetitive behavior legal. Nevertheless, the decision presented a serious challenge to MITI's informal guidance of trade associations to achieve its own policy objectives.[62]

In the wake of the initial scandal over the petroleum cartels, the FTC attempted to use the public's concern with inflation and price-gouging cartels to strengthen the Antimonopoly Law. In October 1973 FTC Head Commissioner Takahashi Toshihide announced plans to establish a study group to examine strengthening the law to permit the FTC to break up firms with near monopolies, force firms to lower prices after ordering price cartels to disband, strengthen penalties, use certain kinds of circumstantial evidence rather than merely direct evidence, and get access to the records of monopolistic firms. This was the first time anyone had attempted to strengthen the Antimonopoly Law.[63]

In December 1973 the Special Committee on the Cost of Living in the Upper House called for the government to instruct the FTC to enforce the Antimonopoly Law more strictly. The opposition parties came up with proposals for tightening antimonopoly policy in 1974.[64] In September the FTC produced a draft proposal for strengthening the Antimonopoly Law, which was based closely on the study group's proposals. In addition to Takahashi's original suggestions, it added strengthened restrictions on shareholding to reduce concentration of economic power in industrial groups.[65]

Consumer groups, the opposition parties, neoclassical economists, and legal scholars all supported the proposed revisions, while business groups, the Ministry of Finance, and, most important, MITI opposed them.[66] The FTC's campaign for a strengthened Antimonopoly Law was helped by the 1974 scandal in which Prime Minister Tanaka Kakuei was accused of graft and tax evasion. The next prime minister, Miki Takeo, attempted to clean up the party's image by pushing for the law revision in the Diet. The Lower House passed the revision as a gesture of respect for Miki but the Upper House refused. In 1977 both houses passed the revision, although in a much watered-down form.[67]

At the same time the Diet finally passed the weakened Antimonopoly

---

[62] Upham, *Law and Social Change*, pp. 184–88.

[63] Misonō, *Nihon no dokusen kinshi seisaku*, pp. 228, 229.

[64] Heiwa Keizai Keikaku Kaigi, *Kokumin no dokusen hakusho*, pp. 167–69.

[65] Misonō, *Nihon no dokusen kinshi seisaku*, p. 238.

[66] Heiwa Keizai Keikaku Kaigi, *Kokumin no dokusen hakusho*, pp. 175–77.

[67] Johnson, *MITI*, pp. 300–301. This was followed in 1979 by clearer guidelines on trade association activities, which distinguished between prohibited activities, those that might be violations of the Antimonopoly Law, and those that are in principle not violations. Wada, "Jigyōsha dantai no kinō," p. 58; translation of guidelines in Iyori and Uesugi, *Antimonopoly Laws*.

Law revision, MITI was proposing sweeping exemptions from the law through the Depressed Industries Law (DIL) to allow it to direct cartels in declining basic materials industries. The aim of industrial policy is to affect the industrial structure of a country—that is, the sectors that compose the economy. MITI has classified these sectors differently over time. In the 1970s, MITI divided industry into basic materials industries and processing and assembly industries. Basic materials included sectors that produced industrial inputs from raw materials (iron and steel; non-ferrous metals; petroleum and coal products; cement, glass, and ceramics; and chemicals). In the 1980s four additional sectors were added to the category that either produce for consumer needs rather than industry (lumber and paper) or do secondary processing of basic materials (rubber and metal products). MITI also cut down its current processing and assembly category to include only machine and precision-instrument production and carved out a third category, life-related industries, which included industries producing nonmachine consumer goods.[68]

Basic materials industries are capital rather than labor intensive. Thus, in 1980, while industrial materials industries represented only 15 percent of total manufacturing employment, they represented 41 percent of tangible assets (see table 2–3). This is particularly true for the core industrial materials industries, which were the principal target of the 1978, 1983, and 1987 laws, and that in 1980 had 27.2 million yen of capital per employee compared to the overall manufacturing average of 3.8 million. However, the basic materials industries were light users of labor. Labor accounted for only 8 percent of the value of industrial basic materials, in contrast to 15 percent for average manufactured products in 1980 (see table 2–4). This relatively light use of labor contrasts with most of Japan's other declining industries, such as lumber, apparel, leather goods, and shipbuilding. Labor intensity in most sectors rose from 1980–92 as wages rose and the cost of materials fell. It rose particularly in sectors such as aluminum and shipbuilding, which experienced rapid decline and had large residual work forces.

Wages were especially high in the industrial basic materials sectors, especially in the core, which in 1992 had wages 51 percent higher than the national manufacturing average (see table 2–5). Again, this was in contrast to the lumber and apparel sectors, although not shipbuilding.

Japanese basic materials production declined due primarily to three changes in the world economy that hit all the advanced industrialized countries. First, dramatic increases in the price of oil in 1973 and 1979 stifled demand in industries which were energy-intensive (such as

[68] MITI, *Kōgyō tōkeihyō, sangyō hen* (Census of manufactures, by product), 1980, 1990.

Table 2–3. Size of work force and value of assets in Japanese manufacturing, 1980, millions of yen

	Number of employees	Percent of total employment	Capital per employee	Share of total assets (in percent)
Industrial basic materials	1,575,209	15.3	10.3	41.1
Chemicals	409,338	4.0	10.1	10.5
Petroleum and coal products	43,955	0.4	39.6	4.4
Cement, glass, ceramics	505,585	4.9	4.4	5.6
Iron and steel	428,957	4.2	15.5	16.9
Nonferrous metals	187,374	1.8	7.8	3.7
Core industrial basic materials	272,550	2.7	27.2	18.8
Petrochemicals	111,725	1.1	18.1	5.1
Cement	13,210	0.1	34.3	1.2
Blast-furnace steel	139,657	1.4	32.9	11.7
Primary aluminum	7,958	0.1	43.6	0.9
Processed and consumer materials	1,538,684	15.0	3.2	12.4
Lumber and wood products	362,254	3.5	2.1	2.0
Pulp, paper, paper products	279,361	2.7	6.7	4.8
Rubber products	152,523	1.5	3.0	1.2
Metal products	744,546	7.2	2.4	4.5
Machines	3,523,085	34.2	2.9	25.6
General machinery	1,026,377	10.0	2.8	7.4
Electrical machinery	1,341,722	13.0	2.1	7.3
Transportation machinery	888,840	8.6	4.3	9.7
Shipbuilding	93,247	0.9	5.5	1.3
Precision instruments	266,146	2.6	1.9	1.3
Nonmachine consumer goods	3,087,025	30.0	2.2	17.4
Food processing (including tobacco)	1,086,035	10.6	3.4	9.3
Textiles (not including clothing)	691,018	6.7	1.8	3.2
Clothing	498,282	4.8	0.7	0.9
Furniture	256,112	2.5	1.6	1.1
Publishing and printing	476,054	4.6	2.3	2.8
Leather products	79,524	0.8	1.1	0.2
Other manufacturing	563,400	5.5	2.4	3.5
All manufacturing	10,291,918	100.0	3.8	100.0

Source: MITI, *Kōgyō tōkei hyō, sangyō hen* (Census of manufactures, report by industries), 1980.

aluminum), which used petroleum as a raw material (petrochemicals), or which made products used in the distribution of petroleum (such as shipbuilding, which made oil tankers). Second, even for basic materials that were not particularly petroleum-dependent (for example, steel), demand was stagnant, because industries were learning to use materials more efficiently and because manufacturing was growing slowly compared to services. Third, the rise of the Asian newly industrializing countries (NICs) provided new competition for many industries producing standardized products. The advantages that made the NICs more competitive were the same ones that had made Japan a strong competitor

Table 2–4. Labor intensiveness by sector, in percent

	1980	1990	1992
Industrial basic materials	8	10	11
Chemicals	8	9	10
Petroleum and coal products	1	2	3
Cement, glass, ceramics	15	16	17
Iron and steel	9	10	12
Nonferrous metals	7	10	12
Core industrial basic materials	7	9	9
Petrochemicals	6	7	8
Cement	5	6	7
Blast-furnace steel	9	11	11
Primary aluminum	5	8	55
Processed and consumer materials	15	16	17
Lumber and wood products	13	16	17
Pulp, paper, paper products	11	12	13
Rubber products	16	18	19
Metal products	18	17	18
Machines	15	13	14
General machinery	18	16	18
Electrical machinery	15	13	14
Transportation machinery	11	10	10
Shipbuilding	16	14	37
Precision instruments	19	19	20
Nonmachine consumer goods	15	15	16
Food processing (including tobacco)	10	10	11
Textiles (not including clothing)	17	19	20
Clothing	23	25	25
Furniture	18	18	20
Publishing and printing	22	21	22
Leather products	16	17	18
Other manufacturing	15	N/A	15
All manufacturing	12	13	15

Source: MITI, Kōgyō tōkei hyō, sangyō hen (Census of manufactures, report by industries), 1980, 1990, 1992.
Note: Labor intensity is calculated by dividing wage cost by value of final product.

in the 1950s and 1960s: cheap capital provided by governments eager to push industrial growth, cheaper labor costs, and sometimes being a late developer with up-to-date plants and equipment. For example, steel production was basically stagnant in Japan, North America, Europe, and Oceania but quadrupled from 43 million tons to 165 million in Africa, South America, and the rest of Asia.

While the oil shocks, stagnant demand, and the rise of the NICs affected the advanced industrialized countries in the 1970s and 80s, Japan's relatively late industrialization made its experience with decline

Table 2–5. Average wages per employee (in millions of yen)

	1980	1992	1992 sectoral wage (as percent of average manufacturing wage)
Industrial basic materials	3.2	5.1	117
Chemicals	3.6	5.6	127
Petroleum and coal products	4.0	6.5	148
Cement, glass, ceramics	2.5	4.1	94
Iron and steel	3.8	5.8	133
Nonferrous metals	3.2	5.0	114
Core industrial basic materials	4.2	6.6	151
Petrochemicals	3.9	6.2	141
Cement	4.0	6.3	144
Blast-furnace steel	4.6	7.3	165
Primary aluminum	3.5	5.9	135
Processed and consumer materials	2.4	4.1	93
Lumber and wood products	2.0	3.3	74
Pulp, paper, paper products	2.7	4.2	95
Rubber products	2.6	4.2	96
Metal products	2.5	4.3	97
Machines	2.8	4.5	103
General machinery	3.1	4.9	111
Electrical machinery	2.5	4.0	92
Transportation machinery	3.1	5.2	118
Shipbuilding	3.0	5.6	126
Precision instruments	2.4	3.9	89
Nonmachine consumer goods	2.0	3.3	74
Food processing (including tobacco)	2.0	3.0	69
Textiles (not including clothing)	1.9	3.0	68
Clothing	1.4	2.1	49
Furniture	2.1	3.5	80
Publishing and printing	3.1	5.0	114
Leather products	1.9	2.9	67
Other manufacturing	2.2	3.7	84
All manufacturing	2.5	4.4	100

Source: MITI, *Kōgyō tōkei hyō, sangyō hen* (Census of manufactures, report by industries), 1980, 1992.

somewhat different from that of other advanced countries. Because Japan's plant and equipment base was newer than that in the U.S. or Great Britain, it was not so quickly overtaken by NIC plants employing the latest technologies. Thus, sectoral decline was delayed. Two other factors stemming from Japan's late-developer status did create adjustment problems for Japan. In the 1970s and 80s Japan was facing new competition from the NICs at the same time that its wage levels were catching up with or surpassing those of the most prosperous Western countries. Although many Japanese firms made great strides in improving productivity, the rise in the yen, which was responsible for much of the relative increase in wages, made some Japanese goods less competitive. Loss of competitiveness does not necessarily lead to loss of markets, but the rise in the yen created great pressure to scrap industries dependent on more expensive Japanese labor and accept that the returns on yen-denominated domestic investments in internationally competing industries would be less than anticipated.

Moreover, the government's catchup strategy of encouraging massive investment in heavy industry while successfully spurring rapid growth often wildly overshot the market and left Japan with difficult problems of overcapacity. A number of factors account for Japan's investment rates of more than 30 percent in its high-growth period of the 1950s and 60s. One was the government's ability to create an implicit guarantee for an industry that would in turn lead all the major financial groups to invest in it. This strategy of granting an implicit government guarantee from risk backfired when some of the worst-case scenarios played themselves out. Japan found itself stuck with major overcapacity in industries such as petrochemicals and aluminum in which it had always had natural disadvantages but where the state had pushed investment for strategic reasons.

To deal with this overcapacity, the Depressed Industries Law of 1978 authorized MITI to draw up a basic stabilization plan for each depressed industry establishing the amounts of capacity to be scrapped, the methods of the cuts, the limits on new capacity, and ways for firms to transfer to new activities. The government would establish a designated depressed industries trust fund largely with Japan Development Bank funds. If industry efforts alone were insufficient to make progress on scrapping, the minister could recommend formation of a cartel with the approval of the FTC.[69]

MITI's original proposal had been much stronger, including four additional points that were later deleted or weakened:

1. The relevant minister could ban new investment by outsiders to the cartel. This proposal was deleted.
2. Exemptions to the Antimonopoly Law would permit mergers and transfer of management between firms in depressed industries. This point was deleted.
3. The relevant minister would only have to *discuss* merger or cartel plans with the FTC. The final version required FTC *approval* of the plans.
4. Only a sizable proportion of companies in an industry would have to

[69] Okabe Naohiro, "Kōzō fukyō gyōshu taisaku wo meguru sho mondai" (Some problems regarding policies toward structurally depressed industries), *Kigyō hō kenkyū* 276 (May 1978): 12.

make a request in order for an industry to be designated as structurally depressed. This was raised to two-thirds of all firms, representing at least two-thirds of market share.[70]

At the time it was thought that the deletion of the restriction on outsiders would greatly weaken the law because uncooperative outsiders could undermine the attempt to restrict production. This was not, in fact, a problem in most of the concentrated basic materials sectors.

The law did not generate fervent interest, either among supporters or opponents, and was not given much press coverage. The FTC was opposed to the entire proposal except for the trust fund because it argued that the existing exemption for depression cartels sufficed. The commission succeeded in blocking the restrictions on outsiders, although the remaining indicative cartel represented an important new policy tool for MITI. The FTC was able to limit the scope of the new law because of broad opposition to attempts to weaken the Antimonopoly Law.[71]

Neoclassical economists criticized the fact that, even in its amended form, the law put key market decisions about how much to produce and invest in the hands of government planners. Mizuno Takeshi, a professor at Seikei University, warned that MITI was simply using structural depression as an excuse to intervene more strongly in industrial policy. The journal *Keizai hyōron* said that arguments that cartels for structurally depressed industries would prevent unemployment were misguided; to deal with unemployment, financial and fiscal measures should be directed at labor and small business. Business, on the other hand, generally supported the Depressed Industries Law. Firms in the declining industries especially favored the law and complained about the revisions.[72]

Both business and MITI pushed the bill to head off bankruptcies among large firms in structurally depressed industries. In 1975 Ataka and Company, Japan's ninth-largest general trading company, failed because of bad debts associated with the oil crisis, which left many frightened that structural depression could produce a string of bankruptcies among Japan's highly leveraged heavy industrial firms and create a crisis for the banks that held the debt. Another worrisome case was Sasebo Heavy Industries, which had asked its lending banks for five billion yen to pay

---

[70] Echigo Kazunori, "Tokutei Fukyō Antei Rinji Sochi Hō no kihon teki seikaku" (The fundamental nature of the Depressed Industries Law), *Kigyōhō kenkyū* 276 (May 1978): 2–6.

[71] Mizuno Takeshi, "Sangyō kōzō seisaku he no fushin—Tokutei Fukyō Antei Rinji Sochi Hō no seiritsu wo megutte" (Distrust of industrial structure policy—On the development of the Depressed Industries Law), *Kigyōhō kenkyū* 276 (May 1978): 8.

[72] Ibid., p. 9; Echigo, "Tokutei Fukyō Antei Rinji Sochi Hō no kihon teki seikaku," pp. 3, 4.

severance pay to discharged workers at its shipbuilding docks. Daiichi Kangyō, Sasebo's main bank, had implicitly guaranteed other banks' loans to the company but had balked at making the bailout loan without a guarantee from the company's main shareholders. The Ministry of Finance, the Ministry of Transportation, and business leaders intervened, and the case was much on the minds of political and financial players.[73]

The Chisso Corporation was another highly visible firm teetering on bankruptcy. Its mercury poisoning of the waters around Minamata village had created the infamous Minamata disease, and the company had thirty billion yen in accumulated losses and faced continued claims by sufferers of the disease. Kumamoto prefecture had bailed out Chisso with loans, but there was concern the corporation still might fail. Banks' exposure to risk because of outstanding loans to troubled firms such as Chisso made one banker lament that banks were Japan's "thirteenth declining industry."[74]

Banks were concerned with the threat of bankruptcy in the basic materials industries because of the enormous size of their investments. But although big business generally supported the DIL in order to avoid bankruptcy in declining industries, business groups were critical of the specifics of the plan. The Keizai Dōyūkai was critical of the law, warning that MITI would pressure industries to go along with it. Moreover, it claimed that the trust fund was likely to balloon, putting a burden on the public treasury. Mizuno commented: "It is noteworthy that the financial world, which approves of the structural depression measures in general, does not approve of any of the specifics. The banks want to avoid suffering the direct losses of a string of major bankruptcies, but they also want to avoid the danger of bearing the indirect burden of preventing it."[75]

Some firms in declining industries, such as Tokyo Steel, a ferro-alloy company, and Nissei Spinning, were relatively strong and wanted a shakeout that would leave markets to them. They, too, were opposed to the DIL. Nevertheless, it did pass the Diet, in part because it had been significantly weakened. In addition, there were signs in 1977 that the economy was improving and the law might not actually be used much.[76] In late 1978 the government passed two companion laws to the DIL that were aimed at the social costs of structural decline. The Industries in Depressed Communities Law and the Workers in Depressed Communities Law provided various benefits to help workers and local areas. The

---

[73] Okumura Hiroshi, "Tokutei Fukyō Sangyō Antei Rinji Sochi Hō no ginkō, shōsha kyūsai hō teki seikaku" (The DIL is a bailout for banks and trading companies), *Kigyō hō kenkyū* 276 (May 1978): 24.

[74] Ibid., p. 25.

[75] Mizuno, "Sangyō kōzō seisaku he no fushin," p. 9.

[76] Ibid., p. 8.

first of these provided tax benefits, low-interest loans, loan guarantees, and extensions of preexisting loans to firms in designated areas.[77] The second law provided training and job-search assistance and subsidies to firms that retrained workers.[78] In terms of direct government expenditures, the Industries in Depressed Communities Law was much more important than the DIL or the Workers in Depressed Communities Law. One hundred billion yen was originally authorized under the DIL and its companion laws; but because falling interest rates made the fixed rates on government loans less attractive, only 23.2 billion yen were actually disbursed, and 64 percent of this money went to severance pay. Forty percent of the assistance went to shipbuilding and 30 percent to textiles.[79] In 1983 the two laws to assist workers were combined into the Employment Assistance Law. Subsidies for worker retraining and employment increased, and job-relocation assistance was offered to 64,000 workers in 1983–87, again largely in textiles and shipbuilding.[80]

Although they did not involve any government expenditures, the capacity-scrapping cartels were the most important part of the DIL. They were more far-reaching than the depression cartels, which generally covered only production and sales. The goal was to achieve permanent cuts in production in industries with long-term forecasts of reduced demand. The effect on production and prices was stronger than in depression cartels because it was harder to cheat on them.[81] In a production or sales cartel there is a strong incentive for members to produce more than their allotted quota to make additional profits from the higher prices established by the cartel. In a capacity-scrapping cartel there is the same incentive, but it is more difficult because equipment is often completely decommissioned or made difficult to use in secret. In the cement industry, for instance, the ends were cut off the cement kilns to make cheating impossible.

Although the DIL was originally expected to be temporary and was

---

[77] I follow J. Mark Ramseyer in using these abbreviations rather than the longer names of the laws. The complete names are the Temporary Measures Law for Small and Medium-sized Industries in Specified Depressed Areas and the Temporary Measures Law for Unemployed Workers in Specified Depressed Areas. Ramseyer, "Comments on Letting Obsolete Firms Die: Trade Adjustment Assistance in the United States and Japan," *Harvard International Law Journal* 22 (Fall 1981): 595–619.

[78] Ibid., p. 608.

[79] Sekiguchi Sueo and Horiuchi Toshihiro, "Bōeki to chōsei enjo" (Trade and adjustment assistance), in *Nihon no sangyō seisaku*, p. 337.

[80] Sekiguchi Sueo, "Japan: A Plethora of Programs," in Hugh Patrick, ed., *Pacific Basin Industries in Distress: Structural Adjustment and Trade Policy in the Nine Industrialized Economies*, Studies of the East Asian Institute (New York: Columbia University Press, 1991). Sekiguchi offers an excellent overview of formal assistance under the DIL and SDIL and a wealth of statistics on changes in industries under the laws.

[81] Itoh Motoshige, Kiyono Kazuharu, Okuno Masahiro, and Suzumura Kōtarō, "Shijō no shippai to hoseiteki sangyō seisaku" (Market failure and compensatory industrial policy), in *Nihon no sangyō seisaku*, p. 228.

only authorized for five years, the second oil shock prolonged and deepened structural problems for most heavy industries. The law was successful in getting sizable capacity reductions in the designated industries, but capacity use rates were still low in the early 1980s.[82] When the DIL was about to expire, MITI sought to extend and broaden it, hoping to give the ministry the power to bring about more fundamental structural change. The initial drafts of the 1983 Structurally Depressed Industries Law (SDIL), also known as the Petrochemical Industry Rescue Law, were worked out through close coordination with the petrochemical industry. Two subcommittees of the Industrial Structure Council, the Petrochemical Industry Structure Subcommittee and the Basic Materials Industry Policy Special Subcommittee, worked in parallel and completed their reports in early December. The SDIL was approved by the cabinet in February and sent to the Diet for debate.[83] That debate was much like the one over the 1978 DIL. Labor and the opposition parties joined MITI and the declining industries in pushing for an extended and strengthened law while the FTC and neoclassical economists argued against extension.[84]

Although the law that emerged did not have the controls on imports or outsiders proposed during the debate, it did considerably expand the scope of depressed industries policy. The SDIL continued the capacity-cutting cartels but added provisions for cooperation between firms in such endeavors as joint production, sales, purchasing, product specialization, mergers, and transfer of management between firms.[85] In addition, the law provided subsidies, Japan Development Bank loans, and tax incentives for energy conversion and research and development. It also provided tax incentives for investment in updated equipment, for capacity scrapping, and for mergers.[86]

The capacity-cutting cartels were most effective in the most concentrated industries, which were best able to make agreements on amounts of capacity to be scrapped because it was easier for them to coordinate for the sake of collective goods. Cuts were deepest in these industries, although both heavily concentrated and less concentrated industries met their goals for capacity cuts.[87] Concentrated industries arrived at agreements on a pro-rata basis: each firm made a roughly equal cut in ca-

---

[82] MITI, *Sankōhō no kaisetsu* (Commentary on the Structurally Depressed Industries Law), 1983, pp. 82–84.

[83] *Kagaku keizai* (Chemical economics) 30 (April 1983), p. 16.

[84] Upham, *Law and Social Change*, pp. 190–91.

[85] MITI, *Sankōhō no kaisetsu*, p. 58.

[86] Ibid., p. 66.

[87] This discussion is largely drawn from Gotō Akira, "Kōzō chōsei to shijō kikō" (Structural adjustment and the market mechanism), *Kōsei torihiki* 441 (July 1987): 44–45.

pacity, thus leaving market shares stable. In less concentrated industries, cuts were achieved through a shakeout of marginal companies. These were often negotiated rather than purely market driven because cartel members paid marginal firms to leave the industry and thus hand over their market share to the remaining members.[88]

The pullback of firms from declining sectors in the 1980s can be seen in the movement of both capital and labor. Textiles and basic materials, along with shipbuilding, lost the largest numbers of workers. Within basic materials, the iron and steel, and cement, glass, and ceramics sectors lost the most workers. The capital-intensive core processing sectors lost large proportions of their labor forces, from 34 percent of steel workers to 76 percent of aluminum workers, although only in the steel industry were the absolute numbers large. Within basic materials industries MITI includes chemicals, petroleum and coal products, kiln products, iron and steel, and nonferrous metals[89]—that is, those sectors that convert raw materials into intermediate industrial materials processed for use by the machinery, textile, construction, or other sectors for final use by the consumer. Business investment in basic materials was slow, building assets by only 30 percent during the 1980s compared with an increase of 156 percent in machinery sectors. The broad definition of these industries includes such sectors as metal rolling, which, according to one representative of an aluminum rolling firm, MITI considered a service industry and not as crucial as the processing of primary aluminum ingots from bauxite. The upstream branches of basic materials, which processed naphtha, bauxite, or limestone into ethylene, aluminum, or cement, were the focus of the capacity cartels. These industries experienced drops in invested capital as firms shut down and wrote off excess capacity. These ranged from 11 percent in cement to 80 percent in aluminum. In the case of aluminum, the shutdowns resulted in the near elimination of domestic manufacturing. In cement and petrochemicals, however, the capacity cartels helped firms survive by moderating price competition. In aluminum, imports took over domestic markets, although MITI and firms worked together to ensure that a large share came from Japanese equity-owned plants overseas. Both petrochemicals and cement, despite high domestic prices, remained net exporters rather than importers.

Under U.S. pressure to abandon the SDIL, MITI switched to the Structural Conversion Facilitation Law (SCFL) of 1987, which continued in force as of 1994.[90] Cuts were made under this law in sixteen industries,

---

[88] Ibid.

[89] MITI, *Kōgyō tōkei hyō* (Census of manufactures, report by industries), 1980.

[90] The full name of the law is Sangyō Kōzō Tenkan Enkatsuka Rinji Sochi Hō (Temporary Measures Law to Facilitate Industrial Structure Conversion).

the largest in steel and cement.[91] Technically, the capacity-cutting process is made up of plans worked out between MITI and individual firms. In practice, it is difficult to say how different the process is from the cartel process under the SDIL, although MITI may play a stronger coordinating role. In the steel industry, cuts were based on an industry-wide consensus about how much the total cuts should be. Some firms, however, used a less drastic target as their guideline.[92] The law provided tax benefits for writing off losses and depreciating equipment for new enterprises, government guarantees for loans against retired equipment, and subsidized Japan Development Bank loans.[93]

U.S. pressure also led to new restrictions on cartels in 1991 and 1992 when Japan tightened its Antimonopoly Law. Nevertheless, the new restrictions were not as stringent as the U.S. government and the FTC wanted; and enforcement has not appeared to produce any dramatic curtailment in the informal use of cartels. One principal reform was to raise administrative surcharges from 1.5 percent of total sales to 6 percent for up to three years. This was lower than the 15–20 percent the U.S. had suggested and the 10 percent the FTC had suggested. There was no broad political support for tougher penalties in Japan; and business opposition, especially from construction, kept the penalties at only 6 percent. Similar business pressure limited an increase in criminal penalties from five million yen up to one hundred million yen instead of the several hundred million yen recommended by the FTC.[94] Additional new FTC policies included publication of guidelines and new measures to encourage private damage suits. In 1991 the commission unleashed a brief spate of dramatic enforcement, focused particularly on the basic materials industries. It hit the cement industry with administrative surcharges larger than all previous ones put together and slapped the plastic-wrap industry, a downstream branch of the petrochemical industry, with the first criminal antimonopoly case in twenty years. Nevertheless, the two cases seem to have had little impact on behavior in the cement or petrochemical industries and have not been followed up by the FTC.

Why has the FTC not enforced the law more vigorously? The Japan Federation of Bar Associations (Nihon Bengoshi Renmei) criticizes the FTC for being too closely linked to the bureaucracy and favoring probusiness Ministry of Finance (MOF) and MITI perspectives rather than consumer welfare.[95] The head commissioners of the FTC have come

---

[91] "Sangyō Kōzō Tenkan Enkatsuka Rinji Sochi Hō no jisshi jōkyō ni tsuite" (On the status of implementation of the Temporary Measures Law to Facilitate Industrial Structure Conversion), unpublished document, MITI, October 1993, pp. 5–6.

[92] Interview with retired steel-firm executive, 1994.

[93] MITI, Policy Bureau (Tsūsanshō Seisaku Kyoku), Kōzō Tenkan Enkatsuka Hō no kaisetsu (Commentary on the Structural Conversion Facilitation Law), 1987, p. 3.

[94] Nihon keizai shinbun, 13 March 1992.

[95] Nihon keizai shinbun, 7 February 1991.

from MOF almost from its inception. According to informal custom, the other four commission posts are held by one other retiree from MOF, one from MITI, one from the Justice Ministry, and one from within the ranks of the FTC.[96] The potential for the FTC to sacrifice consumer and citizen interests because of pressure from other agencies was highlighted by testimony from a former FTC member, who claimed that the FTC had backed down on a criminal investigation of a group of contractors after they gave a large bribe to former Construction Minister Nakamura Kishirō.[97]

Thus, although U.S. pressure did create stronger penalties, they had little political support in Japan. It is true that in the early 1990s the media were critical of Antimonopoly Law violations. This criticism, however, did not itself produce a swell of political support for tougher enforcement. As we shall see, the media were happy to report on FTC actions but continued to cooperate with business by not exposing price-fixing arrangements for fear of losing their sources.

MITI no longer has formal authority to sponsor cartels in basic industries, but a weak Antimonopoly Law and feeble enforcement make it possible for private governance to continue. Although trade associations and MITI can no longer formally work out cartels, under the SCFL industry can work out a consensus, which MITI can implement through individual plans. Formal law has changed; nevertheless, trade associations continue to provide private-interest governance.

[96] Personal communication from Professor Shōda Akira, 1994.
[97] *Japan Times*, 29 July 1994.

CHAPTER THREE

The Aluminum Industry

The energy-intensive Japanese aluminum industry became internationally uncompetitive overnight as a result of the 1973 OPEC oil-price increase. To shore up the most efficient refiners, the government granted subsidies to the industry and authorized a series of plant-scrapping cartels. Nevertheless, by 1987, 97 percent of the domestic industry had been shut down.

As we shall see, aluminum refining was not unique in having very high costs: the steel, cement, and petrochemical industries have succeeded in passing on costs through prices 48–60 percent above import prices. Aluminum, however, which only managed to charge an average of 13 percent above import prices, was run out of business (see figure 3–1). Imports jumped from 40 percent of domestic consumption in 1980 to 97 percent by 1987 (see figure 3–2). Unlike cement users, aluminum buyers had no strong cartel of their own to absorb the prices; and, unlike the steel and petrochemical industries, aluminum refiners had no high-tech products with which to hook their buyers.

The aluminum case has been cited to support the argument that Japanese policy toward declining industries allows the market to determine when and how industries will decline.[1] Paul Sheard, for example, claims that many treatments of Japanese declining industry are misguided because they put excessive emphasis on public assistance. He says that the role of private institutions in helping industries in decline is actually much more important. Sheard argues that bank-centered corporate groups play an important role in assisting firms in declining industrial sectors.[2] His study of the financial burdens assumed by the other

[1] See, for example, Akira Goto, "Japan: A Sunset Industry," in Merton Peck, ed., *The World Aluminum Industry in a Changing Era* (Baltimore: Johns Hopkins University Press for Resources for the Future, 1988).

[2] Paul Sheard, "Corporate Organisation and Industrial Adjustment in the Japanese

Figure 3-1. Ratio of domestic aluminum price to import price

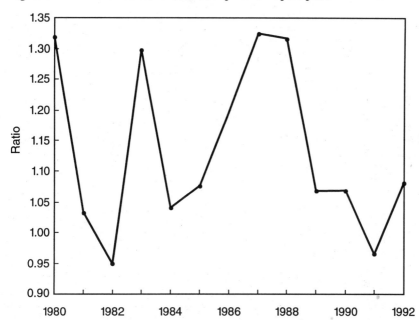

Source: Figures all from Japan Aluminum Federation. Domestic price figures are based on price surveys by the *Nihon tekkō shinbun* (Japan steel newspaper) which sends reporters to the trading companies to ask about their transaction prices. The price cited is an average of these prices and reflects a mixture of spot and other prices.The domestic price includes delivery and a wholesaler's margin, neither of which is included in the import price.

firms in the aluminum-refining firms' corporate groups (commonly known as *keiretsu*) shows that the main banks related to the parent companies of the aluminum firms shouldered the financial burden of shutting down aluminum refining by reducing interest rates. Trading companies assisted by continuing to purchase aluminum from the domestic industry even when it was no longer competitive with imported aluminum. Banks, trading companies, and other keiretsu-related firms in effect gave the parent companies interest-free loans by buying stocks in the aluminum-refining firms and waiting for the parent companies to reimburse them until they liquidated the companies. The bulk of the losses were eventually borne by the parent companies. Sheard shows that direct government subsidies amounted to only a quarter of the losses incurred by the private companies.

Aluminium Industry," in Sheard, ed., *International Adjustment and the Japanese Firm* (St. Leonards, Australia: Allen & Unwin, 1992), pp. 125–39.

Figure 3-2. Import share of the Japanese primary aluminum ingot market

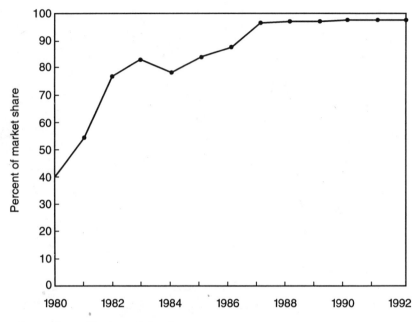

Source: Japan Aluminum Federation.

Sheard's study is valuable in explaining the role of financial-group relationships in facilitating sectoral decline. Nevertheless, he is wrong to conclude that government policy was therefore unimportant. In fact, the state used subsidies to gain bargaining leverage to shape private actions, and the particular pace and manner in which the industry was shut down reflected state priorities. Japanese aluminum refining was not simply shut down but largely replaced, with state and private financing and planning, by Japanese-owned refining capacity overseas. While private assistance was important, it was given partly in response to state pressure on private firms to fulfill their keiretsu obligations in exchange for public subsidies. Moreover, certain financial maneuvers, although they had an economic function, also played a crucial role in the political process of bargaining over government subsidies.

FACTORS BEHIND ALUMINUM'S DECLINE

It is a truism that the reason for the decline of Japanese aluminum refining was the 1973 and 1979 jump in oil prices. The industry was dependent on oil for 71 percent of its energy, in contrast to the U.S. and

Canadian industries, which used almost no petroleum, and European refining, which was dependent on oil for only 11 percent of its needs.[3] Before the oil shock, energy costs accounted for 30 percent of Japanese production costs.[4] This subsequently jumped to 60–70 percent. In 1978 electricity cost 7.6 yen/kilowatt hour in Japan, while Canada, with a bountiful supply of hydroelectric power, had rates as low as 1 yen/kwhr. By the mid-1980s Japanese electricity rates had climbed to 15.5–17 yen/ kwhr. Canada's remained at 1–1.5 yen, and rates in the United States and Australia hovered between 3 and 5 yen.[5] In 1978 the production costs of even the most efficient one-third of Japan's capacity was 297,000 yen/ton; imported aluminum ingots, including a 9-percent tariff as well as freight and insurance charges, cost only 230,000 yen/ton.[6] By 1980 the second oil shock shot Japan's production costs up to 460,000– 560,000 yen/ton, while Canadian and U.S. imports were priced at 370,000 yen/ton.[7]

Certainly the oil crisis caught all advanced industrialized countries by surprise; in this sense Japan was a hapless victim of the winds of economic change. Nevertheless, the price jump only partly explains the industry's troubles. In one sense, it simply exacerbated other problems— some pervasive in all countries' basic materials industries, some peculiar to Japan. Aluminum refining, like other basic materials industries throughout the world, faced stagnant demand in the 1970s because of slower economic and less material-intensive growth and competition from new materials. In addition, the industry typified the problem of government incentives' encouraging rapid investment in Japanese basic materials industries, which left firms with overcapacity in the slow-growing 1970s and 80s.

The government began nurturing the industry in the 1930s and supported it after the war with tax incentives and low-interest Japan Development Bank loans, just as it did other heavy industries.[8] The rapid expansion in investment was also motivated by the full set strategy, the attempt by each keiretsu to enter all industries that enjoy an implicit

[3] Yano Keizai Kenkyūjo (Yano Economic Research Institute), *Arumi shijō no tenbō to senryaku* (Outlook and strategy in the aluminum market), 1985, p. 25.
[4] Anzai Masao, *Arumi kōgyō ron* (The aluminum industry) (Tokyo: Dayamondo Sha, 1971), p. 404.
[5] *Light Metal Tsūshin*, 14 November 1978; *Shūkan dayamondo*, 8 March 1986, p. 83; Yano Keizai Kenkyūjo, *Arumi shijō no tenbō to senryaku*, p. 17.
[6] *Nihon keizai shinbun*, 18 September 1978.
[7] *Nikkan kei kinzoku*, 9 June 1981; *Nihon keizai shinbun*, 20 June 1981.
[8] Sekiguchi Sueo, "Shigen kakō kōgyō no sangyō chōsei" (Industrial adjustment in natural resource processing industries), in Sekiguchi, ed., *Nihon no sangyō chōsei* (Japan's industrial adjustment) (Tokyo: Nihon Keizai Shinbunsha, 1981), p. 202; Shōwa Denkō, *Shōwa Denkō Aruminiumu 50 nen shi* (Fifty-year history of Showa Denko Aluminum), 1984, pp. 81, 192.

government guarantee. Keiretsu expected the government would reward early entrants by freezing production, thus granting them monopoly benefits, or by providing direct state largess.

State encouragement of new investment brought large numbers of new firms into aluminum refining. The fact that refineries must be run consistently at full capacity to maximize efficiency discouraged established refiners from expanding capacity. But MITI promoted new investment in the 1960s with financing and government-negotiated technology transfer from foreign refiners.[9] It appears that the implicit promise of a government guarantee encouraged the industry's continued expansion, even after the OPEC price hike in October 1973. Although the rise in oil prices should have signaled that the oil-dependent industry was hopelessly uncompetitive, between 1975 and 1977 Japanese refiners expanded by 20 percent what was already the world's second largest aluminum-refining industry. It is difficult to research firms' spending for the entire period because the refining divisions were taken off the stock market in 1976 and thus do not show up in securities reports. But partial evidence shows that companies did not simply complete nearly finished projects after October 1973; in at least two cases they made major new expenditures (see table 3–1). Sumitomo Chemical, for instance, had only invested 2.5 billion yen on its new Tōyo plant by December 1973, out of a total budget of twenty-five billion yen. Nevertheless, in spite of an increase in estimated costs to thirty-seven billion during 1974, it brought its new 99,000-ton plant on line, representing a 7-percent increase in Japan's total capacity. Similarly, Mitsubishi Chemical spent 7.5 billion of total projected costs of 17.4 billion to add one hundred thousand tons of capacity by December 1973, but it went on to complete the project. More understandably, because more than 60 percent of a total construction budget of 23.4 billion had been spent by September 1973, Japan Light Metal also completed the expansion of its Niigata plant after the OPEC price hike. Sumitomo Light Metal brought a new plant on line as late as February 1977. Opinions about the wisdom of continuing to build new capacity, however, were by no means uniform. Showa Denko abandoned the planned expansion of its Chiba plant,[10] and two other aluminum rolling companies abandoned their plans to enter the refining industry. It may be unfair to criticize in hindsight the aluminum refiners' investment decisions. Nevertheless, the fact that they were continuing to add capacity even as they discussed government assistance to the industry with MITI and the Diet suggests that they were willing to continue to make

[9] Imai Ken'ichi, *Gendai sangyō soshiki* (Contemporary industrial organization) (Tokyo: Iwanami Shoten, 1976), pp. 108–12.

[10] *Shōwa Denkō Kabushiki Kaisha yūka shōken hōkoku* (Showa Denko securities report), June, December 1974 issues.

Table 3-1. Investment decisions in the aluminum-refining industry after the October 1973 OPEC price hike

Date	Events	Cumulative investment in new projects to increase production capacity (in billions of yen)		
		Sumitomo Chemical	Mitsubishi Chemical	Japan Light Metal
7/73			1.5	
9/73				13.8
10/73	OPEC announces price hike			
11/73	Diet decides emergency measures to cut petroleum and electricity use 10%			
12/73	Government announces state of emergency in energy and policy to restrict overall demand; temporary partial suspension of production by Showa Denko due to electricity shortage	2.5		
1/74			7.5	
3/74	FTC advises aluminum refiners to stop price fixing			
4/74				14.8
5/74	Government permits 57% increase in price of electicity			
6/74		9.8		
7/74	MITI permits aluminum price increaase from 266,700 yen/ton to 312,700 yen/ton		14.2	
9/74	Sumitomo stops production at Kikumoto plant			19.8
10/74	MITI forms Aluminum Subcommittee of Industrial Structure Council to Develop Long-Term Vision for Refining Industry			
12/74	Showa Denko idles part of capacity; Japan Light Metal cancels plans for new additional production capacity	18.9		
1/75	Japan Light Metal and Mitsubishi Chemical idle part of capacity		16.3	
3/75	Sumitomo starts production in part of its Toyo plant			
7/75	Light Metal Refines Association petitions Diet for subsidies			
1/76	Mitsubishi Chemical reports plant completed		19.4	
2/77	Sumikei Aluminum begins production at Sakata plant	37.0		23.4

Source: Japan Light Metal, Yūka shōken hōkokusho sōran (Securities report), 1973–75 issues; Mitsubishi Chemical Indutries, Yūka shōken hōkokusho sōran (Securities report), 1973–76 issues; Sumitomo Chemical Industries, Yūka shōken hōkokusho sōran (Securities report), 1973–75 issues; Showa Denko, Shōwa Denkō Aruminiumu 50 nen shi (A Fifty-year History of the Showa Denko Aluminum Company), 1984, pp. 390–95; Yano Keizai Kenkyūjo (Yano Economic Research Institute), Arumi shijō no tenbō to senryaku (Outlook and strategy in the aluminum market), 1985, p. 55.

Note: Total expenditures and exact dates of completion not available. Latest available projected expenditures listed for 1977, by which date the projects were completed.

large, risky investments because they expected government subsidies or import protection if international market forces continued unfavorable. Eventually, almost all of Japan's refining capacity was scrapped; but in the initial stages of policy discussions, government proposed to scrap the less efficient capacity to enable the most efficient plants to survive. Given this apparent commitment to maintaining some aluminum plants, the makers decided to continue building more efficient plants, even if they were unlikely to prove internationally competitive.

Ironically, another important reason for the decline of the industry was that a number of developing countries followed Japan's development strategy of targeting the basic materials sector. Until the 1970s, an oligopoly of six giant integrated aluminum firms—the "majors," from the United States, Canada, France, and Switzerland—kept prices high and stable by controlling 80 percent of the non-Communist world's aluminum, 80 percent of its bauxite, and 90 percent of its alumina. In the late 1950s Japanese firms paid four times as much for electricity as Canadian firms did and more than twice as much as U.S. or even West German firms did.[11] Nevertheless, the high prices maintained by the six majors, combined with a 15 percent tariff, enabled the Japanese companies to sell at a good profit.

This stable world oligopoly was disrupted in the 1970s by a number of developing countries, such as Brazil and Venezuela, that established state-owned aluminum refining firms to use their abundant hydroelectric power. An official of the Japan Aluminum Federation (JAF) sighed, "There's no way you can compete with state-owned companies that want to produce to earn foreign exchange and will keep producing no matter how much money they lose."[12] But Brazil and Venezuela, of course, were simply trying to hurdle the barriers of technology, capital costs, and economies of scale to break into new industries, in the same way as the Japanese state had supported its private firms during the 1930s, 50s, and 60s. The JAF official's lament was doubly ironic because Japan's own investments in productive capacity in developing countries contributed to the worldwide aluminum glut of the 1980s.

A final problem for the industry was that it had been built, like much of Japanese industry, almost completely on bank loans rather than equity capital. In 1976 outstanding debt stood at six hundred billion yen, compared to only 59.3 billion in put-in capital;[13] and by 1978 debt had grown to eight hundred billion yen as firms borrowed to cover their losses. Although the banks were charging only the prime rate as a way of

[11] Sangyō Kōzō Chōsakai, *Industrial Structure in Japan*, vol. 3 (in Japanese) (Tokyo: Tsūshō Sangyō Kenkyūsho, 1964), cited in Goto, "Japan: A Sunset Industry," pp. 90–120.
[12] Interview, 1987.
[13] *Light Metal Tsūshin*, 9 August 1977.

aiding the industry, the interest charges alone amounted to sixty billion yen/year, or approximately sixty thousand yen/ton of aluminum at a time when import prices were 230,000 yen/ton. By 1981, when it was announced that capacity would be cut to seventy thousand tons/year, refiners were carrying one trillion yen in debt.[14] Who would take responsibility for these bad debts? That was a central question of the aluminum policy negotiations, although it was never publicly stated in such bold terms.

The state targeted aluminum in the 1930s because of its military importance for building aircraft. In the 1950s, 60s, and early 70s MITI encouraged aluminum production because of its importance as an industrial material. During the 1960s, the ministry also supported plans for Japanese overseas investment to take advantage of cheap overseas energy while continuing to encourage domestic investment. Once oil prices skyrocketed in 1973 and 1974, however, MITI's strategic goals shifted to scrapping the least efficient portion of domestic capacity and replacing it with Japanese-owned production facilities overseas.

MITI originally targeted the industry in self-defense against the high prices of the international majors' cartel. After the oil shock the ministry's principal goal in maintaining a domestic refining industry was security of supply at stable prices. MITI thought Japan could bargain for import prices from a stronger position if it provided for some of its needs itself. It also held that maintaining domestic refining would preserve skills that would be needed if the industry had to be reexpanded in the future. Tempering these considerations, however, was a conviction that Japan should not go too far in supporting an industry that wasted scarce electricity.

Starting from these broad goals, MITI encouraged refiners to scrap the least efficient domestic capacity and invest overseas. To encourage compliance, the government provided the following forms of assistance.

1. *Subsidies*. By Sheard's calculation, the industry was granted as much as eighty-two billion yen in subsidies between 1978 and 1985. Most of this (sixty billion yen) was in the form of tariff rebates on imported aluminum. A smaller subsidy (3.6 billion yen) was also provided for stockpiling aluminum during periods of oversupply. Most of the rest was for conversion from oil- to coal-fired electricity production.[15] Over and above the seventy billion yen were subsidies for workers in structurally depressed industries.

2. *Assistance from MITI in pressuring buyers to buy domestic aluminum.*

[14] Ibid., *Nihon keizai shinbun*, 18 August 1978; *Tekkō shinbun*, 23 October 1978; *Nihon keizai shinbun*, 19 October 1978.
[15] Sheard, "Corporate Organisation," p. 130.

3. *Financial assistance in investing overseas.* This assistance came in part from large low-interest loans for the projects (approximately 276 billion yen) and in part from the use of the tariff rebates to provide tariff discrimination in favor of imports from Japanese-owned plants overseas.[16]

4. *Government promotion of production and capacity-scrapping cartels.*

5. *Tax benefits as a designated structurally depressed industry.*[17]

There was considerable debate over how much assistance the industry should receive, and we shall turn to these negotiations shortly. First, however, let us look at the incentives that encouraged Japanese overseas investment in aluminum refining. Planning for overseas investment had begun in the early 1960s among Japanese private firms for projects in New Zealand and Venezuela and by both Japanese firms and the Japanese government for projects in Brazil and Indonesia.[18] None of these projects, however, were brought to fruition until after the oil shock, when plans for switching from domestic aluminum to aluminum produced in Japanese-owned overseas plants were stepped up.

These plans were not intended to secure complete Japanese control over its aluminum supplies. The country had always depended for part of its ingot supplies on purchases from foreign plants, and imports from Japanese-owned overseas plants would not replace these supplies. Moreover, the overseas plants were not to be completely Japanese-owned or managed. The share of Japanese ownership was planned initially to be 75 percent in the Indonesian project; 50 percent in New Zealand, Canada, and Australia; 49 percent in Brazil; 25 percent in the United States; and 20 percent in Venezuela.[19]

MITI wanted these projects to be brought on line as domestic capacity was phased out to provide a smooth transition from Japanese domestic to Japanese overseas aluminum and avoid increasing imports from foreign firms.[20] The Japanese had a specific term for aluminum imported from Japanese-equity plants overseas: "development imports" (*kaihatsu yunyū*). Development imports did not mean imports from developing countries or those from plants set up with government money but specifically aluminum produced in Japanese-owned facilities overseas.[21] As David Arase points out, imports from overseas Japanese projects were

---

[16] Ibid.

[17] Several measures were discussed but not adopted, including higher tariffs, mergers among the refining companies, subsidized electricity, and government-sponsored averaging of domestic and import prices.

[18] Shōwa Denkō, *50 nen shi*, pp. 250–56.

[19] Yano Keizai Kenkyūjo, *Arumi shijō no tenbō to senryaku*, p. 28.

[20] Ibid., p. 26; *Nihon keizai shinbun*, 24 October 1978.

[21] Interview with Japanese chemical company executive, 1992.

called development imports 'because they were developed to supply Japanese industry."[22] It appears that the establishment of secure supplies of basic materials was a more important motive for Japanese government financial support than any interest in the economic development of poorer countries. This is evident in the Overseas Economic Cooperation Fund's (OECF) argument to aluminum smelters that the reason it provided 50 percent of the financing for the Singapore complex, while the Asahan aluminum project only got 40 percent, was that supplies of petrochemicals were more vital to the Japanese economy than were aluminum supplies.[23]

My JAF informant said that MITI and the aluminum industry considered development imports to be essentially equivalent to domestic aluminum because they were produced in Japanese-owned plants.[24] When MOF suggested in 1981 that tariffs be cut to 3 or 4 percent, MITI responded that this would put undue pressure on imports from Japanese-owned plants overseas, implying that the overseas plants could not yet produce enough aluminum to replace the domestic supply and that it would be unacceptable to import additional aluminum produced by foreign firms.[25]

Both MITI and the private firms appear to have shared in planning the overseas projects. Private firms were certainly interested in overseas production, and the Light Metal Smelters' Association played a strong role in lobbying the government, the banks, and the Keidanren to support the overseas projects.[26] But, according to the JAF, the government made the important decisions about whether countries were risky places to invest and chose the host countries in part based on broad foreign-policy considerations. The government also provided considerable financial support for the projects. In both Indonesia and Brazil the OECF initially provided 40 percent of the Japanese equity. In addition both the OECF and the Export-Import Bank made large loans to the aluminum firms for the projects.[27]

Besides direct funding, MITI also used the much contested tariff-rebate system to encourage refiners to invest overseas. Under this program approximately half of the 9-percent tariff during 1978 and 1979, and nearly all of it during 1982–87, was rebated on a portion of Japan's aluminum imports. As we shall see, there was considerable debate in

[22] David Arase, *Buying Power: The Political Economy of Japan's Foreign Aid* (Boulder, Colo.: Lynne Rienner Publishers, 1995), p. 24.
[23] Asahan did eventually get its allotment raised to 50 percent. Interview, JAF official, 1994.
[24] Interview, 1987.
[25] *Nihon keizai shinbun*, 3 October 1981.
[26] Interview with chemical company official, 1992. Interview with JAF official, 1994.
[27] Interviews with JAF official, 1987, 1994.

Japan as to whether this aid should be given to the industry at all; and the U.S. strongly opposed the rebate because it discriminated against U.S. aluminum ingots.

Although the official purpose of the rebate was to subsidize capacity scrapping and help refiners shore up their remaining capacity, it was also used as a carrot to get domestic refiners to invest overseas. When the U.S. criticized Japan for using the rebate to keep out U.S. aluminum ingots, MITI denied that it had tied tariff rebates and overseas investment and said that the Japanese program of investment in overseas aluminum projects was simply a form of foreign aid.[28] My JAF informant, however, said that MITI decided how much tariff rebate each company would receive based on three factors: (1) the amount of capacity scrapped, (2) investment in overseas aluminum smelting, and (3) efforts to maintain domestic capacity. The Mitsubishi affiliate, for instance, was given greater financial rewards because it invested more overseas. The JAF account of the connection between tariff rebates and overseas investment is corroborated by newspaper accounts of the original MITI plan for the tariff quota system.[29]

By 1983 the U.S. government and Alcoa were accusing Japan of using the tariff rebate to keep out imported aluminum ingots produced in foreign-owned plants. As I have explained, the rebate was used to help aluminum refiners invest overseas. But it is difficult to tell whether MITI also used it to get refiners to import from their overseas refineries rather than buy completely foreign ingots. Three facts suggest that MITI could have used the system for this purpose. First, the rebate was not allowed to be used for imports brought in on a spot-market rather than long-term basis. While all imports from Japanese-owned refineries were on long-term contract, most of the aluminum from foreign-owned refineries was bought on a spot basis.[30] Second, the rebate was not given automatically but at the discretion of MITI. Third, MITI had long said openly that it intended to use the tariff rebate as a flexible tool to pressure domestic companies not to buy foreign imports. In 1977, when the rebate was first proposed, it was suggested that it be given to users in exchange for their using domestic aluminum, although this was not done at that time. In 1981, the *Nihon keizai shinbun* reported that, because of opposition within MITI to subsidizing energy or raising the aluminum tariff, the ministry had decided to use the tariff-rebate system to restrict imports.[31] It would allow the importing rollers and trading companies not to pay

[28] Interview with official from MITI Basic Industries Bureau, Nonferrous Metals Division, 1987.
[29] *Light Metal Tsūshin*, 13 October 1981; *Tekkō shinbun*, 14 October 1981.
[30] Yano Keizai Kenkyujō, *Arumi shijō no tenbō to senryaku*, p. 26.
[31] *Nihon keizai shinbun*, 11 July 1981.

the 9-percent tariff but would then "strongly direct them to buy as much domestic aluminum as possible."[32] The deliberation council repeated MITI's proposal, recommending that the tariff-rebate system be used to prevent a rapid increase in imports.[33] When the U.S. government complained that the rebate was keeping out U.S. aluminum imports in favor of Japanese domestic aluminum and Japanese overseas equity aluminum, MITI defended itself by arguing that U.S. aluminum was benefiting disproportionately from the program and coming in under lower-than-average tariffs.[34] Nevertheless, because the rebate was not allocated automatically but at the discretion of MITI, the fact that the rebate might be registered as having been applied to American aluminum ingots did not mean the system encouraged imports from non-Japanese–owned refiners in the U.S. The rebates encouraged exactly what the JAF understood them to encourage: gradual cuts in Japanese domestic capacity combined with continued overseas investment so that domestic supplies would be replaced with Japanese-owned supplies from overseas.

Once the projects were completed, two factors combined to make them less profitable than expected: lower prices and a higher yen. Lower-than-expected prices cut into profit margins, while the higher yen made repaying the large yen loans from the Japanese government much more difficult because the dollar-based revenues from the aluminum sales had declined in value. By early 1987 the industry association was pressuring the government to reduce its interest rates; it argued that it had made the investments not simply for profit but in the national interest.[35] This position seems to exaggerate the industry's reluctance to invest abroad and be another example of the association's using past state incentives as an excuse for demanding that the state share investment risks. Certainly, the government played the role of planner, promoter, and financier of the overseas projects and even provided tariff rebates for investing overseas. Yet given how vocal the refiners were over other issues, it seems likely they would have protested had they really had major objections to overseas investment.

As table 3–2 shows, by 1990 Japan had equity stakes of 20–59 percent in nine aluminum smelters in a wide range of countries. Six were in the

---

[32] Ibid., 20 June 1981; 11 July 1981.

[33] Ibid., 7 October 1981. For a broader discussion of the functions of deliberation councils in the Japanese political economy see Frank Schwartz, "Of Fairy Cloaks and Familiar Talks: The Politics of Consultation," in Gary D. Allinson and Yasunori Sone, eds., *Political Dynamics in Contemporary Japan* (Ithaca: Cornell University Press, 1993), pp. 217–41; and Frank Schwartz, *Advice and Consent: The Politics of Consultation in Japan* (forthcoming).

[34] Interview with official at MITI Basic Industries Bureau, Nonferrous Metals Section, 1987.

[35] Interview with JAF official, 1987.

Table 3–2. Overseas aluminium smelters invested in by Japanese

Project	Japanese equity	Annual capacity (metric tons)	Japanese metal take (metric tons)	Completion	Power
Enzas (New Zealand)	21%	244,000	50,000	1971	Hydro
Venalum (Venezuela)	20%	456,000	170,000	1978	Hydro
Alpack (Canada)	50%	90,000	45,000	1977	Hydro
Asahan (Indonesia)	59%	225,000	135,000	1984	Hydro
Albras (Brazil)	49%	320,000	160,000	1985	Hydro
Boyne (Australia)	50%	230,000	115,000	1982	Coal
Intalco (U.S.)	25%	270,000	68,000	1966	Hydro
Eastalco (U.S.)	25%	170,000	42,000	1970	Coal
Alouette (Canada)	20%	215,000	43,000	1992	Hydro
Portland (Aust)	5%	364,000	32,000	1986	Coal
Total			860,000		

Source: Japan Aluminum Federation, 1990, 1994. My thanks to Mahesh Rajan for sharing this information with me.

politically stable countries of heavy British and French settlement. The three largest projects in terms of the Japanese metal take, however, were in developing nations. The purpose of the overseas investment was not simply to provide profit opportunities for Japanese firms or development opportunities for poor countries. Rather, it was to secure supplies of refined aluminum for Japan. From its peak of 1,193,000 tons in 1977, Japanese aluminum production fell to 18,884 by 1992. By 1993 overseas investment had replaced 78 percent of this lost production with 910,000 tons of development imports.[36]

POLICY-MAKING ARENAS

Although the aluminum industry took much of the initiative for moving production overseas, it was more reluctant to cut domestic capacity. With MITI and MOF, the industry went through a long series of nego-

[36] Estimate by Marubeni Corporation, Light Metal Department, September 1993. Received from JAF.

tiations over how much capacity would be cut and how much subsidy the industry would receive. It pleaded consistently for maximum subsidies and minimum cuts, while cheapskate MOF dug in its heels against subsidies. MITI was initially in favor of maintaining as much domestic capacity as possible. But once it was clear that both MOF and U.S. opposition made it impossible to keep the industry in business on a subsidized basis, MITI switched to cajoling and pressuring the industry to go along with cuts. The ministry used a deliberation council as a public forum for industry opponents to badger its representatives into submitting to the MITI program of plant scrapping. Once it was settled that there would be no complete operating subsidy for the industry, negotiations boiled down to bargaining over how much aid the industry would receive for its capacity cuts.

Most public negotitations centered on direct subsidies. Loans for overseas investment, which were officially considered foreign aid, were not subject to public debate. Attempts to restrict imports through administrative guidance were, of course, also not discussed openly. Permission to engage in cartel activities and receive tax benefits and labor subsidies were all automatic because of aluminum's designation as a structurally depressed industry, although the speed at which the capacity-cutting cartel would proceed and the amount of reward the industry would receive was a matter of negotiation between MITI and the refiners' trade associations.

The bargaining process began in 1975 with the establishment of a deliberation council to discuss the industry; and it lasted until December 1985, when the Japanese government buckled to U.S. pressure and agreed to abolish its tariff on refined aluminum. The most intense bargaining was in 1977 and 1978, when the industry was suffering from falling international prices and a rising yen, and in 1981 and 1982, when it was hit by another sharp drop in prices. Among Japan's declining basic materials, the policy-making process toward aluminum refining was unique in involving this extended public debate. Because the industry was unable to use a cartel successfully to pass its costs on fully to its customers, it alone could demand government subsidies through the Diet.

Bargaining over the terms of assistance was divided between two arenas, each involving different sets of actors and addressing different issues. The Aluminum Subcommittee of the Industrial Structure Council was dominated by MITI and the refining industries, who bargained over the degree to which the industries would go along with MITI's cartel and overseas-investment plans in exchange for how much they would get in the way of subsidies. To an important extent, this negotiation went on in the deliberation council, where the trading companies, rolling firms, and other users of aluminum who paid high prices that resulted from anti competitive activities in the refining industry were also represented. These players sometimes managed to bargain for their own rewards for agreeing, but sometimes they were simply pressured into going along. The banks, interested in funds to keep their loans from going bad, also participated in the deliberation council, although they kept a low public profile. Formally the deliberation council made independent recommendations to MITI. In practice, however, it worked from documents prepared by MITI and, as we shall see, did not deviate far from them. MITI worked out tentative deals with the refining industry over subsidy amounts through the deliberation-council process, but final amounts were decided in a second policy arena through negotiations with politicians and MOF. Although MOF was opposed to subsidizing the industry, the association lobbied local politicians from the LDP and the opposition parties, the Keidanren, and top LDP officials to intervene in its favor.

The MITI-Industry Arena

MITI and the aluminum industry concluded a series of agreements over how much capacity would be scrapped in exchange for what level of financial assistance. From a peak capacity of 1,640,000 tons/year in 1977, a series of four plans cut capacity to 350,000 tons/year before MITI finally ran out of subsidies and capacity dropped to 35,000 (see table 3–3). Which side pushed for capacity scrapping, and which side decided what company would cut how much? My JAF informant said the companies were not forced to cut capacity but had asked the government for help in doing so. Nevertheless, the JAF bargained hard for assistance in exchange for capacity cuts; and both it and MITI made the connection clear between financial rewards and capacity cutting. For instance, JAF president Nakayama Ichirō responded to MITI's August 1978 capacity-cutting proposal by stating that "unless the government sets out very clearly how much subsidy will be provided for industrial restructuring, we can't put forward an industry opinion."[37] MITI's approach was apparent when its basic industries bureau chief, Ueda Moriaki, called together the presidents of the five aluminum smelters in October 1982 to explain the government-subsidized stockpiling system and tell them he wanted to see a restructuring plan.[38] The refiners balked at scrapping as much capacity as MITI suggested. Although in 1978 MITI was offering assistance to help the industry cut back to 750,000 tons of capacity, the JAF refused to make cuts below 1,100,000 tons until 1981.[39]

[37] Tekkō shinbun, 23 August 1978.
[38] Asahi shinbun, 9 October 1982.
[39] Nikkan kei kinzoku, 26 October 1978.

Table 3-3. Change in aluminum refining capacity, 1973-90

	Capacity (in thousands of metric tons)	Restructuring plans/targets
1973	1,238	
1974	1,416	
1975	1,440	Stockpiling plan recommended.
1976	1,588	Light Metal Stockpiling Agency established.
1977	1,641	Capacity to be reduced to 1,250,000 tons.
1978	1,642	Capacity to be reduced to 1,110,000. Tariff-quota scheme established.
1979	1,157	
1980	1,136	
1981	1,136	Capacity to be reduced to 700,000. Tariff-quota scheme replaced by tariff-exemption scheme.
1982	743	
1983	712	
1984	712	Capacity to be reduced to 350,000. Tariff of 1% on the remaining 350,000 tons.
1985	354	
1986	293	
1987	35	Tariff of 1% extended to all aluminum ingot imports.
1990	35	

Source: MITI. My thanks to Mahesh Rajan for sharing this chart with me.

As it did for the cement and petrochemical industries, MITI pushed for the capacity cartels and made hard decisions about allocating cuts among firms. The first capacity-reducing plan was easy to agree on: it merely said that the entire industry would be cut by 24 percent.[40] But firms disagreed over whether the cuts should be distributed evenly. It made most sense to cut back first at the least efficient facilities, and leave economies of scale intact at individual plants. Ultimately the system required companies to submit records showing exactly which capacity they had already idled; then MITI decided which company should scrap how much. The ministry calculated how much subsidy each firm would receive as a reward based on firms' simultaneously scrapping and maintaining domestic capacity and investing overseas.[41]

There are two reasons that explain why MITI took the initiative in pushing the cartels. First, because the industry was holding out for as much aid as it could get, it counted on MITI to do the pushing. The industry appears to have felt it deserved the aid because MITI had

[40] *Light Metal Tsūshin,* 26 May 1978.
[41] Interview with JAF official, 1987.

encouraged investment in aluminum in the first place. As my JAF informant said, "MITI probably felt sympathetic to the plight of the industry
since it had provided incentives for investment."[42] Second, MITI initiated
cartels because refiners were not unified enough to coordinate them on
their own, perhaps in part because of the history of the JAF. Although
the industry association had existed as a control association during the
war, it had not enjoyed a history of long-term relations among a stable
set of firms. Miwa Yoshirō has suggested that old industries often have
more cohesive industrial associations than newer ones because of the
experience of having served as control associations during the war.[43]
Nevertheless, because aluminum's control association had barely started
up before the war, it did not develop the type of cohesive relations among
firms apparent in industries such as steel, which was solidly established at
the time and continued to be stable through the postwar period.

In the late 1930s the military forced the entry of a new firm, Japan
Light Metal, in the face of strong opposition from already existing firms.
The government gave the firm priority for wartime allocation of raw
materials, and it produced nearly 40 percent of Japan's aluminum by the
early 1940s. After the war several firms dropped out of the industry,
leaving only Sumitomo Chemical, Showa Denko, and Japan Light Metal.
During the early 1960s, lured by MITI financial incentives and assistance
in arranging technology transfer from overseas, Mitsubishi Chemical, a
consortium of Mitsui firms, and the Sumitomo rolling company,
Sumitomo Light Metal, entered aluminum refining in the face of strident
opposition by established firms.[44] As we shall see, petrochemicals, a new
postwar industry, and cement, an industry that received many new
entrants after the war, also were unable to coordinate capacity cartels on
their own.

Because of high prices secured by the international aluminum cartel
and rapidly increasing domestic demand, the concentrated Japanese
aluminum industry had little trouble in the 1960s using price leadership
to keep domestic prices high, although no one outside the industry knew
how successful it had been either at that time or during the deliberations
over assistance to the industry. During the deliberations one academic
lamented aiding an industry that had never been very profitable, even
before the oil crisis. Because aluminum-refining operations were only a
part of the larger operations of the parent firms, it was impossible to say
how profitable they were at the time; but industry watchers later learned
that aluminum refining had actually been the most profitable division of

[42] Ibid.
[43] Personal communication.
[44] Anzai, *Arumi kōgyō ron*; Shōwa Denkō, *50 nen shi*; Imai Ken'ichi, *Gendai sangyō
soshiki*, pp. 107–26.

companies such as Mitsubishi Chemical. One official at a downstream rolled-aluminum company remarked with annoyance that a colleague in a refining firm had told him (much after the fact) that, in the late 1960s, production costs had been only 85,000/ton while prices were at two hundred thousand yen.[45]

Immediately after the 1973 oil shock, the refining industry colluded to raise prices in the face of rising costs. In February 1974 the FTC advised it to stop price-fixing activities as part of the commission's general move to slow inflation. By July, however, MITI granted the industry a price increase.[46] Although the refiners were perfectly capable of colluding to set prices, the trade association was not cohesive enough to deal with the 1975–76 drop in domestic demand. Thus, in June 1976 MITI announced that it would watch producers to make sure they observed a 40-percent production cut until stockpiles returned to normal levels. When the process of attempting to form capacity cartels began, the industry also had difficulty coming to agreements, in part because of opposition from Sumitomo Light Metal, which was a user as well as a refiner of aluminum.[47]

Bargaining over capacity scrapping and overseas investment took place between MITI and the refining companies. But the relation between the trading companies and user firms, with both the refiners and MITI was also important because it determined how quickly the market responded to price changes and replaced domestic with foreign aluminum. The Japanese aluminum industry is divided into three major branches: refining (or smelting), initially made up of seven but by the late 1970s composed of five large firms; rolling (or milling), made up of six large firms; and processing, made up of many firms in several fields, which include extruding and dye casting. Two refiners, Japan Light Metal and Sumitomo Light Metal, also rolled aluminum, but most did not. Aluminum rolling accounted for one-third of the demand for new aluminum ingot, while extrusion accounted for approximately one-half. The industry considered the cooperation of the rolling sector key to stabilizing prices in the aluminum ingot market because it was more concentrated than extrusion. But cooperation was difficult, primarily because ties were weak between suppliers and purchasers.[48] The indus-

[45] Interview, 1988.

[46] Shōwa Denkō, *50 nen shi*, p. 393; Chalmers Johnson, *MITI and the Japanese Miracle: The Growth of Industrial Policy, 1925–1975* (Stanford: Stanford University Press, 1982), p. 299.

[47] *Nihon keizai sangyō shinbun*, 25 November 1977; 30 November 1977; *Light Metal Tsūshin*, 26 May 1978.

[48] Richard Samuels also points out that the lack of strong ties between refiners and users was a key factor behind the rapid decline of refining. "The Industrial Destructuring of the Japanese Aluminum Industry," *Pacific Affairs* 56 (Fall 1983): 498.

tries had evolved separately: refining was developed by the large chemical firms; rolling was developed by metalworking, steel, and electric-power companies. In addition, the rollers and refiners had traditionally maintained separate trade associations. During World War II the refining sector was under the Light Metal Control Association, and rolling was under the Metal Industries Control Association. These trade associations had continued separately after the war. The failure to integrate vertically or merge industry associations was widely considered in the smelting industry to be the cause of its woes.[49] MITI tried to build tighter relations among keiretsu-affiliated firms and pushed the trade associations to unite. Reportedly there was some increase in buying within keiretsu groups. But when the price gap grew large between imports and domestic aluminum, this attempt to push stronger keiretsu ties proved to have little effect.

In 1978 the refiners' and rollers' industry associations joined to form the JAF. The rolling industry had been sharing the refiners' troubles because it was unable to pass on high aluminum prices to its consumers: while refiners were losing thirty thousand yen/ton, rollers were losing between forty and fifty thousand. To gain support for a proposed production-cutting cartel, the rollers entered into an alliance with the refiners. To further this alliance, the refiners pushed for the rollers to be included in the Aluminum Subcommittee of the Industrial Structure Deliberation Council, which was formed in 1977. MITI opposed including the processing industry because it was not under the jurisdiction of MITI's Basic Materials Bureau and thus would create organizational problems. As a result, the rollers were included in the main committee but not in the more important Basic Problems Subcommittee. In return for their support for the refiners, MITI granted the rollers a production and price cartel, although only for six months.

The rollers went into the alliance, however, with deep-seated grudges against both the refiners and MITI; and their actual cooperation was limited. The rollers resented what they saw as years of preferential treatment for the refiners as a strategic industry. One rolling-company official quipped that the rollers had acted as a service industry—a play on the Japanese usage of the English term to mean something done for or given to the customer for free. He said that because of MITI pressure the rollers had no choice but to merge the two trade associations, and grumbled that the only assistance they got in return was a six-month cartel. He believed, however, that joining the refiners' trade association and supporting them was a necessary step to getting rid of the domestic

---

[49] See, for instance, *Aruminiumu* 576 (August 1978): 39.

industry once and for all: "We joined the refiners' trade association in order to go to their funeral."[50]

While the rollers did give their political support to the refiners' requests for government assistance, what the refiners really wanted was for the rollers to buy domestic aluminum, even if it were more expensive than imports. There were important limits, however, to the rollers' support for the refiners' cartel. While the rollers were willing to support capacity scrapping as a way of supporting prices and doing away with uncompetitive productive capacity, they did not support the proposal for a joint sales company, which would put upward pressure on prices without necessarily making room for cheaper imports. In spite of pressure from MITI to buy domestic rather than imported aluminum, the rollers paid only small premiums for domestic aluminum.

The trading companies also supported the refiners politically and were willing to buy domestic aluminum at a premium, to fulfill their obligations to the industry based on long-term keiretsu relations. But the unconcentrated extruding industry, which had little hope of forging a cartel, and the aluminum window-sash makers, who were doing quite well on their own, were critical of attempts to protect the refining industry.[51] The trading companies, too, had limits to their sympathy. As the president of one of the major refiners said, it would have been "irresponsible for them to go right out of business and leave their clients high and dry."[52] He alluded to the ethic of relational contracts, which obliged his company to fulfill its commitment to supplying aluminum at the same time that the users' firms were obliged under "gentlemen's agreements" to buy the aluminum. But most users appear to have shared the hardheaded opinion of the chief of the light metal division of Mitsubishi Trading Co: "There is no one who thinks they'd be in trouble if the refining industry disappeared. Rather, everyone is in trouble because there is an unsatisfactory domestic refining industry."[53]

User firms were ultimately unwilling to pay much of a premium for domestic aluminum. The aluminum refiners argued that domestic users should pay a premium for their product because of quality considerations—the rollers should buy domestic aluminum because the domestic refiners could custom-make aluminum to particular specifications and provide after-service. But the rollers scoffed at this suggestion, saying that 99.7-percent pure aluminum was completely standardized inter-

---

[50] Interview, 1987.
[51] Tekkō shinbun, 20 October 1977; Nikkan kinzoku tokuhō, 28 November 1977.
[52] Interview, 1986.
[53] Nikkan kei kinzoku, 22 June 1978.

nationally and that there was no after-service involved with solid metal ingots.[54]

With users reneging on their relational contract obligations, MITI tried to enforce them by pressuring buyers not to purchase imports. In 1978 the ministry said it was asking users voluntarily to restrain their purchases of imports.[55] In April 1981, MITI Basic Industries Bureau Chief Komatsu Kunio said the ministry was using administrative guidance such as surveys of trading companies to discourage imports.[56] MITI had little success in pressuring the rollers to buy domestic, although Sheard found that the trading companies did help the aluminum refiners by paying a premium for their ingots.[57] Indeed, domestic prices averaged 12 percent over import prices from 1980 to 1985, and 15 percent over from 1986 to 1992 (see figure 3–1). Nevertheless, while Sheard has argued that this assistance was evidence of the importance of private relational contracts, the associations did in fact need to be prodded by MITI into fulfilling their contracts.

An important institution in forging the bargain between MITI and the refining industry was the Aluminum Subcommittee of the Industrial Structure Deliberation Council (which I will refer to as the deliberation council). It included representatives from user industries and academics who sharply criticized the refining industry at the beginning of their inclusion in the council in 1977. These critics, however, appear to have had little power and were used by MITI to pressure the refining industry into accepting the ministry's plans.

When the subcommittee was originally convened in 1975, it was headed by Nakayama Ichirō, a refining-industry representative who later became president of JAF. Basically the subcommittee was a forum for the refiners and MITI. In August 1977, when the council was reconvened, Nakayama was replaced by Uchida Tadao, a Tokyo University professor. In addition, the Basic Problems Subcommittee of the Aluminum Subcommittee was headed by Ueno Hiroya, a Seikei University antitrust scholar famous for his opposition to the MITI-engineered Yawata-Fuji steel company merger.[58] More significantly, Ueno, who headed the subcommittee where the actual discussions were to take place, had been involved in planning for the electric-furnace steel industry and recommended capacity scrapping. Thus, MITI's appointments were a signal to the

[54] Interview with rolling-company executive, 1988.

[55] *Asahi shinbun*, 4 July 1978.

[56] *Nikkan kei kinzoku*, 7 April 1981.

[57] Paul Sheard, "How Japanese Firms Manage Industrial Adjustment: A Case Study of Aluminum," paper presented to the AJRC-JARC Joint Meeting, Australian National University, 21–22 August 1987.

[58] Johnson, *MITI*, p. 282.

industry that it was going to be tough in its pressure on the industry to cut back.

Representatives of various user industries sat on the main Aluminum Subcommittee, a rubber stamp for the more important Basic Problems Subcommittee, which was made up of representatives from the refining companies and banks and Professor Ueno.[59] At the first meetings of the Aluminum Subcommittee, the academics and users emphasized that the aluminum industry was no longer viable and that the market must take its course. Uchida stated, "Since Japan has a free economic system, it goes without saying that policy measures are secondary and that it is the industry's own efforts which are important."[60] Ueno and Torino Takuji, a Gakushūin professor, argued that Japan needed to take a hard look at the long-term prospects of the aluminum industry and decide whether it made sense to support the industry.

Torino said, "Japanese aluminum refining is at a comparative disadvantage internationally. It makes sense from the point of view of international economics to import cheap goods. If you decide to maintain domestic refining even though it's expensive, someone is going to bear the burden. I know aluminum needs emergency measures, but we have to take it up as a long-term problem."[61] Ueno warned against being too optimistic about the long-term prospects of the industry and ignoring the short-term problems, "since the medium-to-long term is an accumulation of short-terms."[62] A representative of the electronics-appliance industry, which was not part of the refiner-roller alliance, seconded the academics' opposition to the protection of an uncompetitive refining industry: "In our recommendation we must give due weight to the people's economy and to structural aspects." The journalist who took down the comment reported that "the silence of the majority of the audience was noticeable."[63] The rolling firms, which were allied with the refining industry, were not quoted in the press as criticizing the refiners' requests.

Tekkō shinbun (Steel news) noted that "not only are the academics' ideas different from the industry's, they're also different from those of MITI, which wanted to use the committee to get policy for the industry."[64] The first general meeting of the council, with a broad spectrum of user industries present, let the refiners know quickly that they were not going to get the kind of long-term full-operating subsidies or price

[59] *Light Metal Tsūshin*, 9 August 1977.
[60] *Tekkō shinbun*, 17 September 1977.
[61] *Tekkō shinbun*, 17 September 1977.
[62] Ibid., 14 September 1977.
[63] Ibid., 17 September 1977.
[64] Ibid.

supports that they were requesting. But the mood at the Basic Problems Subcommittee was friendlier. Attention there turned to projections of a worldwide shortage of aluminum in the early 1980s, which served as a rationale for subsidies for the industry.[65]

After another year of low prices and slack demand aluminum users criticized these projections as unrealistic. Officials of Yoshida Kōgyō, one of the large rolling firms, argued in both 1978 and 1981 that the deliberation council's projections of high demand and high prices were exaggerated because users would substitute other materials if prices for aluminum went too high.[66] Nevertheless, these projections were used to justify proposals to give the industry financial aid in exchange for production cuts to keep the rest of the refining capacity in operation.

From their statements in the press, it appears that the academics recommended subsidies for the industry not because the projections changed their minds but because they were relatively powerless. Ueno, for instance, appears to have given in reluctantly. In 1977, after agreeing to the first swap of financial assistance for capacity cutting, he commented: "We set the tariff quota [rebate] program at five years, but it's doubtful whether five years would be long enough to get the industry back on its feet. It may take longer."[67] The following year, with the benefit of hindsight, he said that the process of drawing up a plan "is meaningless since, no matter how you fiddle with the figures, in even just a year things will have changed."[68] Nonetheless, in 1978 and 1981 the council again recommended large subsidies.

Banks were also important in negotiations between MITI and the trade association. Sheard has argued correctly that they gave the aluminum industry important aid during its decline, but it is significant that this assistance was granted as part of a bargained settlement with MITI. Banks were the only institutions except for refiners and an academic who were represented on the Basic Problems Subcommittee of the deliberation council. Although they were rarely mentioned in the press, their position was, not surprisingly, that the government needed to provide buyout funds to pay the industries' debts.[69] It is true that the banks provided discounts on their interest rates to help the industry, but only after MITI publicly demanded that action. Of course, they had their own motives for assisting the refiners. In the late 1970s and early 80s the chemical firms responsible for the debts were in difficult straits, and there was some risk

[65] *Tekkō shinbun*, 17 September 1977; 20 October 1977.
[66] *Nikkan kei kinzoku*, 26 October 1978; 9 June 1981.
[67] *Nikkan kinzoku tokuhō*, 28 November 1977. See also *Nihon keizai sangyō shinbun*, 2 December 1977.
[68] *Nikkan kinzoku tokuhō*, 5 October 1978.
[69] *Nikkan kei kinzoku*, 5 October 1978.

the debts might go bad. Thus, it was in the banks' immediate self-interest to help the refining companies. As Sheard argues, by providing relief the banks were also living up to their implicit agreement to provide assistance in times of adversity. It is important to recognize, however, that MITI used the negotiations over subsidies to bargain with private actors and make sure that assistance was provided in exchange for state support. Thus, although bank assistance was important, it was another case of private institutions' acting within a negotiated and coordinated public-private response to industrial decline.

The Political Arena

The central conflict in the political arena took place between MITI and the industry, which were pushing for substantial financial assistance, and MOF, which opposed it. The conflict was mediated and settled by politicians. JAF acted as a lobbying group on two fronts, one of which involved directly asking local Diet members to press for government assistance to the industry. In addition, JAF pressed the Keidanren to lobby top LDP officials to intervene on its behalf. This approach appears to have been crucial in getting financial aid for the industry, although the aid granted was always much less than MITI's original requests.

MOF was opposed to the tariff rebate for several reasons. First, it considered subsidies for refining a waste of money. The ministry argued that aluminum could be replaced by plastics and steel and that it was no longer in the public interest to protect it. Second, MOF argued that it was inappropriate to subsidize aluminum at the same time aid was being cut to small and medium-sized business and agriculture.[70] It also argued that the tariff rebate constituted an inappropriate avoidance of the normal budgetary process of close political scrutiny and comparison with other demands for government spending. Finally, MOF saw the rebate as a usurpation of its administrative prerogative to appropriate tariff revenues.[71]

Negotiations over the 1977 tariff rebate proposal do not appear to have been highly politicized. The deliberation council proposed a complete rebate of the 9 percent tariff to provide for a complete buyout of the 24 percent of total capacity that was being cut. Industry compromised with MOF at 5.5 percent.[72]

In 1978 the industry made a poorly calculated attempt to bypass completely both bureaucratic channels and the LDP and tried to get the Democratic Socialist party (DSP) to sponsor the JAF's own industry law. The industry was highly dissatisfied with what it saw as an insignificant

---

[70] *Nihon keizai shinbun*, 18 September 1981.
[71] *Nikkan kinzoku tokuhō*, 20 November 1978.
[72] *Nihon kōgyō shinbun*, 7 September 1978.

subsidy provided by the 1977 plan, saying it aimed at euthanizing the industry.[73] Therefore, industry introduced a law that would give it the kind of protection afforded to Japanese wheat farmers: domestic aluminum would be sold at government prices set high enough to ensure a profit, and then these prices would be averaged with cheap import prices for domestic sale.[74] MITI complained that JAF had hardly bothered to consult with the Basic Industries Bureau before proposing policy on its own.[75] By attempting to push legislation directly through the DSP without first trying to mobilize LDP support, JAF found itself politically isolated.[76]

After that failure, JAF set to work mobilizing LDP support, focusing on Diet members from aluminum-producing areas or with ties to aluminum companies. In October 1978, when the deliberation council produced its proposal, an aluminum policy subcommittee was formed under the LDP's Policy Affairs Research Council (PARC) Commerce and Industry Committee. The subcommittee was headed by Yamazaki Hiroshi, who was from Shizuoka, where Japan Light Metal's Kanbara plant was located. Other LDP Diet members who came to the refiners' aid were Harada Shōzō, also from Shizuoka; Watanabe Kōzō, from Fukushima, the site of two refining plants; Hayashi Yoshirō, an ex-MITI official; and Harada Ken. In November 1978 the Commerce and Industry Committee and the Resource and Energy committees of PARC announced they would support the industries' requests for a renewal of the tariff rebate.[77] Over MOF opposition, the tariff rebate was extended for a year at a slightly lower rate of 4.5 percent.

Price recovery in 1979 and 1980 led to the abandonment of the tariff-rebate system. By 1981, however, prices were falling, and again industry campaigned for a tariff rebate. This time the industry successfully enlisted active Keidanren support and won much higher levels of subsidy.

In 1981 MOF again strongly opposed the proposed tariff rebate. It offered some tongue-in-cheek counterproposals, such as giving consumers rather than refiners a rebate by simply cutting the tariff outright, or giving the industry a tariff break on a grade of oil it did not use.[78] JAF appealed to the Keidanren for help; and in late November 1981 a consultation took place between top LDP and Keidanren leaders and Nagano Shigeo, a prominent business leader who headed the MOF-

[73] *Asahi shinbun*, 1 June 1978.
[74] *Nihon keizai shinbun*, 5 June 1978.
[75] *Light Metal Tsūshin*, 27 June 1978.
[76] *Nikkan kinzoku tokuhō*, 23 June 1978.
[77] *Nihon keizai shinbun*, 24 November 1978.
[78] Ibid., 3 October 1981; 15 October 1981.

affiliated tariff deliberation council. This meeting led to Nagano's announcement that a tariff rebate would be granted.[79] In preparation for the subsequent decision about rebate size, JAF lobbied the LDP and all the major opposition parties except the Communist party and persuaded twenty-seven Diet members to form a nonpartisan group, headed by Harada Shōzō, to push for aid to aluminum industry.[80] In both the DSP and the Japan Socialist party (JSP) Diet members cooperated with the refiners in mobilizing support. These included JSP member Takaya Shinnen and DSP member Ozawa Teikō. Ozawa was from Nagano, the site of a Showa Denko plant, and had been a member of the Showa Denko labor union. This broad political support helped engender the decision in late December 1981 to grant 34.8 billion of the ninety billion yen over three years that MITI had requested.[81]

Debate over aid to the industry subsequently quieted down for a few months. JAF continued to push for various subsidies, but they were not taken up by the government. In August 1982, however, discussion began in earnest over further financial assistance. MITI proposed new emergency government financing (five billion yen over three years) in exchange for assistance from the parent firms and banks in shelving the refiners' debt. The ministry also proposed that the government buy up stockpiles of aluminum. MOF was opposed, and MITI said it would appeal to the Basic Materials Subcommittee of LDP's Commerce and Industry Committee.[82] Keidanren president Inayama and vice-president Hanamura met with LDP's three top leaders to argue that assistance to specific depressed industries was more important than general measures to improve the economy, such as public works.[83] The subcommittee did decide to subsidize the stockpiling of aluminum at a cost of 3.6 million yen over three years.[84]

Although the Keidanren and top LDP officials seem to have held the key to breaking deadlocks with MOF, the broader process of creating support also put pressure on top LDP leaders and made sure there would be no embarrassing opposition to what, after all, was a large subsidy to big business. This process included lobbying local Diet members in both the LDP and opposition parties. The deliberation council process, although it gave no real power to critics of MITI policies, did allow those involved to let off a little steam. It also served as a forum for co-opting the rolling industry as well as sympathetically publicizing the industry's

[79] *Light Metal Tsūshin*, 29 September 1981; *Nihon keizai shinbun*, 18 November 1981.
[80] *Nihon keizai shinbun*, 25 November 1981.
[81] Ibid., 18 December 1981; *Asahi shinbun*, 25 December 1981.
[82] *Asahi shinbun*, 28 August 1982.
[83] Ibid., 3 September 1982.
[84] *Nihon keizai shinbun*, 3 September 1982.

situation in the press. While the refining work force was quite small, the labor union also played a minor role in publicizing the industry's needs.

Sympathy for the industry position continued to develop when the parent chemical companies split from their aluminum-refining divisions in 1976 to form separate companies. The parent companies involved were Mitsubishi Chemical, Sumitomo Chemical, and Showa Denko; Mitsui Aluminum had already existed as a separate company.[85] According to industry representatives (and echoed by Sheard), this split kept aluminum's losses from hurting the earnings profiles of the parent firms and thus their stock values as well. Industrial Bank of Japan officials stated that the chemical companies were suffering from problems with the chemical industry and needed time before they could absorb the losses.[86] Although it is difficult to say if this result was intentional, the split also created a set of impoverished companies that could plead for government assistance without reference to the assets of the parent firms. In the hundreds of newspaper articles on the difficulties of the aluminum industry, the larger financial resources of the parent companies were almost never mentioned.

FOREIGN PRESSURE

The United States began complaining in 1981 that the tariff-rebate system, although not precisely conflicting with GATT, would fuel the trade conflict with Japan. Japan's defense was that the rebate would last only three years (it actually lasted six) and that, because it simply reduced the tariff, it did not constitute an import restriction.[87] U.S. pressure on Japan to open its aluminum market intensified; and in December 1985 Japan agreed to abolish its tariff in exchange for continuing its protection of the leather industry, the special preserve of the *hisabetsu burakumin* (discriminated-against villagers). This low-caste group, similar to the untouchables in India, was assigned such taboo but necessary tasks as animal slaughter and leather tanning during the Tokugawa period (1603–1868). Because of the discriminatory barriers to many occupations *burakumin* still face, they defended their jobs in the leather goods industry vociferously. The government was anxious to avoid opening up the domestic leather-goods market because it feared the political heat of this group. The U.S. was threatening a legal action based on section 301 of the Trade Act against Japanese protection of the leather industry and had hinted it might do the same against the aluminum industry. Although plans for 80-percent cuts of Japan's aluminum-refining capacity had

[85] Sheard, "How Japanese Firms Manage Adjustment."
[86] Interview, 1987.
[87] *Nihon keizai shinbun*, 22 October 1981; 7 October 1981.

already been carried out, the 1985 agreement led the aluminum firms to close virtually all their remaining production capacity by early 1987. While specific U.S. pressure ultimately forced Japan to agree to dismantle its tariff-rebate program, general pressure from the U.S. and other trading partners to cut trade surpluses had been an important constraining factor in preventing the adoption of numerous proposals for more protectionist policies (such as higher tariffs).

Aluminum refining has been a principal focus of studies of Japanese declining industries. It is unusual internationally because it was a major industry that was almost completely replaced by imports in little more than a decade. Soon after the 1973 oil shock MITI decided that it would be an unacceptable waste of electricity to protect or subsidize the entire domestic refining industry, and opposition to subsidies from MOF and the electric companies and to import protection from users reinforced this decision.

I disagree with arguments that the aluminum-refining case shows that Japanese policy toward declining industries relies on market forces and the responses of private actors. While it is true that the domestic industry was replaced by imports, the way in which this happened was shaped by MITI strategy. The existence of a large, uncompetitive refining industry was to an important extent the result of MITI's encouragment of massive high-risk investment with the implicit guarantee that the government would provide assistance if necessary. The ministry then used similar incentives to encourage overseas investment as part of a plan to switch from domestic refineries to Japanese-owned refineries overseas, and it used the tariff-rebate program to encourage domestic refiners gradually to phase out domestic supplies as Japanese supplies from overseas came on line. MITI also pressured domestic rolling firms and trading companies to honor their keiretsu ties and buy domestic rather than imported aluminum and bargained with banks to ensure that government aid would be accompanied by bank assistance. The rapid influx of aluminum imports was speeded by the fact that aluminum was a product subject to close U.S. scrutiny and thus an unusual case. Japan has been freer to erect barriers to imports in industries such as cement, petrochemicals, fertilizers, and steel where the U.S. has not expressed interest in exports to Japan.

Refiners' extreme weakness in the marketplace by the mid-1970s put their trade associations in an unusual political situation. While most trade associations in heavy industries are able to exert considerable control over the domestic market, aluminum refiners' loose ties with buyers and extreme lack of international competitiveness forced their trade associations to lobby publicly for government subsidies and protection. With the exception of shipbuilding, the only other declining industries that have had to beg for official import protection or subsidies have been unconcentrated light industry, such as textiles and apparel, and primary-sector producers, such as agriculture and coal mining. Although it was unusual, the aluminum case is instructive because it shows the broad political support available to declining heavy industry in the late 1970s and early 80s, even for one with a small work force and little need to protect jobs. The only strong opposition to sizable subsidies came from MOF. The fact that even members of the Socialist party rallied to support the subsidies was due in part to two tactical moves by MITI and the industry to obscure the nature of the subsidy. First, by splitting off their refining divisions, supposedly for accounting purposes, the parent chemical companies made the refining industry seem more vulnerable and needy. Of course, this did not fool any of the government negotiators, but it dramatically affected how the industry's financial situation was reported in the press and helped it obtain diffuse support. Second, MITI insisted on a form of subsidy that would come from tariff revenues and thus would not appear to be in direct competition with other claims on the general budget.

Ironically, the extreme weakness of the industry's trade association may have been partly due to its excessive strength in the 1960s. As we saw, the refining cartel was able to manage the market easily in the 1960s and early 70s. When faced with declining demand and increasing imports, however, it was unable to organize its own domestic production and capacity-cutting cartels or pressure buyers not to buy imports. MITI fulfilled all these functions instead. The internal weakness of the trade association may have been due to the lack of institutional continuity between the pre- and postwar periods, although this is a characteristic shared by the cement and petrochemical industries. Moreover, the ease with which the association could impose high prices in the 1960s may have prevented it from developing strong ties of mutual obligation with users or the institutional means to enforce discipline in a difficult market. This is in sharp contrast to both the cement and petrochemical industries, which developed elaborate mechanisms for maintaining prices. Another reason aluminum producers were less able than steel or petrochemical makers to command high prices despite cheaper imports was that aluminum refiners produced only standardized goods. Without sophisticated products, domestics buyers' only motivation to keep domestic refiners in business was security of supply, and this alone was not enough.

Conflict between MITI and the refiners' trade associations developed when MITI pushed the refiners to make cuts and the refiners held out for as much subsidy as they could get. Whatever MITI might initially agree to, however, was not necessarily what the refiners would ultimately receive; the subsidies had to be approved by MOF and the politicians. Thus, MITI used criticism in the deliberation council to convince refiners that they were going to have to make difficult structural adjustments. One might ask, "Well, why didn't MITI just let the market take care of the refiners? Why did it have to convince them to scrap uncompetitive plants?" The reason is that MITI's strategic vision for the industry involved restructuring: cutting the most inefficient domestic capacity in an organized fashion without introducing any unnecessary competition among domestic producers, while simultaneously shifting production overseas. As MITI made these strategic decisions and implemented the cartel, the trade association put up the public front—the needy supplicant that could beg for aid from the LDP.

I revisited my informant at JAF in 1994, years after my initial interviews with him in 1987, and found him nostalgic for the good old days when the industry was in the refining business. Since smelting had gone, he lamented, the Japanese aluminum industry was not a basic industry anymore and no longer a full-fledged aluminum industry. He longed for the days when the trade association had power and political battles to fight. "We had real committees then; now we just have safety and recycling. These are 'peacetime activities.' ... It gives you an empty feeling to be just working on recycling. That's what scrap dealers used to do."[88]

[88] Interview, 1994.

The Cement Industry

Because cement is a crucial building material, countries undergoing rapid heavy industrialization generally require a strong cement industry. From early on Japan considered cement a strategic industry because it was one of the few that could produce a manufactured good for export with domestic raw materials. Like most basic materials industries, however, the Japanese cement industry is intrinsically vulnerable to competition from newly industrializing countries. Both the product and the production technology are highly standardized. Although direct labor costs constitute only about 6 percent of total production costs, the quarrying of raw materials and transportation, which account for 10 percent and 20 percent of production costs respectively, are highly labor intensive. Cement producers in developed countries are therefore vulnerable to price competition. Because cement is heavy relative to its value, transportation costs present a certain barrier to international trade. For example, the cost of land transportation effectively closes the inland U.S. market, but ocean transport is cheap enough that cement is readily transportable to coastal markets all over the world. Moreover, most of Japan's population and industry are located near seaports, which makes the Japanese market especially accessible to imports. Half the domestic cement used inside Japan is transported by sea. Because the thriving cement industries of South Korea and Taiwan are not much farther from northern Japanese cement markets than Kyushu is (the source of much of Japan's cement), there are no natural barriers to cement imports.

Japan's success as a cement exporter bears witness to the ease with which the product can be shipped long distances. In 1992 the nation was the world's largest exporter of cement, shipping much of it as far as the Middle East. Japan is the only advanced industrialized country that is a major exporter of cement; the only other countries exporting more than five million tons in any year during the 1970s, 80s, or early 90s, were

Figure 4–1. Japan's international cement trade

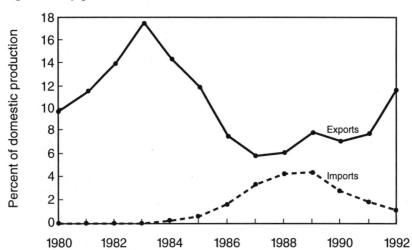

Source: Semento nenkan, 1990, 1993.

Spain, Greece, and South Korea, all of which had considerably less industrial development and lower wages. Japan has also been very successful at competing with imports in its domestic market. Except for a brief episode in 1973, it imported no cement from the end of World War II until 1984; and while imports rose to 4.5 percent of the domestic market in 1988 and 1989, they fell again to 1.2 percent by 1992 (see figure 4–1). Japan's success at resisting cement imports is particularly impressive given that the country's domestic prices are quite high by international standards. From 1980–85 its domestic undelivered cement prices averaged 46 percent over export prices; and with the rise in the yen they averaged 154 percent over export prices from 1986–93 (see figure 4–2). Japan's domestic prices were just 22 percent above the small volume of imports in 1984 and 1985, but from 1986–93 they averaged 68 percent over import prices.

What is surprising about this gap between domestic prices and export-import prices is that Japan has no formal barrier to cement imports. One might imagine that, in the absence of import barriers, cement producers in other countries would want to take advantage of Japan's high prices. One might also be surprised that Japanese producers are willing to sell cement overseas so cheaply when domestic prices are so temptingly high. How has the industry managed to maintain its high domestic prices and compete so successfully in world markets? The answer lies in informal policies to coordinate simultaneously the sale of domestic goods overseas

Figure 4–2. Ratio of Japanese domestic cement prices to import and export prices

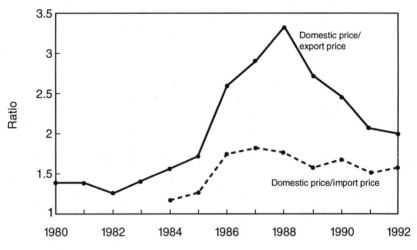

Source: *Semento nenkan,* 1990, 1993.

at low prices while restricting imports into the domestic market. To understand these policies one must look not simply at official state policy but at the informal (although state-supported) policies of trade associations. These informal policies are developed by associations representing the cement and construction industries as part of an intertrade association relational contract to assure stability in the cement market. They possess quasistate authority inasmuch as they are able to use illegal but government-tolerated sanctions to enforce rules that govern the market.

Although we will examine it at greater length later in the chapter, the core policy that restricts the flow of imports into the Japanese market is a refusal-to-deal agreement between the Japanese cement and construction industries. In the interests of stable supply, the construction trade associations agree to buy only from members of the domestic cement trade association, while the members of the cement association sell only to construction-association members that abide by the agreement. If a construction company buys imported cement, domestic companies will no longer sell to that company. Some small construction firms working in restricted local areas have been willing to take this risk, but large firms that operate across a broader area are unwilling to be cut off from domestic supplies.

The state supports this policy by helping to organize domestic cartels that restrict competition and promote cooperation among companies. In doing so, the state supports cement prices and company profits and thus appears to represent interest groups rather than advance national strategic interests. Indeed, the cement industry has used influence with LDP politicians to get government contracts for individual firms. The Construction Ministry, which designates the cement companies from which the government will buy cement, certainly pays attention to the industry's political power; and MITI pays attention to the relative interests of the cement and construction industries in negotiating with them over market controls. Nevertheless, even if MITI has an interest in supporting prices for firms that support the LDP, it also has a clear strategic interest in maintaining production of basic materials. While the ministry assists industry in organizing the market to keep prices high, it does so on the condition that industry use these prices to stay in domestic manufacturing. As we shall see, at one point the Japanese cement industry attempted to use its anticompetitive price supports to make high profits by marketing cheap imports. MITI supported the FTC when the commission forced the industry to abandon the import plan, which did not fit with MITI's structural goal of maintaining domestic manufacturing. Thus, MITI is able to delegate authority to the trade association but at the same time succeeds in fostering state goals and keeping the trade association on a short leash.

Because association governance is informal and lacks legal sanctions, a trade association often requires state backing to come to a consensus on rules and to enforce them. This informality also allows the state to place constraints on the association. Because informal governance of markets requires explicit or implicit suspension of Antimonopoly Law enforcement, the state is able to threaten a return to strict enforcement to pressure the association to act according to state wishes.

The strong cartel in the cement industry is an excellent example of how trade associations form relational contracts between industries and enforce these contracts. The cement case shows the links between official policies to encourage collusion among association members to keep prices high and unofficial refusal-to-deal policies to prevent buyers from purchasing from sources outside the association and the country. Refusals to deal are not an aberration or violation of the spirit of official policies that deal with structural decline but a logical and necessary extension of them. Such control of outsiders is necessary for collusive price-supporting measures to work, just as control of competition within the association is necessary for enforcing refusals to deal. In short, the cement case is especially useful for showing the ways in which MITI policies have supported private-market governance, the degree to which the FTC has tolerated such governance, and the disinterest of the Japanese press in exposing these illegal practices.

The strong cement cartel exemplifies the extreme degree of market controls the Japanese state is willing to support and shows how trade association and state policies can work together to control a market. It is important to note, however, that the cement industry has a number of features that particularly facilitate market controls. First, economies of scale require large plants; therefore, like all heavy industries, cement has relatively few firms. Second, cement is a highly standardized product, which makes it easier for a cartel to arrive at price and volume agreements. Third, because there is no substitute for cement, the industry is not in competition with other industries.[1]

A fourth factor is the cost of overland transportation. In inland areas the cost of overland transportation can effectively restrict the number of firms that can compete; and this makes it easier for a small number of competitors to combine to set prices. Because ocean transport has become cheaper and much of Japan is accessible by sea, transport costs no longer significantly restrict competition over cement sales in much of Japan. But today, most cement is converted into ready-mix concrete before distribution. Ready-mix concrete is expensive to transport, and most of Japan's four thousand plants only transport within a range of fifteen to twenty kilometers. At this stage a small number of ready-mix concrete plants may combine to raise prices. Alternatively, because they are unable to go further afield in search of other markets, they may also try to undercut each other aggressively. If competition can be controlled, however, the high transport costs, which segment the larger market into tiny markets with few sellers, provide an opportunity for local oligopolistic control. The problem is that capital barriers to entry into the ready-mix concrete industry are low, and local oligopolies are always in danger of being upset. As we shall see, MITI and the Cement Association of Japan have worked hard to organize the industry to control such competition.

A fifth factor that makes the cement industry relatively easy to cartelize is that the construction industry, which buys the cement, is also highly cartelized. Prices in the construction industry are governed by *dangō*— that is, price fixing by competitors—before bids are submitted for government construction projects, which account for half of construction jobs. Because the construction firms are not under strong competitive pressure among themselves, they are able to absorb the high cost of domestic cement.

Competition among construction companies is weak for both govern-

---

[1] Kōsei Torihiki Iinkai Jimukyoku Chōsabu (Research Section of the Fair Trade Commission Office), *Semento sangyō ni okeru jigyōsha dantai no kako oyobi genzai* (Trade associations in the cement industry, past and present), 1951, pp. 8–16. FTC publications are hereafter cited as 'FTC' followed by date.

ment and private building contracts. In 1989 Japanese construction costs for a two hundred-square-meter house, not counting the cost of land, were 2.19 times the U.S. cost at 130 yen/dollar.[2] The economic journal *Shūkan tōyō keizai* writes that labor productivity in the construction industry is so low that "it is difficult to believe it is in the same country as the auto and electronics industries."[3] The journal hypothesizes that the lack of competition to spur improved efficiency has spilled over from bureaucrats who discourage productivity increases by fixing cost formulas for public works. This lack of competition also allows firms to buy expensive domestic materials.

Nevertheless, certain factors in the cement industry do encourage competition—at times, intense competition, which in turn has created incentives to establish cartels. For example, low technical and capital barriers to entry have invited large numbers of new entrants to the industry in boom times, as in the 1930s, 50s, and early 60s. As a result, the cement industry, with twenty-three firms, is less concentrated than many basic materials industries, posing a challenge to cartel formation. Another factor promoting competition is cement's short shelf life: it can only be stored a few months before its quality suffers. This makes it hard for firms to hold on to stock in slack times and tends to push them into intense competition to sell it off, no matter how low the price. But these same factors have created a strong incentive for cement companies to combine to moderate competition. Moreover, the lack of a cement substitute, the fact that ready-mix concrete markets are extremely localized, and the fact that the downstream construction industry is tightly cartelized have provided a strong basis for cartelizing the cement industry.

The Japanese cement industry, like most of the country's basic materials industries, was started up by the state in order to reduce dependence on imports of materials vital for industrialization. In 1873 the Home Ministry established a model cement plant that it later sold to a private party, Asano Sōichirō. The company eventually became one of Japan's largest cement firms, Asano Cement, renamed Nihon Cement after the war.[4] A number of coal-mining firms subsequently followed Asano into cement production as a way of using their coal.[5]

---

[2] Uchida Michio and Ōzaki Akiko, "Jūtaku kenchiku hi wa gowari yasuku dekiru" (Construction costs could be 50-percent cheaper), *Shūkan tōyō keizai*, 4 September 1993, p. 7.
[3] Ibid.
[4] FTC, 1951, p. 1.
[5] Ube Cement and Iwaki Cement (later Sumitomo Cement) are examples of coal-mining companies that went into cement production. Sumitomo Semento Kabushiki Kaisha Hensan Iinkai (Sumitomo Cement, Inc., Editorial Committee), *Sumitomo semento 80 nen*

The cement trade association has been quite effective at times, both before and since World War II. It has managed to coordinate strong cartels, although these have sometimes fallen apart during booms or busts. Nevertheless, a few institutional factors made cartelization more difficult in this industry than in other basic materials industries. First, because cement was not dominated by zaibatsu firms before the war, coordination may have become more difficult. In 1930 Asano Cement, which was a core company in one of the lesser zaibatsu (Asano), did control 34 percent of market share; but half the market was controlled by smaller non-zaibatsu companies.[6] Yūi and Hirschmeier write that in the Meiji period (1868–12), industries dominated by zaibatsu firms had little need for formal cartels because these firms "worked under unified control, and among each other they tended to acknowledge some vaguely defined boundaries of competence."[7] Shibagaki Kazuo has also noted that zaibatsu ties have been more important than formal trade-association ties in many industries.[8] The fact that cement was dominated by non-zaibatsu firms made it depend on a strong formal cartel in a way that zaibatsu-dominated industries did not.[9]

In addition, until the period of decline beginning in the mid-1970s, the industry was not amenable to MITI guidance: it used domestic coal and limestone as raw materials and did not rely on MITI import approval to get them.[10] In a sense, this shows trade-association strength vis-à-vis MITI, but the relative weakness of MITI guidance may have made it harder to form effective cartels (for example, during the early 1960s).

Even with these weaknesses, the prewar cement cartel did have considerable strength. It was established in 1924 by the two largest firms,

---

shi (An eighty-year history of Sumitomo Cement) (Tokyo: Sumitomo Cement, 1987), p. 15; Semento Shinbunsha, ed. *Jinbutsu Semento Shiwa*, vol. 2 (Tokyo: Semento Shinbunsha, 1983), p. 24.

[6] Hashimoto Jurō, "Semento rengōkai" (The cement federation), in Hashimoto Jurō and Takeda Haruhito, eds., *Ryōtaisenkanki Nihon no karuteru* (Cartels in interwar Japan) (Tokyo: Ochanomizu Shobō, 1985).

[7] Johannes Hirschmeier and Tsunehiko Yui, *The Development of Japanese Business 1600–1973* (London: George Allen & Unwin, 1975), p. 177.

[8] Shibagaki Kazuo, *Nihon kinyū shihon bunseki* (An analysis of Japanese finance capital) (Tokyo: Tokyo Daigaku Shuppan Kai, 1965), pp. 318–30, cited in Hashimoto, "Semento rengōkai," pp. 128–29.

[9] Although most cement firms were not previously zaibatsu affiliates, after World War II all the major cement companies established relationships with the major bank groups, the postwar successors to the zaibatsu. All six big bank groups became represented in cement—some through new relationships with preexisting firms, some when their coal companies began cement production to use coal. Sumitomo Coal Mining, for instance, went into cement production in Fukushima in 1960 to use coal from the area in the face of declining demand for coal. It intimidated one of the larger pre-war cement firms, Iwaki Cement, into merging with it to avoid competition with powerful old zaibatsu groups entering the industry. Sumitomo Semento, *80 nen shi*, pp. 240–46.

[10] Interview, cement company official, 1988.

Asano and Onoda, which played leadership roles and quelled internal disturbances.[11] By sacrificing their own market share, the two firms managed to stabilize prices in the late 1920s. The cartel fell apart with the crash of 1929, but the resulting shakeout strengthened the market position of the two large firms and laid the ground for the reestablishment of strong market controls, which included production, sales, price, and delivery cartels.[12]

The postwar cement industry grew rapidly during the 1950s and 60s, slowing in the 1965–68 period and again growing quickly until the oil shock of 1973. Cement production grew from twenty-eight million tons in 1960 to seventy-eight million in 1973. Nevertheless, while cement was growing rapidly in absolute terms, it was declining relative to the economy as a whole. As the economy matured, cement consumption declined as a percentage both of GNP and real domestic fixed capital formation. While cement consumption relative to GNP had increased during intensive building in the late 1950s, this ratio declined in the early 1960s. Relative to overall fixed capital formation, cement use declined from 335 tons per 100 million real yen to approximately 270 tons by 1965 and just over 200 tons by 1979.

In the late 1950s, a high level of concentration had enabled the largest firms to keep prices stable. In 1959 the three largest firms in the industry enjoyed a combined market share of 53 percent, which allowed them to maintain some price leadership and restrain price competition.[13] The economic boom of the early 1960s, however, brought new entrants into the industry; and by 1974 the top three firms controlled only 36 percent of the market, upsetting the earlier pattern of stable prices.[14] The combination of expanded production capacity and slower increase in demand led to a drop in capacity use from 75 percent in 1960 to 56 percent in 1965.[15] In turn, the resulting increase in competition pushed prices down from 6,900 yen/ton in 1960 to 5,900 yen/ton in the slow growth year of 1965.[16] While cement company profits were slightly

[11] FTC, 1951, p. 17.

[12] FTC, 1951, foreword; Hashimoto, "Semento rengōkai," p. 168.

[13] Onoda Semento Kabushiki Kaisha, *Onoda semento hyakunen shi* (A One Hundred Year History of the Onoda Cement Company) (Tokyo: Onoda Semento Kabushiki Kaisha, 1981), p. 685.

[14] Ibid.

[15] Eighty-percent use of capacity is considered peak because cement demand varies considerably by season. Interview with cement company officials, 1988; Nihon semento kabushikigaisha, *Hyakunen shi* (One-hundred-year history) (Tokyo: Nihon Semento, 1983), p. 177.

[16] Dokusen Bunseki Kenkyū Kai (Research Group for the Analysis of Monopoly), *Nihon no dokusen kigyō* (Japan's monopoly firms), Vol. 3 (Tokyo: Shin Nihon Shuppansha, 1974), p. 129. While the Japanese economic growth of 5.7 percent was high by later standards, it at that time was the slowest growth Japan had experienced since the war. Onoda Semento, *Hyakunen shi*, p. 618.

Table 4–1. Changes in investment and operating rates in cement industry, 1959–1968

	Plant and equipment investment (in million yen)	Production capacity at year end (1,000 tons)	Operating rate (%)
1959	21,400	23,148	74
1960	33,200	29,020	75
1961	34,200	31,200	73
1962	32,569	35,568	71
1963	44,460	43,200	72
1964	56,605	53,352	63
1965	35,981	58,788	56
1966	29,976	64,140	58
1967	34,908	67,344	62
1968	64,500	70,644	65

Source: Dokusen Bunseki Kenkyū Kai (Research Group for the Analysis of Monopoly), Nihon no dokusen kigyō (Japan's monopoly firms), Vol. 3 (Tokyo: Shin Nihon Shuppansha, 1974), p. 129.

above the average for mining and manufacturing companies in the early 1960s, by 1964 they had fallen below the average; and in 1965 companies were losing money.

Due to cement's poor profit and price situation in 1965, MITI ranked it third on a list of ten recessed industries and used administrative guidance to place the industry in a capacity-freezing cartel. Under this cooperative system firms pledged to follow a scrap-and-build policy whereby for a three-year period any new production facilities would be offset by scrapping old cement kilns.[17] At the same time, four outsider firms to the Cement Association, Myojo Cement, Tōa Cement, Chiyoda Cement, and Mitsui Mining, joined the association. As a result of the agreement, investment cooled down over the next three years; and the expansion of production capacity slowed, although it did not stop. Capacity use rates improved from 56 percent in 1965 to 65 percent in 1968 (see table 4–1).[18] In addition, firms cut costs by concentrating production in their most efficient plants, cutting down on fuel use and reducing the work force.[19]

The late 1960s and early 70s were years of rapid economic growth, increased demand for cement, and sudden expansion of productive capacity. Demand for cement rose an average 12 percent per year between 1965 and 1970, just ahead of average real economic growth of 11.7 percent. Although 1971 was generally a slow year for the economy, 1972 and 1973 were boom years again for the cement industry

[17] Nihon Semento, Hyakunen shi, p. 177.
[18] Dokusen Bunseki Kenkyū Kai, Nihon no dokusen kigyō, p. 129.
[19] Nihon Semento, Hyakunen shi, pp. 179–80.

because of Tanaka Kakuei's Plan to Restructure the Japanese Archipelago, which was fueling a government-sponsored building boom throughout Japan.[20]

Although MITI had earlier tried to organize the cement industry to cool overinvestment, the rise in demand was so great by April 1973 that MITI was pressuring the industry to increase production.[21] The ministry's pressure on the industry was intensified by an FTC investigation in March 1973 that resulted in advice in June to stop price fixing.[22] But the problem of undersupply became moot later that year with the OPEC oil embargo. As it did for many industries, the embargo marked the beginning of decline for Japanese cement—in part because overall economic growth had slowed but also because, as the economy became more sophisticated, demand for basic materials became less important for growth.

These trends cut demand nearly 20 percent, from seventy-seven million tons in 1973 to sixty-four million in 1975. Although prices rose somewhat to reflect higher fuel costs, weak demand during the mid-1970s put downward pressure on cement prices. To boost them, the FTC allowed the Cement Association to form two production-restricting depression cartels, which existed from November 1975 to January 1976 and from June to December 1977. These cartels were successful in raising prices, although prices fell somewhat between the cartels.[23] Because MITI believed that cement prices were being dragged down by excessive competition in the ready-mix concrete industry, it worked to strengthen the Ready-Mix Concrete Federation.

In the 1960s and 70s the cement industry had shifted from selling dry cement directly to construction companies to selling it to ready-mix concrete firms who then sold ready-mix to construction firms. The share of Japanese cement that went through these firms rose from 9 percent in 1960 to 60 percent by 1973 and 70 percent by 1980.[24] To minimize risk and capital outlay, cement makers avoided creating wholly owned ready-mix concrete subsidiaries but instead attempted to get others to invest in ready-mix companies while maximizing cement-company control over them. That is, they formed keiretsu ties with buyers rather than rely on arms-length market relationships. Onoda Cement, for example, invested some equity in the ready-mix concrete firms to which it sold cement and dispatched some of its own employees to them in order to exert some

[20] Ibid., p. 177.
[21] Semento Shinbun Sha (Cement Newspaper Corporation), *Semento nenkan* (Cement annual), 26 (1974): 35.
[22] Cement Association documents.
[23] *Onoda semento hyakunen shi* (A one-hundred year history of the Onoda Cement Company) (Tokyo: Onoda Semento Kabushikigaisha, 1981), p. 687.
[24] Nihon Semento, *Hyakunen shi*, pp. 219, 221.

control.[25] Cement companies also loaned money to create leverage with ready-mix companies. But many of these companies were set up with capital from gravel, construction, and cement sales companies that were quite independent of the cement companies.[26] By 1977 there were 4,212 ready-mix concrete firms, and competition among them was weakening cement prices despite cement company attempts to rein them in.

To reduce competition MITI tried unsuccessfully to use administrative guidance to restrict new entrants into the ready-mix concrete industry. When this approach did not work, MITI tried getting existing firms to scrap capacity and cooperate to keep prices high and boost profits. In February 1976 the ministry proposed several policies aimed at "modernizing" (that is, reducing competition in) the ready-mix concrete industry, including forecasting demand on a quarterly basis, carrying out investment according to plans, and organizing sales through a joint-sales company. In September 1976 MITI joined the Cement Association and the Ready-mix Concrete Federation to form the Committee for the Modernization of the Ready-mix Concrete Industry. The committee recommended that the industry be organized into a nationwide pyramid-style organization with a central federation of industrial unions (kōgyō kumiai) at the national level, nine regional industrial union offices, industrial unions at the prefectural level, and cooperative unions (kyōydō kumiai) at the local market level.[27] The industrial unions were to use government loans and preferential tax measures designed to assist small and medium-sized firms, including the Law for Subsidies and Funds for the Modernization of Small and Medium-sized Firms, the Law for the Promotion of Modernization by Small and Medium-sized Business, and the Special Measures Law to Assist Change in Small and Medium-sized Businesses in order to scrap excess capacity.[28] The cooperative unions were to promote joint sales.[29]

As it would later do with the cement industry, MITI pressured the ready-mix concrete industry to cooperate in making capacity cuts to reduce competition; but few established companies were willing to do so.[30] Nevertheless, the Ready-mix Concrete Federation had considerable success at organizing joint marketing and expanding memberships. Although the cartel restricted membership to small and medium-sized

[25] Onoda Semento, Hyakunen shi, p. 659.
[26] Ibid., p. 685.
[27] Ibid., p. 687.
[28] The Japanese names of the laws are Chūshō Kigyō Kindaika Shikin Tō Josei Hō, Chūshō Kigyo Kindaika Sokushin Hō, and Chūshō Kigyō Tenkan Taisaku Rinji Sochi Hō.
[29] Onoda Semento, Hyakunen shi, pp. 687–88.
[30] Interview, cement company official, 1988. Zenkoku Nama Konkuriito Kōgyō Kumiai Rengōkai (National Federation of Ready-mix Concrete Industrial Unions) uses the amusing acronym, Zennama, or "all raw."

firms, the large ready-mix concrete firms directly owned by the cement companies got around this requirement by splitting up into smaller firms. In the Tokyo area the large cement companies supported the federation by providing money to buy all outstanding ready-mix concrete contracts (which were set at low prices) to give the association a fresh start in negotiating with the construction industry.[31]

By 1979, 75 percent of ready-mix concrete plants belonged to industrial unions, that were to scrap capacity, 69 percent to cooperative unions, and 59 percent to joint sales unions.[32] Because of this expanded participation in trade-association activities, ready-mix concrete prices improved considerably relative to cement prices in the late 1970s; and cement industry officials were satisfied that competition had been considerably reduced.[33]

Although strengthening the Ready-mix Concrete Federation boosted cement prices, the second oil shock of 1979–80 raised costs; and deep cutbacks in public-works spending in 1980 cut demand. The cement industry attempted to overcome these problems with an illegal price cartel. In 1982 the FTC searched company offices, and in 1983 it warned the industry to stop its illegal cartel and fined the companies involved. The commission allowed the industry to form a third depression cartel but warned that this would be the last one it would permit.

Immediately after the FTC ruling, a group of five or six section chiefs from the large cement companies formed the Structural Problems Study Group under the tutelage of a MITI official from the Ceramics and Construction Materials Division of the Consumer Goods Industries Bureau. The official lectured the group on the SDIL and laid out the forms of aid that MITI could provide. At the same time, the FTC warned the cement firms they would not be able to form a production cartel again and advised them to adopt legal measures to reduce competition. According to cement industry officials, the FTC did not directly order firms to submit to a MITI-led capacity-cutting cartel.[34] Nevertheless, by advising them to follow the law and prohibiting them from using production-cutting cartels in the future, the FTC was in effect pushing the trade association into the arms of MITI.

Although the Cement Association did not volunteer to set up an SDIL plan before being pushed into it, cement companies had been talking about the need to deal with structural problems on their own. Company officials emphasize that the industry did not simply go along with the capacity-scrapping cartel and joint sales because MITI told them to. But

[31] Nihon Semento, *Hyakunen shi*, p. 220.
[32] Onoda Semento, *Hyakunen shi*, p. 688.
[33] Interview, cement company official, 1988.
[34] Ibid.

the Cement Association was not able to muster internal discipline and cooperation without FTC and MITI pressure.

It is significant that the FTC wielded the stick that successfully pressured the trade association into going along with MITI. Remarkably, the commission, whose ostensible purpose is to discourage cartels except as exceptions, in this instance pushed the Cement Association into a much stronger capacity-scrapping cartel and joint-sales arrangement by prohibiting it from engaging in a mere price cartel. Thus, while the FTC sometimes acts as a check on trade association and MITI-sponsored attempts to restrict competition, it occasionally pushes associations into legal but stronger restrictions of competition. We do not know whether the FTC was intentionally supporting MITI's policy goals or whether it was simply enforcing the law without reference to MITI's policies. Nevertheless, given that the FTC was generally quite lax in enforcing Antimonopoly Law in the cement industry, its strictness in this instance appears intended to push the industry into the stronger, MITI-sponsored cartel.

One way the Cement Association prepared to form a cartel within MITI guidelines was to hire Ono Masabumi, a retired MITI bureaucrat.[35] Although most trade associations employ retired government bureaucrats, the Cement Association had not hired one because its ties with MITI were not strong. In the cement industry MITI retirees had typically been employed at the large firms rather than at the trade association.[36] Ono had not worked on cement at MITI but had been posted to the FTC for two years and knew Antimonopoly Law well. He joined the association in March 1984, just before the industry was designated a structurally depressed industry under the SDIL. According to an association official, Ono did not act to facilitate communication with MITI so much as advise the association on how to work out the MITI-sponsored cartel within the limits imposed by the FTC. As we shall see, the trade association continued to violate the Antimonopoly Law through its refusal-to-deal system.

The Cement Association also tried to improve its understanding of the Construction Ministry by hiring a retired bureaucrat from that ministry in 1987.[37] This contact was important, as I shall discuss later, because negotiations with the construction industry and the ministry established how far the capacity-cutting cartel could go and thus how much market control the construction industry would allow.

In June 1984, shortly after Ono joined the trade association, a former MITI official, Honda Hiroyasu, and a former inspector from the Con-

---

[35] *Semento nenkan* 38 (1986): 344; interview, Cement Association official, 1988.
[36] Personal communication, Yamazaki Hiroaki.
[37] Interview, Cement Association official, 1988.

struction Ministry, Shirasaki Nisaburō, were invited to join the Ready-mix Concrete Federation, presumably to help the industry figure out how to negotiate market controls with the cement and construction industries and their respective ministries.[38]

In the negotiations over the SDIL measures, the twenty-three individual members of the Cement Association had difficulty agreeing to make individual sacrifices for the sake of collective goods. Understanding how joint action was accomplished is to appreciate one of the association's major achievements. All twenty-three member companies have their headquarters in Tokyo, and their company presidents keep in close touch through monthly meetings.[39] Junior officials meet regularly in other committees and thus get to know one another over the years.[40] Coordination within the Cement Association is enhanced by the fact that a handful of the twenty-three member firms control most of the market. Although many new firms entered the industry in the 1960s and early 70s, in the early 1980s the five biggest companies still controlled 60 percent of market share while two others each had about 6 percent. The five largest firms—Onoda Cement, Nihon Cement, Sumitomo Cement, Mitsubishi Mining and Cement, and Ube Industries—have tended to act as leaders within the trade association; and their presidents usually make up the association's five-member board of directors.

Nevertheless, leadership within the association is not determined simply by market power. For example, Moroi Ken, the president of Chichibu Cement, played a key role in the 1983 negotiations and was a member of the board of directors despite his company's mere 6 percent market share. Moroi was important because he was both an important leader in the Keizai Dōyūkai and "one of the most popular guys in the world of Japanese business leaders."[41] He is also a close friend of Ōshima Kenji, the president of Onoda Cement, having gone to college with him at the Tokyo University Faculty of Economics (their two firms eventually merged in 1994).[42] During the 1983 negotiations over the capacity-cutting cartel, Moroi was key in planning the cartel, while Ōshima worked at consensus building.[43]

Although the large firms acted as leaders in developing consensus for the capacity cuts, they relied on pressure from MITI to give their arguments weight. Total cement capacity in 1983 was officially 130 million

---

[38] *Semento nenkan* 38 (1986): 344.
[39] One firm has its official headquarters elsewhere, but its de facto headquarters are in Tokyo. Interview, Cement Association official, 1988.
[40] Ibid.
[41] *Asahi shinbun*, 25 May 1988, p. 11.
[42] Interview, Cement Association official, 1988.
[43] Ibid.

tons. The first round of cuts of twenty-five million tons was easy because it involved capacity that was no longer economically viable and was only maintained in case of unexpected surges in demand. Thus, cutting it had no real impact on competition. But the Cement Association was initially unable to agree on how to make furthur cuts. The principal participants in the negotiations were the cement company officials. The MITI retiree at the Cement Association was present at the meetings but did not play a leading role, and no active MITI officials attended.[44] MITI pushed negotiations along, however, by issuing orders to the association that its leaders used to pressure members to go along with cuts.

Faced with membership unwillingness to cut more than twenty-five million tons, MITI ordered the association to cut an additional six million. According to one association official, most cement firms thought that the deeper cuts were necessary to bring prices up; but no individual firm wanted to push for them. This official believes that MITI only orders an industry to cut capacity if it perceives the industry would like to make the cuts. But an order from the ministry helps trade association leaders convince reluctant companies to go along. Thus, MITI helped give the association the discipline to make the cuts. Even with this pressure, however, it was difficult to cut capacity; and, as in shipbuilding (see Chapter 7), the biggest companies made disproportionately large cuts. Cement firms were divided into five joint-sales companies, and each made approximately equal cuts. But within the joint-sales firms, the largest seven firms made 87 percent of the cuts in productive capacity that was actually in use, while most of the smallest firms made no cuts (see table 4–2). To reward those that sacrificed individual interests for the sake of the industry, firms made payments to one another to compensate those that made the cuts. Firms paid a small amount for the original twenty-five million tons and larger sums for scrapping the last six million.[45]

Even after the first thirty-one tons of capacity cuts were negotiated, most cement firms thought cuts of an additional ten million tons were necessary to stabilize prices.[46] Cuts stopped at thirty-one million tons, however, in part because cement firms would not cooperate on deeper cuts but also because the construction trade associations and the Construction Ministry were opposed. Cuts were not made unilaterally by the Cement Association but as part of a negotiated relational contract with the construction industry trade associations. The terms of the cuts

[44] Interviews, Cement Association official and MITI official, 1988.
[45] The payments on the last six million tons were based on the average book value of the entire amount so that individual firms would not be rewarded for having built plants later or at greater expense. Interview, Cement Association official, 1988.
[46] Ibid.

Table 4–2. Capacity cuts by firm

Company	Operating-capacity cut	Capacity after cuts
Andes Cement Corporation		
Sumitomo Cement	1,466	10,213
Aso Cement	0	1,316
Denki Kagaku Kogyo	0	2,636
Tōyō Cement	399	0
Nittetsu Cement	0	1,507
Hachinohe Cement	0	1,310
Kanda Cement	0	1,653
Central Cement Company		
Onoda Cement	493	10,200
Nippon Steel Chemical	0	794
Tohso Corporation	0	3,228
Hitachi Cement	441	872
Mitsui Mining	0	2,209
Fuji Cement Company		
Mitsubishi Mining and Cement	1,321	12,799
Tokuyama Soda	0	5,106
Tohoku Kaihatsu	482	2,134
Dainihom Cement Company		
Nihon Cement	792	13,031
Osaka Cement	413	6,760
Daiichi Cement	0	1,092
Myojo Cement	0	2,451
Union Cement		
Ube Industries	363	10,524
Chichibu Cement	582	5,777
Tsuruga Cement	0	1,645
Ryukyu Cement	0	540
Totals	6,752	97,981

Source: Semento nenkan 38 (1986): 15.

were negotiated in a deliberation group made up of construction and cement companies and during discussions between the Construction Ministry and MITI. The construction companies opposed cuts over thirty-one million tons and insisted that MITI promise to use administrative guidance to keep cement prices down and distribute cement if shortages developed. Thus, not only did MITI and the Construction Ministry act as negotiators of the relational contract between the two trade associations, but MITI acted as guarantor of the agreement between the industries.

MITI tried to use other official policies under the SDIL to reduce competition in the cement industry and improve productivity through firm cooperation. These policies ranged from the creation of five joint-sales companies to cooperation between firms on transport and production to reduce costs. As it had with the capacity-cutting cartel, the Cement Association preferred easy ways to keep prices high while MITI pushed for greater sacrifices to support prices and reduce costs.

One policy that interested the cement industry was rationalization of transportation. To cut down on transport costs, the industry devised a system of delivery exchanges between firms. For instance, a cement firm in the north of Japan, selling to a buyer in the south and a southern firm selling to a northern customer would each deliver to one another's customers without giving up their individual relationships with the customers.[47] Weak price competition in the cement industry enabled even high-cost producers to transport cement great distances and still make ends meet. Delivery exchange mitigated the inefficiency stemming from the lack of price competition by essentially creating barter between firms. But MITI pressured them to go further in rationalizing production and transportation by creating a market in what had become a nonmarket system. The ministry wanted firms to sell cement to one another through a system of consignment production. This would have the usual advantages of sales over barter: the cement firm in the north would not have to arrange a trade with a southern firm to supply a southern buyer but could simply pay cash for southern cement. More significantly, it would allow high-cost producers to shut down plants and supply their customers with lower-cost cement. Developing such a system would make it easier for firms to participate in aggressive capacity-cutting cartels because they would not have to worry about being able to supply their customers; the long-term, nonmarket relation between the cement company, the ready-mix concrete company, and the construction company would remain in place. Underneath this facade, however, a shadow market would be created where firms would buy and sell cement at prices that bore a closer resemblance to actual production costs. This system of consignment production would have combined the security of high prices under a tight cartel with the efficiency of a market.

Ultimately, however, MITI had little success in creating the shadow market. Under the Structural Improvement Plan, cement companies agreed to only 4.34 million tons of consignment production and 8.84 million tons of delivery exchanges. By 1987 the firms had only achieved 34 percent of planned levels of consignment production while it achieved 62 percent of its planned delivery exchanges.[48] Consignment production expanded slowly because firms had to know each other's production costs to agree on prices but were unwilling to divulge them, perhaps

[47] Interview, cement company officials, 1988.
[48] Cement Association documents.

fearing that competitors would take advantage of them if the cartel broke down and genuine competition was resumed.[49] Here again, firms were unable to put aside concerns over competitive position for the sake of the interests of the industry as a whole.

The policy that firms were most interested in was the formation of joint-sales companies to reduce competition. But while they liked the idea of reducing competition, individual firms were reluctant to go as far as MITI wanted in giving up firm autonomy to the sales companies. At first the joint-sales firms merely acted as representatives for the cement firms. The cement firms maintained separate rooms at the offices of the sales companies, separate brand names on the cement, separate marking on their delivery trucks, and completely separate sales profits. MITI pressured the industry to move toward brand unification and joint sales.[50] As in the negotiations over capacity scrapping, many thought greater cohesion in the joint-sales companies was in the industry's broader interest yet resisted change because of individual interests. MITI also argued that complete mergers between firms, rather than simple mergers of sales functions, would be in the industry's best interest. The ministry consistently pushed the industry toward harder sacrifices. As one company official said, "the industry says it will do as much as possible, but there is a limit. MITI says to push that limit back."[51] The firms did gradually move toward genuine unification of their sales endeavors, but firms refused to go along with MITI's pressure to merge.

While MITI pushed firms to suppress individual firm autonomy to strengthen the sales companies, the FTC worked at cross-purposes to restrain the power of the sales companies. When the twenty-three cement firms were grouped into five sales firms, the preference of the individual firms was to join firms with which they already had close ties, or that could complement them geographically and allow for nationwide distribution. The FTC, while acquiescing to increased concentration and the goal of reduced competition, limited the size of individual groups to preserve some competition (see table 4–3). The FTC argued that, if the companies with close ties all joined together, the group formed around Onoda Cement would be too large—particularly in the Tokyo area, where it would have a 40-percent market share. The commission demanded that each group have only 20 percent of national market share and that no group control over 25 percent of the metropolitan Tokyo market. This produced a number of artificial combinations that made it harder for the groups to work as integrated entities. For instance,

[49] Interview, MITI official, 1988.
[50] *Semento nenkan* 38 (1986): 11.
[51] Interview, 1988.

Table 4–3. Annotated list of sales groupings

Company	Comment on relationship to group
Andes Cement Corporation (20% share of national market)	
Sumitomo Cement	
Aso Cement	No special relationship with Sumitomo Cement, but main bank is Sumitomo
Denki Kagaku Kogyo	No relation to Sumitomo
Nittetsu Cement	Joint venture of New Japan Steel and Sumitomo Cement
Hachinohe Cement	
Kanda Cement	Subsidiary of Aso
Central Cement Company (19% market share)	
Onoda Cement	Main bank: Mitsui and Industrial Bank of Japan
Nippon Steel Chemical	No special relationship with Onoda but wanted to join
Tohso Corporation	Onoda marketed its cement under Onoda brand, and Onoda sold it technology
Hitachi Cement	No special relationship but relatively close. Now has technical relationship
Mitsui Mining	Onoda sold 85% of its cement and sold it its technology
Fuji Cement Company (20% market share)	
Mitsubishi Mining and Cement	
Tokuyama Soda	Wanted to join Andes because Sumitomo was its main bank, but it was too large
Tohoku Kaihatsu	Was public company established to develop Tohoku region. Privatized in 1986. No relationship with Mitsubishi, but Mitsubishi had long wanted the company to enable it to supply northern Japan
Dainihon Cement Company (21% market share)	
Nihon Cement	Fuyō group
Osaka Cement	Sanwa group, No special relationship
Daiichi Cement	Subsidiary, sold under parent company's brand name (Asano)
Myojo Cement	Subsidiary, sold under parent company's brand name (Asano)
Union Cement (20% market share)	
Ube Industries	Main bank: Industrial Bank of Japan
Chichibu Cement	Really wanted to join Onoda. Was doing delivery exchange with Onoda. Presidents were friends from college. Main bank: Industrial Bank of Japan
Tsuruga Cement	Subsidiary of Chichibu
Ryukyu Cement	Subsidiary of Ube. Had belonged to Kaiser Cement (U.S.)

Source: Market share figures from *Semento sangyō no kōzō kaizen: Kyōdō jigyō kaisha no zenyō* (Structural improvement in the cement industry: An overview of the joint operations firms), Japan Cement Association. Comments from interview with cement company official, 1988.

Note: The name *Andes* doesn't come from any South American connection but from the first letters or syllables of the names of the members: Aso, Nittetsu, Denki Kagaku, and Sumitomo.

Tokuyama Soda wanted to join Sumitomo Cement's group because both were part of the Sumitomo Bank financial group (keiretsu) but was blocked because the resulting sales group would be too large. Similarly, Chichibu Cement wanted to be in Onoda Cement's group because the two firms were involved in delivery exchanges and the presidents were good friends, but Chichibu would have made Onoda's group too large. When the FTC told Onoda it would have to discontinue its delivery exchanges with Chichibu under the new system, Onoda protested but backed down when the commission told it to choose between five equal-sized groupings or none at all.[52] In this way the FTC exercised its power to maintain certain conditions to promote competition. One cement company official noted that the FTC also insisted that there be no talking between groups, hoping to make sure that firms did not use their close ties with companies in other joint-sales groups to produce intergroup cooperation. He thought the FTC had been "very strict with the cement industry."[53] Nevertheless, despite FTC limits on the joint-sales companies and the problems of coordinating sales, cement company officials argued that the joint-sales companies had helped support prices.

While the official may have genuinely felt the FTC was "very strict" in forbidding cooperation between joint-sales groups, in practice the Cement Association provided an important unofficial setting for cooperation between the groups. Although there was no official connection, the presidents of each of the five sales companies (who were the representative or managing directors from the five largest cement companies) made up the Distribution Committee of the Cement Association and met regularly on that basis.[54] Thus, the sales companies offered a way for each of the five major companies to rein in competition from the smaller companies, while the trade association offered a setting for these five companies to work together to control the market.[55]

The Distribution Committee's most important function was to represent the cement industry in implementing its refusal-to-deal agreements with the construction industry. The five members of the committee met monthly with representatives of the five big construction trade associations and separately with representatives of the Ready-mix Concrete Federation.[56] In the relational contract between the construction and cement trade associations, the cement industry promised the smooth

---

[52] Interview, cement company officials.
[53] Interview.
[54] *Jōmu* and *senmu riji* translate as "representative director" and "managing director."
[55] Interview, MITI official, 1988.
[56] Interview, cement company officials, 1988.

delivery of cement at stable prices in return for the construction industry's loyalty as a customer. The cement industry's commitment to stable prices included a promise to control attempts by local ready-mix concrete cooperative unions to exploit their local monopolies to raise prices. The tactic these local cooperative unions often use is to stop production to force construction firms to pay higher prices. The monthly meetings between the construction trade associations and the Distribution Committee provided a forum for the construction trade associations to ask the Cement Association to pressure local ready-mix concrete cooperative unions to resume production.

In return for the Cement Association's control of the ready-mix cooperative unions, the construction trade associations promised that their members would only buy cement from members of the Cement Association, which includes only domestic firms. The association enforced this agreement through two layers of refusals to deal. If a construction firm bought ready-mix concrete from an outsider to the Ready-mix Concrete Federation, then insiders in the federation refused to deal with that firm. The Cement Association members agreed among themselves not to sell to outsiders to the Ready-mix Concrete Federation in order to choke off the outsiders' supply.[57] Thus, if a construction firm wanted to be able to buy domestic cement, it had to refrain from buying imported cement. Small construction firms working in certain urban areas were willing to risk being cut off from domestic supplies, but not large construction companies that work in more than one locale and which need access to ready-mix concrete in different areas. They were unwilling to risk losing supplies from members of the Ready-mix Concrete Federation. Thus, the threat of refusals to deal did not always prevent small firms from buying from outsiders, but it has kept the vast majority of the domestic cement market under the control of the Cement Association.

It is crucial to recognize that this unofficial trade association policy did not work on its own but was facilitated by restrictions on competition aggressively pushed by MITI. Thus, the trade association's refusals to deal were not a violation of the spirit of MITI policy but a logical and necessary extension. The joint-sales companies and capacity cartels were important for reducing competition among cement firms, and a strong ready-mix concrete cartel was important for controlling competition in the intermediary industry. Only by restricting competition among the members of the trade associations could refusal-to-deal agreements between trade associations become possible. At the same time it was only

---

[57] Interview, Cement Association official, 1988. Use of refusals to deal against construction firms that buy imports was confirmed in *Semento nenkan* 37 (1985): 28; and 38 (1986): 16, 17.

by unofficially excluding association outsiders from the market that official policies to control competition and maintain high prices could really work.[58]

The MITI-sponsored official system of capacity-cutting cartels and joint-sales companies, along with the unofficial refusal-to-deal pact, were developed to reduce domestic competition. But this system restricted competition from overseas as well. The appearance of significant quantities of imported cement in the domestic market in 1984 caught the Japanese cement industry and MITI by surprise. When asked about imports from Korea and Taiwan, one MITI official commented that cement imports into Japan made no sense: cement was one of the few industries in which Japan had its own raw materials, and it was too heavy to be shipped internationally.[59] This was a silly thing to say, of course, given that Japan at the time was busily exporting much of its own cement. It was also ironic that the official should suggest that cement imports were economically irrational: an earlier Japanese government had actively encouraged Japanese imports from colonial Korea. In fact, one impetus for the original development of the Korean cement industry was a chance to serve as an export platform into the high-priced and strongly cartelized Japanese market of the 1930s.

Onoda Cement, the first company to invest in cement manufacturing in Korea, exported to the Japanese market from its Korean plant in the early 1930s as a way of getting around the government-mandated domestic cartel. The Japanese government, eager to foster industrialization in Korea, applauded Onoda's action and exhorted the other cement manufacturers to do the same.[60]

After the war South Korea and Taiwan rebuilt their cement industries and by the end of the 1970s had built up enough capacity to begin considerable exports. In their early stages of industrialization they both imported cement from Japan to develop industrial infrastructure. By 1979, however, South Korea had become a strong competitor to Japan in

[58] This account of the administration of refusals to deal is based on a 1988 interview with senior officials of one of Japan's largest cement companies. Nevertheless, such refusals to deal may continue, despite the 1991 FTC ruling against the industry (which did not mention refusals to deal). The fact that imports have dropped rather than expanded, although domestic prices continue to be high, also suggests continued refusals to deal. As we shall see, a 1993 FTC discovery that a ready-mix concrete industrial union in Saga prefecture had hired gangsters to force import-using competitors to sell out suggests that illegal governance to block imports continued at least into that year. *Asahi shinbun*, 20 August 1993.

[59] Interview, 1987.

[60] Semento Shinbunsha, *Jinbutsu semento shiwa* (Biographies of cement industry leaders), Vol. 2 (Tokyo: Semento Shinbun Sha, 1983), pp. 51–54.

exporting to the Middle East, and by 1981 Taiwan had also became a strong competitor.[61]

Along with French and British firms, Japan played a key role in developing the South Korean cement industry. Because the South Korean government required firms to export some of the cement they produced, Ssangyong Cement built docks to handle exports in the early 1970s. The Japanese government and Japanese trading companies lent money to Ssangyong Cement to build export docks, and Japanese trading firms promoted South Korean cement exports to third countries.[62] Japanese firms sold South Korea their most advanced production technology and equipment. At first the Japanese did not expect South Korea to be an important exporter because of South Korea's strong domestic demand.[63] And the Japanese never expected South Korea and Taiwan to export to Japan.[64] But South Korea and Taiwan did begin to compete with Japan in third-country markets as well as the Japanese home market because of their labor-cost advantage. As I noted earlier, direct labor costs constitute only 6 percent of total cement production costs.[65] Approximately 20 percent of these costs are made up by transport; 20 percent for energy; 10 percent for raw materials; and 40 percent for capital costs, depreciation, and overhead.[66] But while direct labor costs were small, much of the cost of transportation was the labor of running ships, and much of the cost of raw materials was the labor to dig and transport limestone. Thus, the total real labor component was much larger. South Korean wages were one-sixth those of Japan in the mid-1980s, and Taiwan's were also lower than Japan's, giving both South Korea and Taiwan a cost advantage.[67]

Japan was an important exporter of cement in East Asia in the 1950s and 60s. Although Japanese cement was more expensive than Europe's, transportation costs gave it a comparative advantage in regional markets. In the early 1950s the Korean War precipitated strong demand for Japanese cement; and the 1957 closing of the Suez Canal increased Japan's comparative advantage in Asian markets, making it the world's largest cement exporter.[68] The country continued to be a major exporter through the 1960s, although cement exports dropped in the early 1970s because of intense domestic demand created by the Tanaka government's building drive. But the OPEC price increase of 1973–74 led to steep decline in domestic demand, while creating new markets in the Middle

---

[61] Nihon Semento, *Hyakunen shi*, p. 456.
[62] *Semento nenkan* 26 (1974): 42.
[63] Ibid.
[64] Interview, Japanese journalist specializing in cement, 1988.
[65] MITI, *Kōgyō tōkeihyō* (Industrial statistics sourcebook), 1980.
[66] Interview, MITI official, 1988.
[67] *Asahi shinbun*, 19 January 1988.
[68] Dokusen Bunseki Kenkyū kai, *Nihon no dokusen kigyō*, p. 125.

East. This new demand, coupled with more efficient ships, led to a period of strong exports from 1975 to 1986. During 1979–86 Japan was once again the world's largest cement exporter.[69] Exports dropped in the late 1980s but rose with the recession of the early 1990s, again making Japan the largest exporter.

During the 1970s and 80s Japanese cement export prices were considerably lower than domestic prices for undelivered cement, which grew to over three times the export prices by 1988 with the success of the domestic cartel and the rise in the yen. Recession brought domestic prices down to just over twice the export price by 1992 (see figure 4–1).[70] We have seen how cartel activities in the domestic cement industry supported domestic prices. Selling below home-market price and production cost was a way of getting rid of surplus production so that firms would not drive down prices at home by unloading it in the domestic market. Production costs were estimated to be approximately twelve thousand yen per ton for cement manufacturers in the early 1980s.[71] Of this, just half was variable costs, and cement exporters were satisfied if export prices covered them. As in many industries, however, an export cartel was used to keep cement makers from competing among themselves and pushing export prices down any further than necessary.

The success of the domestic cartel in the 1980s created an enormous gap between Japanese and international cement prices. One might expect that in a freely competitive market, cheaper imports would flood into the Japanese market and pull domestic prices down. But the elaborate restrictions created to limit domestic competition served also to limit imports. Japan had imported cement during its early industrialization. Once the domestic industry was solidly established, however, imports stopped completely. There were no imports into Japan from 1913 until 1973 except for those from Japan's colonies between 1923 and 1944. In 1973 there was a very short spurt of imports followed by zero imports again until the early 1980s.

The 1973 import episode is the exception that proves the rule in keeping the Japanese cement market so tightly closed. In the spring of that year a government construction boom caused a cement shortage. On 2 April MITI called in all cement-company presidents to pressure them to increase production. The industry balked, and on 8 April MITI Minister Nakasone Yasuhiro telephoned South Korean Prime Minister Kim Jong Pil to ask for an emergency shipment of Korean cement. The fact that the

[69] *Semento nenkan*, various issues.

[70] Industry sources suggest that reported sales prices may be exaggerated by one thousand yen/ton in order to cheat on the price cartel. Nevertheless, even discounting for possible cheating of 6 to 10 percent, domestic prices are still very high compared to exports.

[71] *Nihon keizai sangyō shinbun*, 2 November 1984.

Japanese government only imported thirteen thousand tons of Korean cement into mainland Japan, representing 0.02 percent of annual demand, suggests that Nakasone's primary goal was to shock the domestic industry into raising production. In addition, Nihon Cement sponsored a shipment of 167,000 tons of Korean cement to Okinawa, which had just been returned to Japan, but did not bring any of this cement into the mainland market.[72]

Although the Japanese government does not appear to have had a genuine interest in introducing large amounts of imports, the official threat unwittingly unleashed a wave of imports from all over East Asia. Small trading companies responded to the government signal by rushing cement from the Philippines, Taiwan, South Korea, Thailand, and North Korea into Japanese ports. The Japanese response to these imports shows the power of trade-association control over the market. The 1974 *Cement Annual* reported that trading company attempts to import cement into Japan failed because they were done "hastily, on a speculative basis, and without preliminary surveys" of the market.[73] What the trading companies should have learned beforehand was that tight industry control of the market would prevent imports. At the port of Kobe the dock workers' union "formally refused to unload the cement."[74] At other ports longshoremen showed up the first day to unload but "failed to report to work the following day."[75] The cement sat in port, resulting in charges of six hundred thousand yen per day to the shipping companies. Much of the cement became unusable as it effloresced, or hardened, during the long wait in port.

The only cement that successfully bypassed the longshoremen was a scant six thousand tons unloaded by laborers from anxious construction firms.[76] The tiny amount of cement unloaded by longshoremen the first day went largely unsold despite deep price cuts by desperate trading companies. Some companies begged the Japanese cement manufacturers to buy the cement but were told, "We cannot take it even if you pay us."[77] Despite the acute shortage, twenty-two thousand tons of cement were reexported because no buyers could be found.[78] Although the *Cement Annual* does not explain why the dock workers refused to unload foreign cement, later importers' experience suggests that they were probably pressured by domestic cement firms. It was rumored at the

[72] *Semento nenkan* 26 (1974): 54.
[73] Ibid.
[74] Ibid.
[75] Ibid.
[76] Ibid.
[77] Ibid.
[78] Ibid., 37 (1985): 28.

time that the reason trading companies would not bring in imports was that they feared boycotts from domestic cement makers.[79]

The 1973 episode shows two important things. First, government support for the industry cartels was based on an understanding that the purpose of the cartel was to help industry produce sufficient cement for domestic construction, not gouge its buyers. When the industry held back production despite shortages, MITI used imports to remind industry that it could go around private-market controls. Thus, the ministry balanced cement-industry interests against those of the construction industry. Second, the incident shows that private controls exerted by the cement industry kept Japan hermetically sealed from imports during the 1970s.

The market remained tightly closed to imports through the 1970s and early 80s, although one South Korean cement-company official posted in Tokyo in 1978 said that "everyone wanted to sell cement in Japan."[80] Domestic ready-mix concrete firms were afraid of the Cement Association's sanctions against buying foreign cement, but outsiders to the ready-mix cartel wanted alternative supplies from overseas.

In 1980 a Korean resident in Japan who owned a ready-mix concrete company in Abashiri on the northern island of Hokkaido came to Tokyo to ask the South Korean firm, Ssangyong Cement, to sell it cement. The firm wanted South Korean cement because it was an outsider to the Ready-mix Concrete Federation and was unable to get a stable supply of cement from Japanese suppliers. Ssangyong agreed to send the firm one shipload of cement, although it tried to keep the shipment a secret. On the third day after the shipment went out, the Ssangyong office in Tokyo got a call from a Japanese cement company asking Ssangyong not to make the sale. According to the Ssangyong representative, the Japanese cement company "spoke as though the Japanese cement industry was the father and the Korean cement industry was the child and told us not to make trouble."[81] Friends in the Japanese cement industry told the Ssangyong representative not to go to the delivery site because his life would be in danger from gangsters connected to the cement industry. According to the Ssangyong representative, when the shipment arrived in Hokkaido, "the cement companies acted like another bomb had been dropped on Hiroshima." He received death threats over the telephone, and Japanese cement companies called the Ssangyong headquarters in Korea.[82]

[79] *Nihon keizai shinbun*, 2 July 1973.
[80] Interview, 1988.
[81] Ibid.
[82] Ibid.

The Japanese cement industry's threats convinced Ssangyong to give up selling cement to Japan for several years. In the meantime, however, the firm expanded its production capacity and prepared to launch a second sales campaign in the market. Because domestic cement makers continued to refuse cement to ready-mix concrete companies outside the joint cooperatives, these outsiders continued to try to get imported cement.[83] Some outsider firms managed to import tiny amounts of Taiwanese cement in 1982 and 1983.[84]

In 1984 both South Korean and Taiwanese firms began campaigns to sell larger amounts of cement to firms shut out of the Japanese cement market. Although they managed to sell some cement, they encountered a series of barriers that limited their success—some put up by the Japanese cement industry, some by the government. The first barrier was the one which had kept cement imports out in 1973: refusals to deal by longshoring companies. Ssangyong contracted with a longshoring firm to unload its first shipment to Osaka, but the day before the shipment's arrival the longshoring company said it could not do the work because Japanese cement companies had told it they would no longer give the company work if it handled foreign cement. This was a serious threat to the longshoring companies; they handled not only cement companies' exports but much of their domestic shipping as well because half of Japan's domestic cement distribution is by sea. Nevertheless, a friendly longshoring company told Ssangyong that under the government licensing system the longshoring firm could not refuse its services. Although Ssangyong was able to threaten that it would get the longshoring firm's license revoked to force the issue, for two years the firm struggled anew at each new port.[85]

According to a South Korean government official handling trade matters in Japan, Korean cement companies encountered similar problems with trucking firms that had been pressured by Japanese cement manufacturers not to handle cement imports. Korean firms complained to the FTC, but the trucking firms were unwilling to testify and simply said they did not want to handle imports.[86] Trucking firms were vulnerable because delivery exchanges reduced the cement industry's use of trucking services. The Cement Association was engaged in a relational contract with the Truckers' Association and supported the truckers by recognizing their cartel: a system of registration designed to restrict trucking business

---

[83] *Nihon keizai shinbun*, 29 May 1985; *Semento nenkan* 37 (1985): 28.

[84] The imports purchased by Kusama Shōten, a ready-mix concrete company that was refused supplies by the Japanese cement industry, amounted to only fifteen thousand tons in 1982 and ten thousand tons in 1983. *Semento nenkan* 37 (1985): 28.

[85] Interview, Ssangyong official, 1988.

[86] Interview, South Korean trade official, 1988.

to members of the Truckers' Association. The Truckers' Association often complained to the cement companies that nonmembers were taking their business, and it was dependent on the Cement Association to recognize it and enforce its regulations.[87] The Cement Association had its own motives for cracking down on outsiders to the trucking cartel because it suspected that unregistered trucks were carrying cement of uncertain origin. Although the Truckers' Association and the Cement Association were not completely successful in cracking down on outsider trucks, their pressure on truckers not to carry imports presented a significant barrier to Korean cement companies.

If the cement importers did manage to find a truck, domestic cement makers would track it to find out which ready-mix firms were buying imports so that they could intimidate them into stopping. When the first sizable quantities of imports entered Japan in 1984, the *Nihon keizai sangyō shinbun* reported that "the Japanese cement firms are excitedly looking for the 'criminals' who are buying imported cement."[88] The firms did this by sending cars out to tail truckloads of imported cement to find out who was buying it and taking pictures of the delivery. They would then cut off cement to the companies involved.[89]

Like ready-mix concrete companies, truckers, and longshoremen, trading companies also had long-term relations with the cement companies, which they were reluctant to jeopardize by getting involved with cement imports. Even three and a half years after large-scale imports began, Sumitomo Trading Company said, "Given our relationship with the domestic producers we cannot start importing immediately. But the import business is certainly attractive."[90] Eventually, however, major trading companies that were not involved with domestic cement manufacturers did cooperate with cement imports. For example, Hanwa Company, a big steel trading company, joined with Ssangyong to build a silo in Chiba for distribution in the Kanto area.[91]

The Cement Association's response to imports was openly hostile. Moroi Ken, one of the driving forces behind the industry's SDIL plan, said, "Since it looks like demand will continue to stagnate or decline over the long term, we are working to establish a hundred year plan of industrial restructuring. Given this, in principle there should be zero imports. If other countries continue exporting, then it follows that we'll have to export too, but it would not make any sense to go and throw

[87] *Semento nenkan* 38 (1986): 16, 43, 45.

[88] *Nihon keizai sangyō shinbun*, 1 November 1984.

[89] Uesugi Yoshimasa, *NIES seihin de nihon no sangyō wa dō naruka* (What will imports from the NIES do to Japanese industry?) (Tokyo: Eeru Shuppansha [Yell Books], 1988), p. 50; interview, South Korean cement company official, 1988.

[90] *Nihon keizai shinbun*, 10 November 1987.

[91] Ibid.

each others' markets into disarray."[92] In the spring of 1984 the Cement Association formed the Committee on Special Measures to Deal with Imports and Exports, headed by Ōshima Kenji with Imamura Kazusuke as acting head. The *Nihon keizai sangyō shinbun* noted that, although the stated purpose was to look at export conditions, "it is thought that it is actually concerned with a response to be taken against imports."[93] One of the committee's responses was to declare that none of the twenty-three Japanese cement companies would cooperate with importers. Imamura announced, "Japanese importers will have to bear all the costs of facilities for imports and sales on their own. They will have no support from [domestic cement] makers. Even if they bring in cheaper imports, there will be high costs for them, and the price will end up being the same as for domestic cement."[94] Thus, despite the fact that Japanese firms were not competitive with imports, there was no chance that South Korean firms would be able to form joint ventures with Japanese firms to use their distribution facilities, contacts, and networks to distribute South Korean cement much less buy out a Japanese cement maker to achieve the same goal. No Japanese cement firm had to rush to form a joint-venture contract with a South Korean firm for fear they would be left behind because the trade association was able to forge an agreement ensuring no firm would cooperate.

The marketing of cement requires considerable investment in distribution infrastructure. For instance, silos are necessary to store bulk cement. Because the entire network of silos owned by the twenty-three Japanese cement firms was closed to South Korean and Taiwanese firms, they would have to build their own silos if they wanted to enter the Japanese market. When Ssangyong tried to build a silo, it ran into a series of governmental barriers. First, it had a difficult time buying land on which to build because most harbor land is owned by local government authorities, who refused to sell to it. Ssangyong officials believed the local authorities refused to sell to them because they were opposed to imports. But the firm found some private land where the water was too shallow for ship access and had it dredged. After the firm built the silo, it took three months to get a license from the port authority to use it.[95]

Next, Ssangyong ran into opposition from the Customs Bureau. Cement is shipped in bulk, and the standard international practice for establishing the volume of a shipment is to use a draft survey. This survey calculates the weight of the cargo by seeing how low the ship rides in the water; figuring out how much water is being displaced; calculating the

[92] *Nihon keizai sangyō shinbun*, 2 November 1984.
[93] Ibid., 1 November 1984.
[94] Ibid., 27 May 1986.
[95] Interview, Ssangyong official, 1988.

total weight of the load on board; and then subtracting the weight of the fuel, personnel, and so on. It is considered accurate and is used in all the countries to which Japan exports cement. The Japanese customs agents, however, told Ssangyong that they could not use this standard method but would have to weigh all their cement on a scale. The only available scales were truck scales, and to use these would have been prohibitively expensive. Ssangyong complained without result to the South Korean and Japanese governments but finally got around this nontariff barrier by having a hopper scale custom built for fifty million yen (approximately $250,000). Cement was dropped into the hopper, which then weighed the cement before releasing it. It took three months to have the scale built, and then Ssangyong had to use it for another three months before MITI finally gave in and allowed the normal draft survey to be used.[96] The Tokyo office of the Customs Bureau reported that, although the draft survey is the customary method of assessing the weight of imports, deciding whether to allow it is at the discretion of the bureau.[97]

Once the cement was finally imported, MITI again supported the trade association by creating testing procedures that were more cumbersome and expensive for imports than for domestic cement. When Japan first began importing cement, the procedure for receiving Japanese Industrial Standards (JIS) approval was the same for both foreign and Japanese cement. The procedure for a Japanese cement manufacturer is to do in-house tests once a year and give the results to MITI.[98] In December 1984 MITI issued a policy statement titled "Regarding the Treatment of JIS approval for Ready-mix Concrete Companies That Use Imported Cement," which mandated that imported cement be tested twice a year.[99] Furthermore, each ready-mix company that wanted to use foreign cement had to arrange and pay for tests given by one of the semi-public organizations that do the testing. The tests took forty-five days and cost 200 to 250 thousand yen (approximately $1,400–$1,700). Because Japan's four thousand ready-mix concrete companies are small firms, the expense and trouble of having imported cement tested were significant.[100]

The JIS inspection procedure also made it easier for Japanese cement manufacturers to figure out which ready-mix companies were buying imports. Japanese ready-mix companies pass a JIS inspection given by MITI and receive JIS approval for their concrete on the condition that

[96] Ibid.
[97] Telephone interview, 1988.
[98] Interviews, officials from South Korean Ministry of Commerce and Industry and Ssangyong, 1988.
[99] *Semento Nenkan* 37 (1985): 30–31.
[100] Interview, Ssangyong official, 1988.

they use cement from a specific company. If they want to use another company's cement they have to reregister, thus subjecting themselves to the scrutiny of the cement cartel.[101] In short, MITI's procedures helped the Cement Association check up on the ready-mix concrete companies so that they could enforce relational contracts.

Although the Cement Association protected the market with government support, imports managed to take 0.3 percent of the market in 1984. The association continued to enforce its relational contracts with ready-mix concrete companies, longshoremen, truckers, and construction companies. Simultaneously, however, it responded to the imports by negotiating with South Korean and Taiwanese cement trade associations to convince them to restrain their exports and support Japanese cement prices. The Cement Association's Committee on Special Measures to Deal with Imports and Exports decided in May 1984 to work out a deal with the South Korean and Taiwanese trade associations in exchange for Japan's ceding of export markets in third countries to them. Furthermore, the committee proposed that the Japanese trade association would import South Korean cement and distribute it through the Japanese network to reduce the effect of imports on the domestic market.[102]

The president of the Cement Association, Kobayashi Hisaaki; the chair of the Import Committee, Ōshima Kenji; and the vice-chair of the committee, Fukushima Kōichi, went to South Korea in November 1984 to talk to the heads of the Korean cement association and the two largest firms, Ssangyong and Tongyang. They asked that the South Korean trade association restrain exports to Japan in exchange for Japanese discretion in Southeast Asia and the Middle East. The South Korean trade association expressed its understanding but made no promises except to join with the Japanese in restraining competition in the Hong Kong market.[103] The Japan Cement Association also sent Kanemori Tsutomu of Nihon Cement to talk with Taiwan Cement, which was the successor firm to the pre-war Asano Cement (predecessor to Nihon Cement) plant in Taiwan. But because the Taiwanese trade association was largely composed of small firms and was poorly coordinated, it was not possible to negotiate with the industry.[104]

Although the South Koreans would not agree to restrain exports to Japan in 1984, they did agree to do so later when they established a stronger foothold in the Japanese market. In the fall of 1986 the South Korean and Japanese cement trade associations agreed that Japanese

[101] Ibid.
[102] *Semento nenkan*, 37 (1985): 30.
[103] Ibid.
[104] Ibid.

cement companies would import one million tons per year of South Korean cement while the South Koreans would import an additional 1.2 million tons of cement into Japan.[105] The Cement Association's hope was that, if guaranteed a certain level of exports, the South Koreans would cooperate in "developing an orderly market."[106] That is, they would help keep prices up.

The majority share being given to the South Koreans was a concession to the Japanese FTC, which said it would not allow the Cement Association to control over half of South Korean cement imports into Japan. Nevertheless, even with this precondition the deal did not go through because of FTC and, more important, MITI disapproval. A MITI official's comment was that "for domestic producers to import when they've lost the ability to sell their own cement is doubtful from the point of view of structural adjustment."[107] By opposing the industry's plan, MITI made clear it was against firms' using structural adjustment policies to abandon basic manufacturing to foreign countries. MITI opposed the cement industry's exploitation of market-control mechanisms (which MITI had helped foster over the years) merely to generate profits from cheap imports. The ministry's opposition to imports shows that its policies supporting high cement prices were not aimed simply at filling cement company coffers but at maintaining domestic cement manufacture. A possible alternative explanation might be that MITI was concerned with protecting the jobs or business interests of upstream industries such as limestone quarrying, but this seems unlikely given that such interests were never mentioned in discussions of measures to support the cement industry. The most plausible explanation is that MITI had strategic goals for the basic materials industries.

Although the Cement Association was not allowed to broker South Korean imports, it did convince South Korean cement companies and their agents to cooperate with the domestic cartel by keeping their prices fairly high. Ishihara Mitsue, the department head of the building materials division of the Hanwa Company, the steel trading company that handled Ssangyong's cement imports, stated clearly that his firm would not compete too hard with Japanese firms on price: "It is true that the sales price of imported cement is cheaper than that for domestic cement, but we will not set prices so as to provoke domestic manufacturers. It is a distribution company's duty to make sure a situation does not develop where bad money drives out good money by selling cheaply and driving down prices, and I intend to live up to this duty." Of course, Ishihara's client had introduced some change into the market. But Ishihara was

[105] *Nihon keizai shinbun*, 2 September 1986.
[106] Ibid., 1 September 1986.
[107] *Nihon keizai sangyō shinbun*, 9 October 1986.

invoking the ideology of relational contracts in his suggestion that collu-sion among sellers to avoid driving down prices was an ethical good and announcing that his company would take the moral course by following this principle. Such statements do not normally produce an outcry from consumers or an FTC investigation but are part of the everyday language of public discourse about the economy in Japan.

Ssangyong and other exporters to Japan priced their goods more cheaply than domestic goods, but comfortably above the prevailing international price for cement, to profit from the Japanese cartelized market. Thus, while the Japanese did suffer some intrusion on the mar-ket, by reaching an understanding with some importers they were able to keep prices higher than straightforward market competition would have produced.

While the cement industry's trade association has made and imple-mented core policies that keep prices high, MITI has supported those policies, provided leadership to facilitate cooperation among firms, and guided association policies to fit MITI's strategic goals. Politicians have also supported market governance, primarily by padding construction industry profits. Construction companies use *dangō*, prebidding nego-tiations among themselves, to keep prices high. A government audit found that dangō was used in over 90 percent of projects funded by various national and local government agencies in 1992 and 1993.[108] The LDP has long protected the use of dangō in the construction industry, which has been attacked by the FTC. In 1984 the commission attempted to restrict the industry's use of dangō and was opposed by the Construc-tion Ministry. LDP leaders with close ties to construction intervened and forced the FTC to back down by threatening to rewrite the Antimonopoly Law.[109] As we saw in Chapter 2, the LDP's construction minister, Nakamura Kishirō, convinced the FTC in 1992 not to file a criminal prosecution against a group of Saitama Construction com-panies.[110] The LDP also supports the industry by handing out lucrative public-works contracts in exchange for campaign contributions. Accord-ing to one construction firm director, in 1993 it was standard for politi-cians to receive 1 percent of the value of a government contract as a kickback from construction companies. These kickbacks were also often awarded for private-sector contracts.[111] The corrupt relationship of top

---

[108] *Nihon keizai shinbun*, 4 November 1993, cited in *Weekly Japan Digest*, 8 November 1993.

[109] *Semento nenkan* 37 (1985): 6.

[110] *Japan Times*, 29 July 1994; *Japan Digest*, 14 March 1994, p. 18.

[111] Itagaki Hidenori, *Zoku no kenkyū: Sei kan zai wo gyūjiru seikai jitsuryokusha shūdan no jittai* (A study of the tribes: The reality of the groups of powerholders who control the worlds of politics, the bureaucracy, and finance) (Tokyo: Keizaikai, 1987), p. 73; Jun Mamiya, "The Iron Triangle and Corruption in the Construction Industry," *Tokyo Business Today* 61 (November 1993): 10–13.

LDP leaders to construction firms was one of the main factors leading to the fall of the party from power in 1993.

Thus, politicians' support has enabled the construction industry to pay high prices for cement. The tieing of cement contracts to campaign contributions has also excluded imports from the public-works market, which makes up half of all construction. LDP protection of construction industry profits has provided the basis for a strong cement cartel; and because a portion of cement profits from government contracts are recycled into LDP campaign contributions, the party has been in favor of policies that support cement prices. One might cynically suppose that LDP interest in generating campaign donations, rather than MITI's strategic goals, accounts for Japan's strong policies supporting and protecting the industry.

Yet cartel arrangements have been worked out entirely by the trade associations and MITI. Conflict over terms have been negotiated between the associations with Construction Ministry and MITI assistance and MITI guarantees to the construction industry that it would not allow the cement industry to abuse its power. While campaign contributions might give the LDP strong reasons to support the cement industry's high prices, MITI's unwillingness to let the industry use market controls to profit from imports shows that the ministry is concerned with maintaining domestic production, not just industry profits.

The dominant explanation given by the Japanese press for the reluctance of ready-mix concrete makers to buy inexpensive cement from Taiwan and South Korea is that domestic construction and ready-mix concrete firms worry that its quality is inferior to Japanese cement.[112] The Japanese cement industry has argued that imported cement is unreliable. One of the Ready-mix Concrete Federation's first moves against cement imports was to mount a campaign warning local government officials not to buy imported cement because of inferior quality. The South Korean and Taiwanese cement industries countered that their cement was made with the latest Japanese technology and equipment and had passed all Japan's quality tests.[113] One Japanese journalist specializing in cement said that Japanese cement buyers were genuinely concerned that, even if imported cement passed all the tests, it might not stand up for fifty or sixty years as Japanese-made cement would.[114]

Nevertheless, a highly placed executive in one of Japan's largest

[112] Through the use of the Nikkei Telecom computer retrieval system, I was able to read all the articles on cement imports in the two principal Japanese newspapers that dealt with economic affairs between 1984 and early 1988: *Nihon keizai shinbun* and *Nihon keizai sangyō shinbun*. In addition, I read the *Cement Annuals* (Semento Nenkan) published by the principal newspaper specializing in cement, the *Semento Shinbun*. I also read through articles from the *Asahi Shinbun*, although it had less information on the cement industry.

[113] *Nihon keizai shinbun*, 22 August 1987; interview, Ssangyong official, 1988.

[114] Interview, 1988.

cement companies said in an interview that there is no real difference in cement quality except for color.[115] The fact that Japanese cement makers were proposing as early as 1984 to broker South Korean cement imports themselves is further evidence that the industry was not really concerned with the quality of South Korean cement. The Cement Association's brokerage proposal implied that through scientific testing one could indeed verify quality and durability. Of course, even if there is no genuine difference in cement quality, the Japanese industry may have succeeded in convincing its buyers that there is one. But in that case, however, Japanese buyers would have no interest in imports; and MITI and the Cement Association would have no need to harass importers. If the quality of imported cement were not good enough to attract buyers, MITI's and the Cement Association's anti-import measures would have been unnecessary.

In the 1980s the Japanese press supported the cement industry's argument that imports were making slow inroads into the economy because of domestic concern with quality and consequently did not report some important governmental and private barriers to imports. The press made occasional mention of cement makers' refusals to deal with ready-mix concrete makers, but neither the *Cement Annual* nor any newspaper ever suggested that ready-mix companies were reluctant to buy imports because of fear of future refusals to deal. The *Nihon keizai sangyō shinbun* once reported that ready-mix companies were attracted by the low prices of imported cement but were worried about "security of supply."[116] Although security of supply was the broader reason for MITI's and the construction trade associations' support of the cement cartel, individual ready-mix firms were clearly more worried about being shut out of the domestic cement market than they were about the development of overall shortages.

The 1974 *Cement Annual* did report the refusals of longshoring companies to handle imported cement. Although Korean cement company officials reported similar problems with longshoring and trucking firms in the 1980s, the Japanese media never reported such problems in its extensive coverage of cement imports. Similarly, South Korean cement company and government officials reported the refusal of Japanese customs officials to use the draft survey method to process Korean cement, and the hopper-scale incident was covered on Korean television. The Japanese media, however, never mentioned it.

I think that the *Cement Annual* and the *Nikkei shinbun*, as well as the major Japanese newspapers, were unwilling to report on informal barri-

---

[115] Interview, cement company official, 1988.
[116] *Nihon keizai sangyō shinbun*, 2 November 1984.

ers to imports by 1984 because the press was becoming sensitive to foreign criticism of Japanese nontariff barriers. This avoidance is in striking contrast to the matter-of-fact way in which one pulp press book on imports from the NICs dealt with nontariff barriers to cement imports. *NIES seihin de nihon no sangyō wa dō naruka* (What will imports from the NIES do to Japanese industry?) was an informal book put out as part of the Yell Books series. It bluntly describes the cement industry's tailing of cement trucks and its use of refusals to deal against construction companies as tactics to keep imports out of the market.[117] Thus, it seems that the establishment press was purposely avoiding the topic.

A journalist specializing in chemical prices for one of Japan's largest and most respected business newspapers explained that journalists in both industry-specific and general newspapers have to be very careful about telling the real story for fear of retribution from the industries. He noted that, because industry-specific newspapers (such as *Semento shinbun*) are dependent on their industries for advertising, they avoid revealing industry secrets or being critical of industry practices. Larger, more general newspapers are less dependent on specific industries but are limited in what they can write because they fear that industry might stop sharing information with them.

The newspapers' recent spotlight on political corruption in the construction industry has also illuminated some of the irregularities in the cement and ready-mix concrete industries. A 1993 *Asahi shinbun* article broke new ground by suggesting that "although some say concern with quality is the reason [for the lack of imports] the real reason appears to be the fear that imports would trigger a collapse in the price of ready-mix concrete."[118] Thus, the particular political pressures on the construction industry have brought some measure of critical attention to cement, although the problem of journalist fear appears to impede our general understanding of Japanese industry.

The FTC and MITI both restricted the cement cartel in the 1990s, although the basic market structure shows little change. The *Japan Economic Journal* reported that in 1990 the industry was relieved of restrictions on capacity expansion imposed by MITI under the Structural Conversion Facilitation Law (SCFL) of 1987, which was not supposed to function as a cartel law.[119] In 1991 the FTC cracked down on the

---

[117] As its name suggests, the Yell Books series is lively and fun to read, with lots of anecdotes and no heavy footnotes. Yoshimasa, *NIES seihin de nihon no sangyō wa dō naruka*, p. 50.

[118] *Asahi shinbun*, 20 August 1993.

[119] *Japan Economic Journal*, 1992, p. 150

industry's price cartel and levied the heaviest fine ever for violation of the Antimonopoly Law. The commission found that joint-sales companies in Hokkaido and the Chūgoku region in Western Japan were holding back production and fixing prices. The FTC appears to have been prompted both by general U.S. pressure to get rid of structural protection and by U.S. Commerce Department findings that Japanese firms were dumping cement in the U.S. market. Another factor involved accusations that the industry's cartel practices were increasing the costs of the new Kansai International Airport. In addition to fining the firms involved, the FTC dissolved two joint-sales companies—those led by Ube Industries and Onoda Cement.[120]

One result of the FTC crackdown was to push the largest firms into mergers. In 1991 Mitsubishi Materials acquired Tōhoku Kaihatsu, and in late 1993 Onoda and Chichibu Cement announced they would merge.[121] The FTC ruling, along with a fall in demand for cement due to economic recession, also reduced domestic cement prices by 2.2 percent from 1990 to 1992 (see figure 4–3).[122] Nevertheless, the impact of the ruling appears to have been limited because it overlooked the trade association's boycott of firms buying imported cement. As a result, the gap between domestic and import price remained just as wide, and imports actually dropped (see figures 4–1 and 4–2). The direct cause of the drop in imports was increased demand in other Asian countries. But the continued price gap between imported and domestic cement suggests that the threat of boycotts still scares domestic builders away from buying imports.

Moreover, the cement industry was still protected by the powerful ready-mix concrete cartel that was built up by MITI and the Cement Association in the 1970s. Ready-mix companies are under no pressure to buy imports because, due to their joint-sales operations, they do not compete over prices. The only price competitors are outsiders to the industrial unions, who rely on imports. The ready-mix cartel uses powerful informal governance to suppress competition from outsiders who import cheap cement. A March 1993 investigation by the FTC and the Saga prefectural police found that the Saga Ready-mix Concrete Industrial Union used gangsters several times, beginning in 1984, to force outsiders to sell their operations to union members. Later in 1993 the Nagoya Ready-mix Concrete Cooperative Union decided that members

---

[120] *Japan Economic Almanac*, 1992, p. 150.

[121] *Japan Economic Journal*, 1992, p. 150; *Nihon keizai shinbun*, 12 November 1993, cited in *Weekly Japan Digest*, 15 November 1993.

[122] The falling price was for delivered cement, which is the price-indicator commodity in the market. Prices of undelivered cement showed a sharp drop of 14 percent from 1990 to 1992, although this reflected an unusual jump in the price in 1990.

Figure 4–3. Japanese cement prices (in thousands of yen)

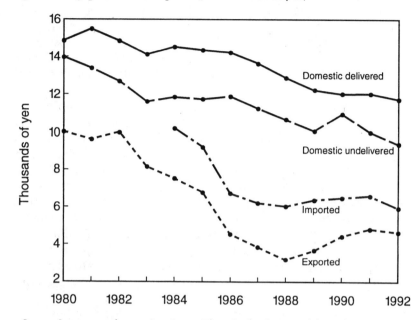

Source: *Semento nenkan*, various issues. The price for domestic delivered cement may be overstated at times by some one thousand yen because of cheating on the domestic price cartel.

would cut prices by 11 percent to undercut outsiders' prices and drive them out of business. Although members complained this would push prices below production costs, the ready-mix concrete companies were not left to fight off cheap imports alone. The industrial union arranged to borrow money from financial institutions to compensate member firms for two-thirds of the price cut.[123] This revelation suggests that informal governance of the cement market was still thriving in 1993.

The crackdown by the FTC and the U.S. government also made the cement industry more circumspect about publicizing its cartel activities. *The One-Hundred Year History of the Onoda Cement Company*, published in 1981, lauded the success of MITI-sponsored cartels in "modernizing" (i.e., reducing competition in) the ready-mix concrete industry. It backed this up with a graph that showed very nicely that the depression cartels during the 1970s had raised ready-mix concrete and cement prices.[124] In 1995, however, when I asked the Chichibu Onoda Cement

[123] *Asahi shinbun*, 20 August 1993.
[124] *Onoda semento hyakunen shi* (A one-hundred year history of the Onoda Cement Company), (Tokyo: Onoda Semento Kabushikigaisha, 1981), p. 687.

Corporation for permission to include the graph in this book, it flatly refused. Its stated reason was that the graph was based on statistics gathered by third parties, like the Bank of Japan, and that readers might mistakenly think that Onoda itself had collected them. Since most graphs incorporate data produced by a third party, I would guess that the more likely reason is that Chichibu Onoda wanted to discourage publicizing the cartels.

The official policy toward Japan's declining industries has been to use capacity cuts and joint sales to reduce competition and support prices but to avoid any restrictions on imports. Like most of Japan's declining basic materials industries, however, the cement industry has experienced relatively little competition from imports despite high domestic prices. The reason for imports' slow inroads into the cement market does not involve any natural immunity to imports due to dyadic relational contracts between firms but instead a system of market controls established by trade associations with strong backing by MITI. Although many have argued that MITI's strategic goal for declining industries is to allow them to shut down to make way for rising industries, MITI was so concerned with preserving the domestic capacity to produce cement that it opposed the domestic makers' own efforts to replace some domestic production with imports.

Policy toward the industry has been worked out through a combination of strong MITI leadership on formal policy and private governance to create informal policy. The Cement Association has carried out the core official and unofficial policies to reduce competition. On the official plane, the association coordinated a capacity-cutting cartel and a system of joint-sales companies. Unofficially, the association used refusals to deal to ensure that buyers would be forced to buy solely from the trade association and thus be obliged to pay the association members' high prices.

Internal cohesion within the Cement Association was necessary to forge the capacity-cutting cartel, agree on the joint-sales companies, and enforce refusals to deal. It was also important for ensuring that no members would let foreign competitors use their existing distribution facilities to bring in imports. In the period of structural decline MITI played a key role in helping the association create a consensus on cooperation. Its pressure facilitated agreement on capacity cuts and the establishment and strengthening of joint-sales companies.

The system of controls developed by the cement industry was based not only on consensus within the industry but on a relational contract with the construction industry. Specific measures to reduce competition in the cement industry and support prices were not taken unilaterally but in consultation with the construction industry. In exchange for the construction industry's support for market controls, the cement industry agreed not to exploit its position and to provide a stable supply of cement. The core policy of refusals to deal were worked out through regular direct meetings between the Cement Association and the construction trade associations.

Nevertheless, this relationship alone was not enough to maintain strong control over the market. In the 1970s competition in the intermediary ready-mix concrete industry undercut the cement industry's efforts to raise prices. Strengthening the Ready-mix Concrete Federation was an important factor in strengthening the cement industry's market controls. Just as the cement and construction industries developed a relational contract, the Ready-mix Concrete Federation developed a relational contract with both the cement and the construction trade associations, although it relied on pressure from the Cement Association to force local cooperative unions to honor their agreement with the construction industry. In addition to the ready-mix industry, there were several other layers of relational contracts in the distribution of cement that added rigidity to the market. Longshoring companies and the trucking association were bound by agreements not to handle cement produced by outsiders to the Cement Association—that is, imports. Trading companies had firm-level relational contracts with cement firms, which prevented them from handling imports.

The necessary variables for the success of informal market governance to exclude imports from the cement market are the concentration of the cement sector itself and the powerful cartel of the downstream construction industry. The cement industry had no technological hook that would have bound construction firms to them if they had been under intense competitive pressure. While relational contracting at the trade-association level supported the principal controls in the cement market, MITI strengthened and supervised these relationships. It strengthened the Ready-mix Concrete Federation in the late 1970s; and when the cement and construction industries negotiated over the cement cartel in 1983, MITI guaranteed that the cement industry would maintain steady production at reasonable prices. Thus, the state made intratrade-association cohesion possible and facilitated relational contracting between associations. Although cement is a relatively easy industry to cartelize, the state has played an important role in making sure that cartels work well.

MITI and customs officials also backed up market controls by setting up nontariff barriers to keep out imports. Customs officials stalled Korean imports by imposing cumbersome customs procedures, and MITI imposed expensive and time-consuming testing procedures. Although not designed specifically to deal with imports, the requirement that ready-mix concrete firms register their manufacturers' names helped deter imports by subjecting importing firms to scrutiny by domestic cement companies.

MITI delegated policy-making to private institutions and helped make policy work by using pressure to help the trade association conclude collective goods pacts. Here there was no basic conflict of interest: MITI sought to strengthen domestic manufacturing by supporting prices of manufactured goods. Thus, pressure did not force firms to do something they did not want to do but helped them cooperate in something that would benefit all firms as long as cheating was kept to a minimum. Firms did not always go along with all of MITI's proposals; but when they did, both their interests and MITI's strategic goals were furthered.

While market controls can help buoy a declining industry, those that work too well can destroy incentives for efficiency. MITI tried to finesse the problem by creating a shadow market between cement producers who would buy and sell cement at prices corresponding to production costs while selling to construction companies at inflated cartel prices. Firms were reluctant, however, because they feared divulging costs to potential competitors.

Although FTC enforcement in the cement industry has been lax, the commission has put some limits on MITI's push for collusion and controls. For instance, it has limited the anticompetitive impact of joint-sales companies by restricting their size. Paradoxically, however, FTC enforcement sometimes has had the effect of pushing the Cement Association to go along with strongly anticompetitive MITI policies, as in 1983 when the FTC pushed the industry into the capacity cartel and joint-sales companies that were recommended by MITI.

Although MITI and the trade associations played the central role in making policy for the cement industry, LDP politicians supported the industry by doling out government contracts at inflated prices to both construction and cement firms in return for campaign contributions and by opposing the FTC's attempt to regulate the construction industry more strictly. In this way the LDP made it easier for the construction industry to accept high domestic prices for cement. The party did not, however, act as an arbiter between the cement and construction industries, a role played by MITI and the Construction Ministry. Nor did it serve as a vehicle for translating cement interests into policy. If there is one thing the cement case makes clear, it is that MITI did not support the protection of the cement industry from imports because of industry pressure. The cement case, indeed, does not make sense if one attempts to analyze it from an American pluralist perspective. There is no scenario more implausible in American politics than that which occurred in the Japanese cement industry, where a humdrum basic materials industry proposes to substitute imports for a portion of its own domestic production and is turned down by the government because of concerns about maintaining domestic supply. Like any capitalist state, Japan relies on the profit motive to get private firms to further its economic goals. What is striking about the cement case is that MITI fostered cartels to shape profit incentives and, due to the informal character of its policies, was able to intervene flexibly and effectively when the cartel organizations did not further the ministry's goals of boosting manufacturing production.

As of 1994, the cartels in the cement and ready-mix concrete industry continued to control markets effectively. Ultimately, however, their power rests on the ability and willingness of the construction industry to pay their high prices. Attacks on the cozy relationship between the construction industry and politicians threaten the construction industry's price cartel and could conceivably push construction firms to aggressively seek cheaper cement. Foreign pressure on Japan to open the construction market is another force that might ultimately destroy the cement cartel. Although the United States is creating the most pressure, the general opinion in Japan is that, while U.S. firms are unlikely to make great inroads into the Japanese construction market, South Korean firms could do very well because of their low management costs, technological sophistication, and overseas experience. A major cost advantage for South Korean builders is that they would bring in cheap cement, steel, and other building materials. Cement insiders worry that the entry of South Korean construction companies could in this fashion destroy the Japanese cement price structure.

The Petrochemical Sector

We have looked so far at two sharply contrasting cases of internationally uncompetitive industries. Aluminum refiners had no technological hook to hold on to customers. Buyers are unwilling to pay a high premium for a good that is completely standardized, readily transportable, and easily storable and that makes up a high proportion of the cost of the finished good. In the cement market, builders will pay high prices for the domestic material because their own strong domestic cartel allows them to do so. They have cooperated with cement producers to keep out imports. Aluminum and cement frame a spectrum of ways in which cartel policy can affect an uncompetitive industry. In aluminum refining, Japanese cartel policy helped the industry ease out of domestic production when domestic buyers had no interest in paying the prices to keep it in business. By contrast, the cooperation between buyers and sellers to protect the domestic cement market is a classic example of interindustry relational contracting to preserve an uncompetitive industry.

Petrochemicals is a more complex case. Like aluminum and cement, Japan's petrochemical industry is internationally uncompetitive. The country lacks energy resources and is forced to rely on petroleum-based raw materials that are more expensive than those used in North American and Middle Eastern industries. Japan's lack of competitiveness is also due to cartel policies that have discouraged shakeouts and inadvertently encouraged inefficiency. But petrochemical firms produce sophisticated goods that give customers reason to support them with relational contracting. Thus, the industry has a technological hook. I have seen no evidence, however, that it exploits this hook to coerce buyers. Rather, dyadic relational contracts appear intrinsically powerful, and in this sense the industry has what Ronald Dore calls a "natural immunity to imports." Nevertheless, because dyadic relational contracts alone have failed to maintain prices, they have been supplemented by various cartel

122

Figure 5-1. Ratio of domestic price to import and export prices for ethylene-based petrochemicals

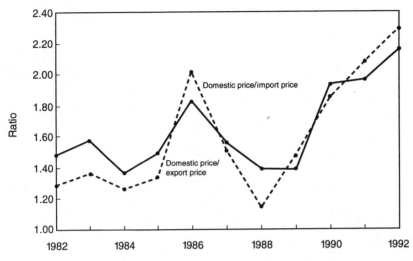

Note: This figure summarizes material from tables 5-7 and 5-10, and includes all the standardized ethylene-based chemicals produced in Japan in quantities over 500,000 tons.

arrangements that reinforce the bargaining position of the petrochemical producers. As in cement and aluminum, these have included legally based, government-sponsored cartels as well as informal, extralegal government policy to coordinate the industry. MITI has led, although not forced, the industry in the formation and implementation of policy. In addition, industry has worked out its own elaborate and informal mechanism that establishes rules for pricing under relational contracts.

Informal governance has helped keep petrochemical prices high compared to both export and import prices, as it has in cement. Domestic prices for all the major standardized ethylene-based petrochemicals averaged 60 percent over export prices for 1980–92 and 64 percent over import prices (see figure 5-1). Nevertheless, Japan remains a net exporter of ethylene-based goods (see figure 5-2).

Petrochemicals are chemicals made from petroleum. The two principal feedstocks are naphtha and ethane. Ethane is made from natural gas and is not as readily transportable as naphtha. Japanese petrochemical production, like most of Europe's, is based on the more expensive naphtha, most of which is now imported from Middle Eastern oil refineries. Naphtha is "cracked" to make a variety of products; the most important to petrochemicals are ethylene and propylene. Both ethylene and propylene are monomers: that is, they are composed of a single molecule. These

Figure 5–2. Japan's international trade in ethylene-based goods

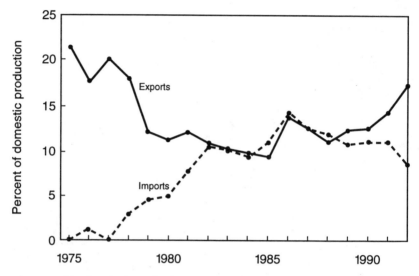

Source: Sekigu kagaku kōgyō kyōkai (Japan Petrchemical Industry Association), *Petro-chemical Industry of Japan,* 1991, 1993.; *Kagaku keizai* (Aug 1984); *Kagaku keizai* 39 (August 1992):26.

two monomers are made into a variety of polymers (chemicals composed of chains of multiple molecules) such as polyethylene, polyvinyl chloride, and polypropylene, which are in turn molded or extruded and sold to producers of finished goods such as cars and consumer electronics. As figure 5–3 shows, plastics are by far the most important form of petrochemicals, accounting for 61 percent of the market. Textiles and synthetic rubber are the other two important products.

Table 5–1 shows the major derivatives of ethylene and propylene and their uses. Half of ethylene is made into low- or high-density polyethylene, both of which have a wide range of applications. One-third of high-density polyethylene is used for film and another third for molded goods such as bottles and containers. Most low-density polyethylene is made into film or used to coat paper. Other major ethylene derivatives include polyvinyl chloride monomer, the raw material for polyvinyl chloride (PVC) pipe used in construction; ethylene oxide, about half of which is made into polyester fiber; and styrene monomer, two-thirds of which is made into polystyrene for use in electronics and household goods. Nearly half of propylene, the other major product of naphtha cracking, is turned into polypropylene, most of which is molded into parts for electronics and other industries.

Figure 5-3. The Japanese petrochemical market

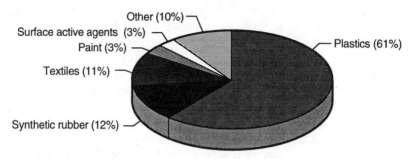

Source: Sekiyu Kagaku Kōgyō Kyōkai (Japan Petrochemical Industry Association), *Sekiyu kagaku kōgyō no genjō* (The current situation in the petrochemical industry) (Tokyo: Sekiyu kagaku kōgyō kyōkai, 1991), p. 12.

Table 5-1. Major derivatives of ethylene and propylene, 1990

Product	Production volume	Percentage ethylene or propylene used	Major uses
Derivatives of ethylene			
Low-density polyethylene	1,785	30%	Film, laminates, wire wire housings
High-density polyethylene	1,103	19%	Molded goods, film, pipe
Vinyl chloride monomer*	2,288	14%	Polyvinyl chloride (used for pipes for construction)
Ethylene oxide*	674	10%	Polyester fiber, surface active agents
Acetaldehyde*	383	4%	Acetic acid, ethyl acetate
Styrene Monomer*	1,417	10%	Polystyrene, synthetic rubber, polyester resins
Other		13%	
Derivatives of propylene			
Polypropylene	1,942	46%	Molded goods, film, synthetic fibers
Acrylonitrile*	592	15%	Acrylic fiber, synthetic resin. synthetic rubber
Propylene oxide*	336	7%	Polyurethane, polyester fiber
Other		32%	

Source: Sekiyu kagaku kōgyō no genjō (The current situation in the petrochemical industry) (Tokyo: Sekiyu kagaku kōgyō kyōkai, 1991), p. 12.
Note: Asterisk indicates that good is standardized and easily transportable.

Many buyers in the petrochemical market are strongly committed to relational contracting for reasons that depend on the sector of the market. First, in the upstream market most firms are connected by pipeline. Petrochemical production is highly vertically integrated in the

United States and Western Europe and has become more so in recent years.[1] Japan, on the other hand, built its industry around complexes (*kombinaato*) of various factories performing different stages of production, which were often connected by pipeline and owned by different companies. Thus, companies sank great investments into plants in which they were virtually locked into a sales relationship with other firms.[2] The original reason for this approach was the riskiness of investments: Japanese firms were dependent on the West for technology, and the market was small. To minimize risk, companies have limited their investments to certain stages of production.[3] Often work even in a single stage of production is shared among a number of companies. For example, at Mitsubishi Yuka's Kagoshima complex, Shin-Etsu Chemical, Asahi Chemical, and Kanegafuchi Chemical all make polyvinyl chloride, while at Tonen's Kawasaki complex, Nitto Chemical, Asahi Chemical, and Showa Denko all make acrylonitrile. All these firms are members of different *keiretsu*.[4]

Second, relational contracting is important because, in some downstream markets, users want to give suppliers enough stability to produce finely differentiated products. For instance, Japanese automakers routinely ask resin makers to produce different grades of material for car seat arms, and backs, and seats. Buyers want manufacturers to make a dedicated investment to particular production techniques and relational contracting is necessary to promise rewards for dedicated investments in physical plant or know-how. A third reason for relational contracting is a desire for security and convenience of supply.

In the case of the cement industry, both the state and trade associations worked to back up dyadic relational contracts and support prices. The cement industry produces a single standardized good. The state supports production and price cartels while intertrade-association cooperation focuses on keeping out cheaper imports. The petrochemical industry, in contrast, produces an enormous variety of different products. Thus, cooperating to support prices is much more complicated. As it did for cement, the state has often helped the industry coordinate cartels to reduce price competition. The much greater complexity of petrochemical prices, however, makes the task of setting them more difficult. The solution has been industry-wide negotiation of basic chemical prices to

[1] Walter Vergara and Donald Brown, *The New Face of the World Petrochemical Sector* (Washington, D.C.: World Bank, 1988), p. 12.

[2] This is the classic motive for relational contracting, cited by Oliver Williamson, *The Economic Institutions of Capitalism: Firms, Markets, Relational Contracting* (New York: Free Press, 1985).

[3] *Kagaku kōgyō nenkan* (Chemical Industry Annual), 1976, 78.

[4] Itami Hiroyuki, *Nihon no kagaku sangyō, naze sekai ni tachiokureta no ka* (Japan's chemical industry: Why is it behind the rest of the world?) (Tokyo: NTT Shuppan, 1990), p. 125.

create a consensus for the price levels of derivatives. The initiative for this price-setting framework came from upstream petrochemical firms but is based on interindustry relational contracting because it is largely accepted by downstream industries.

MITI has played an important role in the initial growth of the industry, its retrenchment in the early 1980s, and its regrowth in the late 1980s. The industry was established in the 1950s with government support. MITI initially expressed interest by issuing a 1951 report urging the establishment of a petrochemical industry. In 1955 the ministry established an infant industry policy to encourage the development of petrochemicals. The government's stated goal was to replace imports with domestic goods and assure sufficient, cheaper supplies of the raw materials necessary for the development of high-polymer petrochemicals. Thus, the industry was intended to strengthen international competitiveness and upgrade Japan's industrial structure. Various policy tools supported the new industry, including preferential lending by the Japan Development Bank and tax benefits.[5] To compensate for Japan's lack of plentiful, cheap natural gas, which the United States enjoyed, and for the inefficiency of its relatively small-scale plants, the government established a two-tiered market in the refined-petroleum market, with high-priced gasoline for consumers and cheap naphtha for the petrochemical industry.[6] In addition, MITI protected the domestic petrochemical market with tariffs and the Foreign Exchange Control Law and kept technologically advanced American and European companies from setting up competing subsidiaries in Japan. As it did for other industries, MITI helped the industry get technology cheaply from foreign companies by intervening in negotiations over technology transfer.[7]

Cartel policy also played a key role in the development of the industry. Although there have been widespread complaints in industry and government circles about excess competition in the petrochemical industry, a study by the Kagaku Keizai Kenkyū Jo (Chemical Economics Institute) argues that the tremendous surge of investment in the 1950s and 1960s was made possible by the system of industrial cooperation established in one of the earliest branches of the petrochemical industry—polyvinyl chloride. The fourteen PVC manufacturers alternated between extreme competition and cooperation under the auspices of the PVC Association, established in 1953. The association sponsored five recession cartels and

[5] Kudō Akira, "Sekiyu kagaku" (Petrochemicals), in Yonekawa Shin'ichi, Shimokawa Kōichi, and Yamazaki Hiroaki, eds., *Sengo nihon kei'ei shi* (Postwar Japanese business history), Vol. 2 (Tokyo: Tōyō Keizai Shinpō Sha, 1990), p. 283.

[6] Watanabe Tokuji and Saeki Yasuharu, *Tenki ni tatsu sekiyu kagaku kōgyō* (The petrochemical industry at the crossroads) (Tokyo: Iwanami Shoten, 1984), pp. 80, 103.

[7] Itami, *Nihon no kagaku sangyō*, p. 68; James C. Abegglen and George Stalk, Jr., *Kaisha: The Japanese Corporation* (New York: Basic Books, 1985), pp. 128, 220.

pioneered a cooperative system to manage competition among a large number of firms. It was later copied by other petrochemical industries such as high-density polyethylene, polystyrene, acrylonitrile butadiene styrene, polypropylene, and low-density polyethylene. In subsequent expansions, new entrants calculated that, although their own entry might push prices down, there was a good chance that the system of industrial cooperation would ultimately bring prices back up.[8] The particular forms of interfirm coordination pioneered by PVC firms (such as production cartels and ways to share information about users) were later used by the high-density polyethylene and polystyrene industries to raise prices in the late 1960s.[9] Although cartels did not always work, especially in periods of rapid expansion, firms believed they could fall back on cartels with MITI's blessing if competition became too severe. Depression cartels could be used to support prices in downswings, and investment cartels could be used to manage rapid expansion.

MITI used investment cartels to regulate investment and thus prevent overcapacity and excess competition. This move was prompted by the challenge of imminent trade and capital liberalization in the 1960s. Through the Petrochemical Cooperation Council (Sekiyu Kagaku Kyōchō Kondankai), MITI and business coordinated firms to facilitate investment at optimum scale. Companies agreed to take turns investing in new capacity so that each could get maximum economies of scale without producing a glut on the market. The council was to decide on rules for building new capacity for ethylene and the principal derivatives, while section committees decided on demand projections for individual products.[10] These policies of the late 1960s are now broadly criticized in Japanese industry circles for having created an industrial structure that was internationally uncompetitive. The cartel structure allowed a very large number of firms to survive, all producing in plants that were small by North American and European standards.[11]

In addition to depression and investment cartels, the industry used export cartels to establish floor prices. The first export cartel, for PVC resins, operated continuously from 1957 to 1972. Others, for low- and

---

[8] Kagaku Keizai Kenkyū Jo (Chemical Economics Institute), *Sekiyu kagaku kōgyō no kōzō kaizen to sekiyu kagaku seihin kakō ryūtsūgyō no arikata* (Structural improvement in the petrochemical industry and the nature of the petrochemicals processing and distribution industries), (Tokyo: Kagaku Keizai Kenkyū Jo, 1984), p. 51.

[9] Kagaku Keizai Kenkyū Jo, *Sekiyu kagaku kōgyō no kōzō kaizen*, pp. 51, 62.

[10] *Kagaku kōgyō nenkan*, 1976, p. 78.

[11] On my research trip in February 1992, every chemical industry official I interviewed brought a copy of Itami's very critical book (*Nihon no kagaku sangyō*) and expressed agreement with it. One high-level executive expressed a single reservation: because the book was written by an academic, it did not include the *ura* (behind the scenes) part of the picture and was therefore somewhat misleading. Various interviews, 1992.

high-density polyethylene, polypropylene, and various other goods, operated from the late 1960s through 1976.[12] As we shall see, although Japanese industry has long sold plastics more cheaply overseas than at home; it used the export cartel to make sure that competition among Japanese firms did not drive prices any lower than was necessary to compete abroad.

The 1970s started with a slowdown in the Japanese economy that prompted the use of depression cartels in the PVC, polypropylene, and medium- and low-density polyethylene industries to stop the fall of domestic prices.[13] This slowdown was followed by overheating in 1973; but after rapid growth in the 1960s and early 1970s, the petrochemical industry was hit in the fall of 1973 with the first oil shock. A second and even more devastating oil shock followed in 1979–80. The dramatic rise in the price of oil raised costs and pushed down demand, leaving petrochemical firms with excess capacity and high materials costs. The oil shocks were particularly hard for Japan and most European countries, which used petroleum-based naphtha as their feedstock rather than the cheaper natural-gas–based ethane.

The reasons for the structural decline of the petrochemical industry in the 1970s and 80s are similar to those behind aluminum refining's decline. Just as the oil shocks put the Japanese aluminum industry at a disadvantage relative to countries that had nonpetroleum sources of energy, they put the Japanese and European petrochemical industries at a disadvantage relative to countries with ample natural-gas supplies. This newly intensified price disadvantage was compounded by new petrochemical plants in natural-gas–rich countries such as Canada and Saudi Arabia. In addition, rising prices put a damper on demand, which intensified competition among producers.

Petrochemical companies feared that higher oil prices would produce a tidal wave of cheap imports. As figure 5–2 shows, Japan's balance of trade in ethylene-based petrochemicals did move slightly into the red in the mid-1980s. Japan ran a deficit of 1.5 percent of total production in 1985 but by 1991 was back to a trade surplus of 3.2 percent of total production—even though its domestic prices were internationally uncompetitive.

The oil shocks upset the domestic system of relational contracting for three reasons. First, the jump in oil prices forced petrochemical makers to

[12] Sekiyu kagaku kōgyō kyōkai (Japan Petrochemical Industry Association), *Sekiyu kagaku kōgyō 30 nen no ayumi* (Thirty years of progress in the petrochemical industry), (Tokyo: Japan Petrochemical Industry Association), 1989, p. 209; *Kagaku kōgyō nenkan*, 1976, p. 135.

[13] *Sumitomo Kagaku Kōgyō Kabushiki Kaisha Shi* (History of the Sumitomo Chemical Company) (Osaka: Sumitomo Kagaku Kōgyō Kabushiki Kaisha, 1981), p. 612; *Kagaku kōgyō nenkan*, p. 79.

convince buyers of the need for higher prices. Second, price increases depressed demand and increased competition among producers. Third, the general economic slowdowns following the shocks made it harder for buyers to absorb price increases even if they wanted to. At these crisis points government and the trade associations actively began establishing new market rules to reinforce the norms of relational contracting and strengthen the bargaining position of the petrochemical industry.

Prices rose quickly when the first oil shock hit; and MITI responded by freezing prices on fifty-three goods, including most major petrochemicals, to cool inflation. At the same time, the investment cartel managed by the Cooperation Council was disbanded because of concern about high prices and Antimonopoly Law violations by big business. Industry watchers hoped that production cutbacks resulting from new antipollution regulations would create supply shortages.[14] MITI lifted its price freeze in August 1974, although the ministry continued to use administrative guidance to keep prices down.[15] Because of recession and higher prices, demand for petrochemicals plummeted; capacity use dropped from 90.5 percent in August 1974 to 54.5 percent by March 1975.[16] Prices fell correspondingly, and both industry and MITI worked to raise them. Industry negotiated with buyers to get higher prices that compensated for the rise in the price of naphtha, but it met considerable user resistance. Therefore, MITI intervened, using administrative guidance to cut the supply of petrochemicals. The ministry followed a guideline system: it announced quarterly demand projections and told firms how much to cut production. The guidelines were applied to most of the major polymers: high- and low-density polyethylene, polypropylene, polystyrene, and polyvinyl chloride. In December 1975 the industry finally managed to negotiate price increases to compensate for the October 1974 rise in the naphtha price and moved to establish a new pricing system.[17] Once the new prices came into effect, MITI discouraged firms from expanding capacity.[18] Thus, the ministry hovered over the market during this crisis, using administratively guided cartels to reduce competition and support prices.

In 1979 and 1980, the industry was hit by another rise in petroleum prices. Although panic in the market meant they were initially able to raise prices faster than their costs were rising , by 1981 petrochemical producers were losing money because they could not get buyers to cover

[14] *Kagaku kōgyō nenkan*, 1976, p. 102.
[15] Ibid., p. 80.
[16] Mitsui Sekiyu Kagaku Kōgyō Kabushiki Kaisha (Mitsui Petrochemical Industries), *Mitsui Sekiyu Kagaku Kōgyō 20 nen shi* (A twenty-year history of Mitsui Petrochemical Industries), (Tokyo: Mitsui Sekiyu Kagaku Kōgyō Kabushiki Kaisha, 1978), p. 186.
[17] Ibid., p. 187.
[18] Ibid.

Figure 5-4. Ethylene producer profits (in billions of yen)

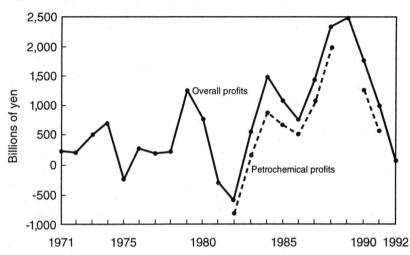

Source: Sekiyu kagaku kōgyō kyōkai (Japan Petrochemical Industry Association), *Sekiyu kagaku kōgyō 30 nen no ayumi* (Thirty years of progress in the petrochemical industry) (Tokyo: Sekiyu Kagaku Kōgyō Kyōkai, 1989); *Kagaku keizai* 40 (August 1993): 27.

their costs (see figure 5-4). In 1982, even as petrochemical companies were selling assets to minimize their losses, they lost 882 billion yen. Although industry structure was ideal for stable relational contracting, both government and industry felt these individual contracts were too fragile to stand alone and needed to be reinforced by market governance to prevent downstream buyers from pressuring suppliers into reducing prices to dangerously low levels. Governance was done formally and informally, by both the state and trade associations.

Government assistance principally involved official cartel policies. The most important were capacity-cutting cartels from 1983 to 1987 and joint-sales companies from 1982 to the present. Outside the bounds of these legal cartels, however, MITI also used administrative guidance to pressure the industry to keep prices up and restrict production.

The producers' principal policy objective was to bring down naphtha prices, which had begun to subsidize gasoline prices after the first oil shock. MITI was split: the Basic Industries Bureau, which had jurisdiction over chemicals, wanted cheaper prices, while the energy agency, which had jurisdiction over petroleum refining, wanted to support the refiners. The bureau wanted industry to use capacity cuts and mergers to reduce competition and support prices.[19]

[19] Frank K. Upham, *Law and Social Change in Postwar Japan* (Cambridge: Harvard University Press, 1987); *Kagaku keizai*, April 1983, p. 15.

The process of negotiating capacity cuts and joint-sales companies took two years. Industry knew production needed to be cut; but while everyone was happy to have price cartels, companies were reluctant to make the permanent capacity cuts that MITI felt were necessary to solve the long-term problems of excess competition. Firms also resisted mergers for fear of undermining company culture or damaging keiretsu ties.

MITI began by submitting a report, "Policy toward the Petrochemical Industry in the 1980s," to the Industrial Structure Council in April 1981. It was deliberated on by the Chemical Industry Subcommittee chaired by Arisawa Hiromi, one of the principal architects of MITI's postwar policies, with all twenty presidents of the major petrochemical producers in attendance.[20] The industry's initial position was to push for cheaper raw materials and resist capacity cuts, but there was considerable industry concern about reducing competition. Both the main petrochemical companies and the PVC companies that bought ethylene from them called for joint-sales companies, joint imports, and capacity cuts. It is significant that the downstream PVC industry, which plays a key role in the system of interindustry relational contracting, did not oppose the establishment of upstream cartels but was pressing for its own cartel.

Suzuki Masao, president of Showa Denko, one of the largest petrochemical producers, complained that, although everyone acknowledged the need for capacity cuts, individual firms were unwilling to make them. He called on the FTC to permit cartels in the industry: "We're not talking about a highly profitable industry even in normal times. Since it's just a question of a bunch of poor people talking together there's no need to have a police guard watching over us."[21] There were many complaints about excess competition and price cutting to gain market share. At least one important participant at a later meeting of the subcommittee believed that MITI direction would be necessary to bring about industry agreements. Kishimoto Yasunobe, also of Showa Denko, said, "It's clear that firms are not going to be able to deal with these problems on their own, so unfortunately government intervention will probably be necessary."[22] Because industry officials had such a difficult time coming to a consensus on capacity cuts, MITI sent the heads of the major companies on a trip to Europe, ostensibly to observe European structural adjustment but really to develop trust and establish consensus.[23] Ultimately, the presidents of the sixteen big petrochemical firms agreed to go along with MITI on capacity cuts.[24]

[20] Kagaku Keizai Kenkyū Jo, *Sekiyu kagaku kōgyō no kōzō kaizen*, p. 26.
[21] *Nikkei sangyō shinbun*, 3 December 1981.
[22] *Nihon keizai shinbun*, 8 July 1982.
[23] Ibid.; Upham, *Law and Social Change*.
[24] *Nihon keizai shinbun*, 28 May 1982.

In April 1982, when negotiations were well under way, MITI finally granted liberalized naphtha prices.[25] And in October, when it looked like the industry had agreed to capacity cuts, MITI and the FTC rewarded it with a depression cartel in ethylene. The next step was for individual sectors to decide how much capacity each firm would cut. As was the case with cement, the capacity cuts were made across the board. Ethylene producers, for example, agreed that each company would cut approximately 30 percent of its capacity. Although actual cuts were close to a pro-rated standard, arrangements were made for companies to sell surpluses over their quotas to companies that cut more than their pro-rata share.[26] MITI failed to get cement companies to engage in consignment production, but ethylene producers did agree to sell to one another so that individual firms could continue established relations with individual buyers.

Another adjustment of the pro-rata cut allowed some firms to mothball their plants rather than permanently scrap them. Permission was given to the most vulnerable firms (those that could not write off plants without creating big short-term losses) and firms that were spreading out cuts within their keiretsu. About two million tons of ethylene capacity was cut, half of which was idled rather than scrapped. Some companies resented those firms that received special breaks, especially when they were allowed to restart their plants in 1988.[27]

Capacity cartels were applied to all the major resin industries: high- and low-density polyethylene, polypropylene, ethylene oxide, styrene monomer, and polyvinyl chloride.[28] Although joint-sales companies were not used in ethylene, the industry-restructuring plan called for them to be used in derivative industries to facilitate capacity cuts as well as rationalize production and distribution and reduce competition.[29]

While the capacity-cut agreement went relatively smoothly in the ethylene industry, more and less efficient firms in the high- and medium-density polyethylene industries fought over how much capacity to cut. Firms that had independently cut production early on wanted these cuts taken into account when calculating how large their next cuts should be. MITI intervened to break the deadlock by establishing a formula for capacity cuts that compromised between production- and capacity-based calculations.[30] As table 5–2 shows, the capacity-cut plans were ambitious

[25] Naphtha prices were not completely freed, although imports were freed and by 1990 took three-quarters of the market. The price of domestic naphtha, however, is set under the authority of the Petroleum Industries Law at two thousand yen above the import price.

[26] Kagaku Keizai Kenkyū Jo, *Sekiyu kagaku kōgyō no kōzō kaizen*, p. 31.

[27] *Kagaku kōgyō nenkan*, 1989, p. 190.

[28] *Kagaku kōgyō nenkan*, 1988, p. 200.

[29] Kagaku Keizai Kenkyū Jo, *Sekiyu kagaku kōgyō no kōzō kaizen*, p. 27.

[30] Each firm was to make cuts based on the average of three factors: capacity share as of the end of August 1981, average production share for 1979–81, and share of production

Table 5–2. Capacity cuts in the petrochemical industry (in tons per year)

Product	Capacity before cuts, 1983	Targeted cuts (yen)	Actual cuts (yen)	Capacity by 1985	Capacity targeted for cuts	Cuts achieved	Capacity after cuts
Ethylene	6,347	2,293	2,020	4,327	36%	88%	68%
Polyolefins	4,125	901	851	3,274	22%	94%	79%
LDPE	1,741	637	547	1,194	37%	86%	69%
HDPE	1,052	265	304	748	25%	115%	71%
Polypropylene	1,332	0	0	1,332	—	—	100%
PVC resins	2,007	490	450	1,557	24%	92%	78%
Ethylene oxide	743	201	122	621	27%	61%	84%
Styrene monomer	1,799	468	340	1,459	26%	73%	81%

Source: *Kagaku kōgyō nenkan*, (Chemical Industry Annual) (Tokyo: Kagaku Kōgyō Nippō Sha, 1988, 1991).

and successful. In most targeted branches of industry, a quarter or more of capacity was slated for cuts; and most were carried out.

Although the first task of the joint-sales firms was to coordinate capacity cuts, their most important ongoing purpose was to improve the bargaining position of the petrochemical firms and reduce competition by consolidating market power. They have been fairly successful at this task. MITI has continuously pushed these firms to strengthen their market power by consolidating their activities as much as possible. The FTC, in contrast, has attempted to constrain their power by limiting their concentration of market share, just as it did in the cement industry. It ordered, for instance, that the three appointed companies in polyolefins be increased to four to avoid excessive market concentration.[31]

Originally the polyolefin industry proposed three companies, each centered on one of the powerful old-line zaibatsu: Mitsubishi, Mitsui, and Sumitomo. The FTC objected to this level of concentration, and companies of unrelated keiretsu were split off to form a fourth group. The resulting joint-sales firms were a group of four Mitsui firms with 23 percent of market share; a group of seven Sumitomo and Industrial Bank of Japan companies (33-percent share); a group with two Mitsubishi-related firms (18-percent share); and a group of five others (26-percent

---

for 1981. Cuts were to average 27 percent, but firms that had already cut production were still in the position of having to make deeper-than-average cuts and refused to go along. A compromise was worked out to keep the original target cuts but allow companies to make only 95 percent of them. The high- and medium-density polyethylene industry was to make actual cuts of only 90.2 percent, and the 4.8 percent difference between individual cut levels and the industry-scrapping level was given to the three firms that had made early, deep production cuts. *Kagaku keizai*, July 1983, p. 46.

[31] *Polyolefin* means oil-based polymers. Upham, *Law and Social Change*, p. 197.

Table 5-3. Polyolefin joint-sales companies (established 1983)

Company	Daiya Polymer	Ace Polymer	Union Polymer	Mitsui Nisseki Polymer
Market share	18%	26%	33%	23%
Member firms	Mitsubishi Petrochemical	Asahi Chemical	Ube Kosan	Nippon Petrochemical
	Mitsubishi Chemical	Idemitsu Petrochemical	Sumitomo Chemical	Mitsui Petrochemical
			Chisso	
		Showa Denko	Tohsoh	Mitsui Toatsu Chemicals
		Tonen Petrochemical	Tokuyama Soda	Mitsui Dupont Polychemical
		Nihon Unica	Nissan Maruzen Polyethylene	

Source: Itami Hiroyuki, *Nihon no kagaku sangyo, naze sekai ni tachiokureta no ka* (Japan's chemical industry: Why is it behind the rest of the world?) (Tokyo: NTT Shuppan, 1990), p. 150; *Kagaku keizai* 30 (May 1983): 46.

share) (see table 5-3).[32] One might wonder why it was necessary to form joint-sales companies based on keiretsu ties, which alone might suffice to get firms to cooperate. But there have been numerous examples of different firms from the same keiretsu competing in plastics sales.[33]

At the same time that it tried to guard against excessive market power, however, the FTC said it would make sure that the joint-sales companies worked to increase efficiency in exchange for their enhanced ability to support prices. This goal was clear in the remarks of an FTC official speaking about joint-sales companies' early lackluster progress on joint sales, joint transport, and standardization of grades: "We want to watch how the joint sales firms are linked to strengthening international competitiveness. If all they want to do is 'eat at the restaurant and run off without paying the bill' by just having price agreements, then there is a problem."[34] This was much the same approach that the FTC took when it pressed the cement industry to go along with structural improvement under SDIL. Far from merely policing against violations of the law, the FTC clearly intended to make sure that cartels were used to increase industry competitiveness.

In the PVC industry, as in cement, suspicion and continued compe-

[32] *Kagaku keizai*, May 1983, p. 46.
[33] Kagaku Keizai Kenkyū Jo, *Sekiyu kagaku kōgyō no kōzō kaizen*, 59.
[34] *Asahi shinbun*, 12 March 1983.

Table 5–4. Polyvinyl chloride joint-sales companies (established 1982)

Company	Daichi PVC	Nihon PVC	Chuo PVC	Kyodo PVC
Member firms	Kureha Chemical	Kanegafuchi Chemical	Asahi Chemical	Central Glass
	Sumitomo Chemical	Denki Kagaku	Shin-Etsu Chemical	Chisso
				Tohsoh
	Nippon Zeon	Toagosei Chemical	Kasei Vinyl	Nissan Chemical
	San Aro Chemical	Mitsui Toatsu Chemicals		Tokuyama Sekisui Chemical

Source: Itami Hiroyuki, *Nihon no kagaku sangyo, naze sekai ni tachiokureta no ka* (Japan's chemical industry: Why is it behind the rest of the world?) (Tokyo: NTT Shuppan, 1990), p.150.

tition between firms hampered efforts to consolidate sales. There was competition between new entrants to the industry who wanted to use the system to expand their market share and longer-established firms that were content with the status quo. This was particularly true in 1983, when demand was very weak.[35] But by 1984, sales were up and joint-sales firms were making progress in consolidating sales and consigning production (see table 5–4).[36] Later, the joint-sales company continued to expand its activities by standardizing product grades while continuing to support prices and arranging for firms to sell goods on one another's behalf.[37]

Another reason for the success of the PVC joint-sales companies was that the downstream PVC pipe industry was also cartelized to increase its power in bargaining with the construction industry for higher prices. PVC pipe is sold primarily to construction companies for plumbing and drainage systems. Powerful cartels in the construction industry help firms pay good prices for PVC pipe, just as they do for cement. The economic journal *Shūkan tōyō keizai*, argues that construction companies handling water and sewer lines and plumbing are able to charge high cartel prices because only firms designated by the local municipality may engage in this work.[38] Nevertheless, competition among PVC pipe companies de-

[35] *Asahi shinbun*, 12 March 1983.
[36] *Kagaku keizai*, Special Issue, August 1984, p. 73. The 1985 *Kagaku kōgyō nenkan* (p. 261) also agreed that the joint-sales companies had succeeded in cutting competition among PVC makers.
[37] *Kagaku kōgyō nenkan*, 1986, p. 274.
[38] Uchida Michio and Ōzaki Akiko, "Jūtaku kenchiku hi wa gowari yasuku dekiru" (Construction costs could be 50-percent cheaper), *Shūkan tōyō keizai*, 4 September 1993, p. 7.

pressed prices and made it harder for them to pay high prices to their suppliers, the PVC firms.

The pipe makers were granted a depression cartel in 1984 and 1985 to reduce competition. When this cartel was discontinued in 1985, MITI took unofficial steps to strengthen the industry. Although officially the FTC authorized joint-sales companies only for the plastics companies, not for downstream industries that sold products made from them, MITI unofficially organized joint-sales companies for the downstream PVC pipe industry. The ministry organized producers into four joint-sales companies, set up so that each had factories throughout Japan to enable individual firms to exchange products through consignment production. Seven firms account for 92 percent of PVC pipe production. MITI put one of each of the three largest firms in each company and two medium-sized firms in the fourth. Sekisui Chemical (with 23 percent of total market share) was combined with Komatsu Chemical and Nippon Roru; Kubota (21 percent) with Nippon Plastics and Maezawa Chemical; Mitsubishi Plastics (16 percent) with Shin-Etsu Polymer; and C. I. Chemical (11 percent) with Aron Chemical (9 percent) and Asahi Organic Chemicals.[39]

As in the case of cement, companies sell to construction companies that operate nationwide and want to deal with a single materials supplier with quality guarantees. Nevertheless, nationwide distribution of PVC pipe from a single factory is costly because the pipe's hollowness and bulk make it expensive to transport. To save on transport costs, companies deliver goods where they have a factory, using the name of partner companies that have relationships with the construction company ordering the pipes. This arrangement helps companies cut costs, and it also reduces the temptation for competitors to undercut one another's prices by selling more cheaply to buyers close to their plants. Moreover, it supports the broader dangō relationship that exists between the PVC pipe industry and the construction industry. The FTC cracked down on the industry in 1991, but as of spring 1992 the system still continued.[40]

The polypropylene industry, which began its joint sales in 1984, experienced some success from the start in using joint sales to raise prices.[41] By 1987, after several years of joint-sales company efforts, the *Kagaku*

[39] Market shares are from Yano Keizai Kenkyū Jo (Yano Research Institute), *Nihon maketto shea jiten* (Japan market share sourcebook) (Tokyo: Yano Keizai Kenkyū, 1993). Company groupings are from a 1992 interview with a journalist specializing in chemical prices at one of Japan's major newspapers.

[40] My source on the existence of this informal system of joint-sales companies was a newspaper reporter specializing in chemical prices. He said that the pipe companies deny the existence of the system but that he learned of it from trading companies and PVC companies. Interview, 1992.

[41] *Kagaku keizai*, August 1984.

kōgyō nenkan (Chemical industry annual) concluded that the "establishment of the joint sales system led to the rejection of senseless excessive competition."[42] Nevertheless, MITI continued to be active in pushing joint-sales firms to work more cohesively and less like loose groupings of individual firms. The ministry drew up lists of specific measures the joint-sales companies should take, and individual firms responded with action plans.[43]

In addition to simply reducing competition, the joint-sales companies have alleviated some of the distribution inefficiencies implicit in Japan's keiretsu system of business transactions. One chemical-firm official pointed out that "the Mitsubishi Corporation [the main trading firm of the Mitsubishi group] has a special relationship with Mitsubishi Chemical and comes to it first for a product. Mitsui & Co. has the same relationship with Mitsui Petrochemicals, and the same is true for the other groups."[44] Joint-sales firms have been able to introduce some transportation efficiency in a market where firms have a strong bias toward contracting with keiretsu affiliates, even if another firm might supply them more efficiently. To sum up, the joint-sales companies have been successful in forming capacity-cutting cartels, supporting prices, and cutting distribution costs. Mistrust among individual firms has, at times, been an obstacle to cooperation; but MITI has stepped in to push for consensus and, in the case of the PVC industry, to form an informal downstream joint-sales company to support the upstream one.

In addition to cutting back at home, Japanese petrochemical companies invested overseas. The initiative for overseas investment came from trading companies, which wanted to secure oil supplies and establish bases for overseas sales, and the government, which wanted to strengthen relations with OPEC nations.[45] The government supported overseas investment with financial, tax, and insurance assistance through Japan's foreign-aid program. Although the petrochemical firms did not take the initiative in starting projects, they were interested in the promise of secure access to raw materials and overseas markets.[46] They did not consider the overseas investment drive a way of replacing production for the Japanese market, and these imports have not taken a large part of the Japanese petrochemical market.

---

[42] *Kagaku kōgyō nenkan*, 1987, p. 230.

[43] Ibid., p. 183.

[44] Interview, 1992.

[45] Much of the material on overseas investment is based on an interview with an official of the Kagaku Keizai Kenkyū Jo, 1992.

[46] Kikkawa Takeo, "Nihon ni okeru kigyō shūdan, gyōkai dantai oyobi seifu—sekiyu kagaku kōgyō no ba'ai" (Company groups, industry associations, and government in Japan: The case of the petrochemical industry), *Kei'ei shi gaku*, 30 October 1991, pp. 13, 14.

The most important projects were in Iran, Saudi Arabia, and Singapore. Mitsui & Company, the Mitsui group's trading firm, was the driving force behind the Bandar Khomeini project in Iran. Its goals were to secure oil and natural gas, sell Japanese industrial machinery, and sell the plant's products in overseas markets. Building started in 1976 but was interrupted first by the 1979 Iranian Revolution and then by bombing during the Iran-Iraq war. In addition to this ill-fated project, the Mitsui group undertook a project in South Korea. Meanwhile, the Sumitomo Corporation undertook a large project in Singapore to produce for the Southeast Asian market. This was done in consortium with the Singapore government, and the Japanese government put up 20 percent of the Japanese funds.[47]

The Mitsubishi corporation has had much better luck in the Middle East than the Mitsui group and has enjoyed genuine commercial success with its Saudi Arabia project. The trading company primarily wanted to produce cheap goods for overseas sales, while the Japanese government gave enthusiastic support in order to strengthen ties with Saudi Arabia. The half-Japanese-owned plant began production in 1987, and by 1990 Saudi Arabia was the source of one-third of Japan's ethylene-based imports.[48] Nevertheless, Japan's overall ethylene-based imports have increased only slightly since the Saudi plant came on line and by 1991 had decreased to 11.2 percent as a share of domestic consumption (see figure 5–2). Thus, overseas production has not resulted in any large-scale displacement of domestic production, and any displacement has been more than offset by increased exports.

The system of capacity-cutting cartels, joint-sales companies, and informal price cartels supported prices and maintained industry health through the early and mid-1980s. By the late 1980s the industry was ready for a comeback; and, as table 5–5 shows, capacity for all petrochemicals cut back in 1983–85 was expanded beyond 1983 levels. Thus, the 1983 SDIL did not ease firms out of an uncompetitive industry but helped the industry to support prices and gain strength for renewed growth.

MITI stayed active in maintaining the capacity cartels, even through the new expansion. Although the ministry scrapped the official cartel policies of SDIL in response to U.S. pressure, it continued to use capacity

[47] Tsūshō Sangyō Chōsakai (Research group on trade and industry), *Keizai kyōryoku no genjō to mondaiten* (Current conditions and problems in economic cooperation) (Tokyo: MITI, 1989), pp. 88.

[48] Sekiyu kagaku kōgyō kyōkai (Japan Petrochemical Industry Association) *Sekiyu kagaku kōgyō no genjō,* (Current conditions in the petrochemical industry) (Tokyo: Sekiyu kagaku kōgyō kyōkai, 1991), p. 11.

Table 5-5. Capacity increases in the petrochemical industry in the late 1980s (in tons per year)

Product	Capacity, before cuts, 1983	Capacity, 1992	Capacity increase, 1985–92 (%)	Net increase, 1983–92 (%)
Ethylene	6,347	6,464	49	2
Polyolefin	4,125	4,961	52	20
LDPE	1,741	2,258	89	30
HDPE	1,052	1,261	69	20
Polypropylene	1,332	2,389	79	79
PVC	2,007	2,154	38	7
Ethylene oxide	743	883	42	19
Styrene monomer	1,799	2,478	70	38

Source: Kagaku kōgyō nenkan (Chemical Industry Annual) (Tokyo: kagaku kōgyō Nippō Sha, 1988); Japan Petrochemical Industry Association (Tokyo: Japan Petrochemical Industry Assocation, 1993).

cartels informally. Just as it had done during the industrial expansion of the 1960s, MITI created an unofficial investment cartel in the late 1980s to enable industry to invest in plants with economies of scale but without excessive competition.

The SDIL ended for the ethylene industry in March 1986 and for the polyolefin industry in September 1987. Because the petrochemical industry was doing quite well and had already shed excess capacity, the Structural Conversion Facilitation Law (SCFL) was not applied to petrochemicals.[49] But, in place of official policy, industries turned to informal cartel policy.

With the end of the SDIL, the capacity-cutting cartel was formally ended and companies were free to increase capacity. Firms quickly made plans to bring mothballed ethylene capacity back on line. MITI, however, argued that, even though the law had officially been abolished, it should be unofficially observed until June 1988, its original expiration date.[50] To extend this limit on expansion further, MITI put the industry under a prior notification system that was to last for two years. Under this system, firms had to notify MITI six months before beginning new capacity expansion projects of greater than thirty thousand tons and three months before restarting thirty thousand tons or more of mothballed capacity. The presidents of the twelve producers agreed to these rules and communicated their decision to MITI through the Ethylene Subcommittee of the Industrial Structure Council.[51] The same system was also applied to the polyolefin industry in March 1988, soon after the

[49] *Kagaku kōgyō nenkan,* 1987, p. 183.
[50] *Nihon keizai shinbun,* 14 November 1987.
[51] Ibid.

September 1987 lapse of the SDIL, because of fears that complete liberalization would lead to excess competition.[52]

In 1988 and 1989, MITI continued to push the ethylene industry to exercise restraint. Ethylene users protested that capacity cuts during the industry recession had been too deep and that more capacity was needed to prevent shortages. MITI's Basic Materials Industry Bureau stated that there was already ample capacity. Expansion threatened to create oversupply problems in the future, and in any case, it was not forcing firms to comply with its suggestions.[53] Recognizing that MITI was indeed using informal guidance to hold back expansion, the Bank of Japan asked the ministry in 1988 to encourage industry to restart idled capacity to prevent supply bottlenecks from fueling inflation. MITI rebuffed the bank's request, although idle capacity was subsequently brought back on line.[54]

Negotiations over what was essentially a new indicative cartel were carried out in the forum where discussions of the SDIL cartel took place: the Chemical Industry Subcommittee of the Industrial Structure Council. The ethylene industry supported MITI's call to restrain expansion, although it was not as conservative in its projection of how much new production the market could absorb. Rather, it argued that the industry could limit expansion by self-regulation. While MITI held that the industry should add only one more plant, consensus in the industry was for two.[55] MITI's attitude about guiding the industry was summed up by Hatayama Yuzuru, a MITI official: "We have no intention of controlling the industry; however, it would also be inappropriate for us to simply tell [industry] to go off and handle things however it wishes."[56]

MITI established a panel, which in June 1989 recommended that only one 400,000-ton plant be permitted. Six firms submitted proposals to MITI, and the ministry negotiated with industry leaders over which one to support.[57] In the end, Mitsubishi Chemical was selected. Company president Yoshida Masaki claimed that the company had formulated its investment proposal on its own, but the *Japan Economic Journal* reported that "it is widely believed the company tailored its proposal in order to obtain a consensus among MITI and the other five groups."[58] The journal also reported that industry sources said the FTC was concerned with "the close-knit nature" of the decision-making process be-

[52] *Kagaku kōgyō nenkan*, 1988, p. 200.
[53] *Nihon keizai shinbun*, 26 April 1988.
[54] Ibid., 25 April 1988.
[55] Ibid., 25 May 1989.
[56] "Katte ni yatte kudasai to iu wake ni mo ikanai darō." *Nihon keizai shinbun*, 5 May 1989.
[57] *Japan Economic Journal*, 20 January 1990.
[58] Ibid.

cause of "continuing charges from abroad that Japanese business practices often border on outright collusion."[59] Yet, although the FTC wanted MITI to end its guidelines requiring firms to report plant construction plans to the ministry, it was either unable or unwilling to prevent MITI from coordinating the investment cartel. Thus, MITI still appears to flout the Antimonopoly Law and guide industrial development with cartels in the face of a toothless FTC.

The petrochemical industry has also used informal governance to moderate price competition. In an industry characterized by relational contracting and cost-based pricing, the trade association has established rules on how the costs of basic feedstocks are calculated; and industry leaders often negotiate actual prices on an industry-wide basis.

In both the United States and Japan, pricing under long-term contracts is contingent and cost-based. In principle, contingent price contracts can be negotiated on a firm-to-firm basis. Individual U.S. petroleum firms do negotiate contracts to tie prices to the cost of raw materials.[60] In Japan, however, petrochemical prices are not negotiated simply between the individual parties to a particular transaction. Industry-wide negotiation also plays an important role in setting prices. While prices in the West are contingent on shifts in feedstock prices, they are decided before goods are delivered. But in Japan prices depend on an industry-wide decision-making process that can often be very lengthy. Prices are many times left undetermined for as long as a year after actual product delivery.[61] This system of deciding prices well after delivery is called *atogime*, or postsale pricing. Materials are delivered with only a provisional price; final pricing is postponed until the cost of the entire industry's raw materials is determined and industry-wide negotiation can take place. In addition, because relational contracting takes both buyers' and sellers' needs into account, after-sales pricing also considers the buyer. Because of the volatility of petroleum prices, most emphasis is on cost. But pricing is also determined by the price that the downstream buyer is able to get for the end product sold to consumers.[62] In principle, after-sales pricing might be done simply between the two individual firms involved. In practice, however, it depends on the negotiation of intermediate good prices at an industry-wide level because individual downstream firms need to be sure that their generosity in honoring the relational contract does not disadvantage them in relation to their competitors. The delay

---

[59] *Japan Economic Journal*, 20 January 1990.

[60] Ward Hansen alerted me to this comparison with the U.S. industry.

[61] *Nihon keizai shinbun*, 11 May 1989.

[62] One chemical manufacturer implied that the end price was taken into account through the aftersales pricing system in his complaint that the system needed to be abandoned to keep downstream management on its toes. *Nihon keizai shinbun*, 11 May 1989.

of as much as a year indicates the fundamental weakness of price competition in the industry and the strength of interindustry relational contracting.

Final pricing in Japan's petrochemical markets always awaits publication of average naphtha prices, on which ethylene and propylene prices are calculated. But calculation is not simple. How does one establish the *appropriate* price for ethylene? Each pair of buyers and sellers could decide alone, but they would risk introducing excessive competition and endangering Japan's fundamentally weak industry. The solution has been for the trade association to establish industry-wide rules that determine feedstock prices, which then become the standard on which the derivatives prices are calculated.

Pricing has been cost-based in the petrochemical market since the 1960s, but after the oil-shock crises industry leaders tried to find new ways to convince buyers to agree with this approach.[63] In tandem with the MITI-backed indicative production cartel, which supported prices following the first oil crisis, industry leaders worked informally to increase cooperation in the petrochemical industry and convince buyers of the need for higher prices. In 1975–76 the *Sekiyu kagaku kōgyō shinbun* (Petrochemical industry newspaper) published long group discussion pieces in which petrochemical company presidents spoke about these issues.[64] MITI officials, who occasionally participated in these discussions, said that prices needed to be raised to shift costs downstream to consumers.[65] The institution that actually created the pricing rules for the new system was the Chemical Economics Institute, a think tank that publishes the major policy journal on the industry and regularly sponsors studies that promote the development of chemical industry policies.

The basis for setting standard prices was established by a subcommittee of the Petroleum Deliberation Council, which was formed to set standard prices for refined petroleum products in the wake of the oil shock. In 1975, under the authority of the Petroleum Industry Law, the council set standard prices for refined petroleum goods at an average 9.5 percent above current prices. Its method was to survey manufacturers' costs and calculate what prices would enable firms to cover their costs. Naphtha was among the goods for which a price was set.[66]

In November of 1975 the Chemical Economic Institute used the same method to establish recommended prices for petrochemical goods. It did so "to respond to numerous appeals to the institute to do survey research

[63] Interview, petrochemical executive, 1992.
[64] See, for example, *Sekiyu kagaku kōgyō shinbun*, 11 August 1975; 1 January 1976.
[65] Ibid., 31 July 1975.
[66] "Sekiyu seihin no shin kakaku taisei" (A new price structure for petroleum products), *Kagaku keizai* (Jan. 1976): 65–66.

which would produce an index of the effect of the rise in raw materials and fuel on prices for petrochemical goods."[67] The institute surveyed rises in material and fuel costs for each individual petrochemical product from October 1974 to October 1975. Because naphtha rose five thousand yen/kiloliter during that period, the institute divided the costs by five and projected that manufacturers' costs would rise or fall by that amount for each change in the naphtha price of one thousand yen/ kiloliter. Production of different commodities uses different amounts of ethylene and fuels. Therefore, the institute calculated the differential effects that naphtha price changes would have on different petrochemicals. For example, it established that a kilo of ethylene should rise 2.8– 2.91 yen for each one thousand yen rise in the price of a kiloliter of naphtha, while high-density polyethylene should rise from 3.05 to 3.16 yen because it takes 1.07 tons of ethylene to produce a ton of high-density polyethylene, a process that also consumes additional fuel. Polyvinyl chloride would rise only 1.83 to 1.88 yen because it is partly made from chlorine, and so on.

This formula operationalized and standardized the norm of relational contracting for the entire petrochemical industry and thus provided a basis for governance of the domestic market in succeeding years. Although the formula was adopted by the petrochemical industry in 1976, it was not fully implemented during the 1970s. True implementation did not come until after the 1979–80 oil shock, when the industry was strengthened by the SDIL cartel of 1983. As we shall see, the formula has not been precisely observed; nevertheless, it has helped stabilize prices in the face of cheap imports.

Significantly, this central rule did not simply develop through the trial and error of independent market actors but through the efforts of the same institutions that made official policy. The initiative came from discussions among trade association leaders, who turned to the think tank that commonly develops official industry policy proposals. The Chemical Economics Institute then piggybacked the new pricing system onto the system developed by the Petroleum Deliberation Council under the authority of the Petroleum Industry Law.

During the rapid naphtha price increases in 1979 and 1980, ethylene makers appear to have presented a united front on price increases. They abandoned postsales pricing, however, and instead pushed up prices as fast as or faster than their materials costs rose.[68] But postsales pricing

    [67] "Sekiyu seihin neage ni yoru sekiyu kagaku seihin kakaku he no eikyō" (The effects of petroleum product price increases on prices of petrochemical products), *Kagaku keizai* (January 1976): 62–67.
    [68] *Nihon keizai shinbun*, 9 September 1979; 27 March 1980.

continued to be used in downstream industries.[69] From 1981 to 1983, ethylene prices were set by the price leadership of the two largest producers, Nihon Petrochemical and Mitsubishi Petrochemical, which negotiated with Kawajima Vinyl Chloride Monomer but failed to cover the cost of naphtha.[70]

As I have noted, petrochemical companies were hurting and looking for ways to raise prices in 1981–83. While the principal official measures were the creation of joint-sales companies and capacity-cutting cartels, industry was also informally trying to get its buyers to return to the cost-based price formula for petrochemical goods. The petrochemical industry reinstated the formula for cost-based pricing of ethylene and propylene in September 1983. The formula was put forward by the largest producer, Mitsubishi Yuka, although the *Nikkei shinbun* reported that the other ethylene producers were also participating.[71] Two full-time chemicals buyers for one of Japan's largest auto firms confirmed in an interview that all the petrochemical firms were involved in creating the price formula. They said that the formula was created in "the same sphere where capacity and production cartels are set."[72] We saw earlier that the original price formula was developed in 1975 by the same institutions that developed official policy. It is clear that the formula was also put in practice by the industry representatives who created the official capacity-cutting cartels.

The petrochemicals buyers considered the price formula a rule established by "the petrochemical industry as a whole," one that was observed rigorously by all petrochemical firms in pricing ethylene derivatives. "When a new company comes in as a supplier, it goes by the same formula as the other petrochemical makers. The petrochemical industry (*gyōkai*) has this rule. So new entrants to the relationship abide by the same rule."[73] Thus, while informal, the price formula is considered binding for all firms in the industry.

A chemicals buyer for another large auto company confirmed this account and made it clear that he knew the price formula was not exactly legal. I called him at his noisy office and had an interview by phone, although I despaired of getting frank information under such conditions. When I asked him about petrochemical pricing, at he first refused to answer but then told me to guess. I proceeded to give him the other buyers' story, line by line, and he confirmed, "Deep Throat style," that

[69] Ibid., 10 January 1980.
[70] Ibid., 30 September 1981, p. 7; 9 September 1986.
[71] *Nikkei sangyō shinbun*, 6 September 1983.
[72] Interview, 1992. An executive at a major electronics firm confirmed that petrochemical makers took the initiative in establishing the price formula after the second oil shock. Interview, 1994.
[73] Interview, 1992.

his company followed exactly the same pricing procedures.[74] Thus, it was not accidental that the new price system followed soon after the establishment of the capacity cartel. It was intended to function as an informal governing rule by the same industry representatives, who were supported by the new market power that the petrochemical companies were trying to base on their new official cartel. Though informal, the rule has been long-lasting and powerful.

The specifics of the formula were similar to those of the original 1975 formula, although they required firms to be thriftier with their use of naphtha, which was justified: since that time, yields and fuel efficiency have improved throughout the industry.[75] The formula set ethylene at 155 yen/kilogram when naphtha was at fifty thousand yen/kiloliter. For each one thousand-yen change in the price of naphtha, ethylene was supposed to go up or down 2.5 yen.[76] Propylene was to be set at twenty-five yen below ethylene. The price formula has been remarkably stable, although it was modified slightly in 1986 so that for each one thousand yen naphtha went over forty thousand yen per kiloliter, ethylene would vary only by 2 yen instead of by 2.5 yen/kilo.[77] It reflected buyers' concerns with the high naphtha prices in 1979–85, but prices never rose into this range again. In another minor change, the formula was originally based on the price of naphtha in the previous quarter, but it later changed to one-third the previous quarter's price plus two-thirds of the current quarter's.[78] Otherwise, as of 1992, the formula has remained the same.[79] The ethylene price formula has been the centerpiece of cost-base pricing as the reference point for all derivative prices.

The creation of the cost-based price formula for ethylene was based on interindustry relational contracting. The original initiative did not come solely from upstream chemical makers but had support from downstream buyers as well. An executive at a major electronics firm told me he was busy after the first oil shock finding out where petrochemical makers bought their oil and trying to calculate what their raw materials costs really were. His firm made a cost table and tried to use cost-based pricing to get petrochemical companies to lower their prices.[80] It is true that the system was not fully implemented until petrochemical makers were hurting in the early 1980s, and that users complained in negotiations that the

---

[74] Interview, 1994.

[75] Vergara and Brown, *The New Face of the World Petrochemical Sector*, p. 15.

[76] *Nikkei sangyō shinbun*, 6 September 1983.

[77] The base price of naphtha was to be established as one-third of the average price of naphtha for the quarter previous to the ethylene sales to be priced and two-thirds of the average price of naphtha during the quarter. *Kagaku kōgyō nenkan*, 1988, p. 203.

[78] *Kagaku kōgyō nenkan*, 1988; *Nihon Keizai Shinbun*, 16 July, 1988.

[79] *Nihon keizai shinbun*, 10 April 1991, Interview with car executives, 1992.

[80] Interview, 1994.

formula set prices too high.[81] But users agreed because they saw it as a means of guarding against chemical companies who might take advantage of shortages to raise prices unfairly.[82] Buyers particularly expressed their support for cost-based, post sales pricing when they were vulnerable, as when petrochemical makers threatened to do away with the system during the Gulf War to speed up price increases.[83] Chemicals buyers for an auto firm (cited previously) said that the car company supports the chemical industry's use of cost-based pricing rules. It does not complain about their colluding to set the price because it wants its suppliers to make ends meet. "If they did not use the formula it would create problems for the chemical manufacturers and might push them out of business." The buyers also made clear that the price formula was done in a "separate world which we have no control over." Thus, the governing rule originates upstream in the petrochemical industry but is supported downstream to ensure the survival of suppliers and give some price stability. Although all buyers do not directly participate in the formation of central pricing rules, important downstream firms consent to these rules in ways consistent with relational contracting.

A basic agreement on cost-based pricing does not mean there is no negotiation over prices. Instead, the formula provides a theoretical price that is modified through negotiations to reflect the market power of buyers and sellers at a particular time. These negotiations are often tough and drawn out. Typically, the side in the stronger position at the moment argues that price determination should follow international market trends, whereas the weaker party emphasizes fairness, costs, and prior sacrifices that must now be compensated for. The price arrived at is usually a compromise between cost-based pricing and market pricing. This negotiation, however, is done on an industry-wide basis to lessen the threat of competition's dragging down prices so low that chemical firms are run out of business. During these negotiations, as in the formal cartel, individual firms are reluctant to take on the leadership role. For example, the ethylene price negotiated by the PVC industry is generally accepted as the standard price because PVC is the most important sector that buys ethylene directly. Nevertheless, just as firms are reluctant to lead capacity-cutting cartels, individual PVC companies are hesitant to lead price negotiations. A production consignment company, Kajima Vinyl Chloride Monomer, had been providing price leadership for the industry, but once the new price formula was established in 1983, each of the three member companies—Shin-Etsu Chemical, Kanegafuchi Chemical, and

---

[81] *Nikkei sangyō shinbun*, 6 September 1983. Also reported in *Kagaku kōgyō nenkan*, 1985, p. 204.
[82] *Nihon keizai shinbun*, 27 April 1988.
[83] Ibid., 7 November 1990.

Asahi Glass—began its own negotiations. Next year Kanegafuchi Chemical represented the buyers in negotiations; in 1985 Shin-Etsu Chemical took on this role. But as the *Nikkei shinbun* put it, "neither of these companies likes being the one to set the standard price and did not like standing out in front."[84] Nevertheless, the PVC companies have continued to act as price leaders for the entire petrochemical market in their negotiations with Mitsubishi Petrochemical. Because their ethylene price serves as an indicator price for the whole petrochemical market, stalls in their negotiations paralyze price talks throughout the industry. In 1983, for instance, the PVC industry dragged out negotiations on ethylene so that they were done on an annual basis; other sectors followed suit. In 1987 the industry switched back to quarterly negotiations so it would know its final costs more quickly, and other sectors followed its lead.[85] Thus, MITI's attempt to support PVC prices by informally organizing the PVC pipe industry into joint-sales companies takes on added importance.

In addition to setting prices through price leadership, the petrochemical producers appear to consult with one another on ethylene bargaining positions—at least at times. They seem to have been cooperating on price negotiations even before the new formula was established. The *Nikkei shinbun* of 1 April 1981 reported that the various ethylene makers had "firmed up a decision to raise prices 10 yen/kilo for the January–March period and have entered into negotiations with the derivative makers." Thus, it appears that the industry colluded to set prices rather than simply engaged in price leadership. The petrochemical companies were also working together to negotiate prices in late 1983. The firms offered the same price of 150 yen in their negotiations over ethylene prices for the April–September period, and all agreed on a price of 145 yen on the same day.[86] It became common in later years for all the ethylene companies to ask for the same price on the same day.[87]

I read newspaper reports describing this situation to a senior chemical-company executive and asked if it indicated collusion. He flaty denied collusion, saying that even if prices were decided by a group of petrocheminal firms, they would be attacked if the story came out. His explanation was that buyers are probably resigned to the price, which seems like a way of acknowledging the lack of competition among chemical firms.[88]

Another chemical-company executive admitted that there was a consensus on a price formula among chemical firms. But when I confronted

[84] *Nihon keizai shinbun*, 9 October 1986.
[85] *Nikkei sangyō shinbun*, 8 April 1987.
[86] *Nihon keizai shinbun*, 22 December 1983.
[87] See, for example, ibid., 9 September 1987; 11 August 1989.
[88] Interview, 1992.

him with a 1985 report from the *Kagaku nenkan* (Chemical annual), a standard industry source, that all ethylene prices for the previous year had been decided "at once," he said it was impossible, that the reporter was mistaken. He also denied the minimal interpretation that price leadership rather than collusion might have explained the remarkable pattern.[89]

In keeping with the spirit of the relational contract between the petrochemical industry and its buyers, Mitsubishi Petrochemical plays a leadership role in not only raising prices but sometimes restraining them. Following the 1990 Iraqi invasion of Kuwait, the petrochemical producers displayed their unity in pricing their wide range of derivative products. With rising naphtha prices, chemical firms were itching to raise their own prices. Nevertheless, they were careful not to push ahead until Mitsubishi Petrochemical gave the signal. In mid-September 1990, rumors were flying around the industry that Mitsubishi Petrochemical would raise the price of ethylene on 17 September. Mitsubishi, however, decided to delay the increase until 19 September as a gesture to show that the industry did not intend to take undue advantage of the situation. Industry unity on price increases was underscored by other companies' intense pressure on Mitsubishi to go ahead and raise the price. As the *Nikkei sangyō shinbun* reported, "On the 17th, the telephone of Kodama Tōru, head of the First Business Affairs Department of the Chemical Goods Department, was ringing off the hook. Everybody was pressuring him to raise the price."[90] Prices are governed by price leadership in the sense that Mitsubishi Petrochemical has final authority over price changes. But this is not the tacit price leadership of those who are afraid of accusations of antitrust violations. Rather, it involves intense communication between competing firms in advance of price changes.

I have discussed the creation of the cost-based price formula for ethylene and the method by which the formula is translated into actual prices. How closely has the formula been followed in practice? Table 5–6 shows actual Japanese ethylene prices as well as the price had the formula been followed to the letter. The table also shows the ratio of the actual price to the theoretical price. The formula expressed fairly closely the historical relation of the ethylene price to the domestic naphtha price. Actual ethylene prices ranged from 93 to 97 percent of the theoretical price from 1974 to 1984, except during the second oil shock, when chemical companies took advantage of fears of shortages to push prices just above the theoretical price. In the first years of the new price formula (1984–85),

---

[89] Interview, senior chemical industry official, 1992.
[90] *Nikkei sangyō shinbun*, 29 September 1990.

Table 5–6. Actual Japanese ethylene prices compared to theoretical and U.S. prices

	Actual price (A)	Theoretical price (B)	U.S. price (C)	A/B	A/C
1973	37	49	20	0.75	1.89
1974	71	77	48	0.93	1.48
1975	89	94	58	0.94	1.54
1976	98	101	73	0.96	1.33
1977	97	101	71	0.97	1.38
1978	82	87	57	0.95	1.43
1979	119	116	77	1.02	1.55
1980	181	173	110	1.04	1.64
1981	174	172	122	1.01	1.43
1982	166	173	104	0.96	1.59
1983	145	155	100	0.94	1.46
1984	139	143	99	0.97	1.39
1985	130	140	74	0.93	1.77
1986	90	80	52	1.12	1.73
1987	88	77	45	1.14	1.97
1988	88	68	71	1.29	1.25
1989	96	74	72	1.29	1.34
1990	108	89	71	1.21	1.52
1991	107	89	NA	1.20	NA

Source: Actual ethylene prices are from *Kagaku keizai* and *Kagaku kōgyō nenkan*, various issues. Theoretical price is based on the formula reported in the *Nihon keizai shinbun*, and naphtha prices are from *Kagaku keizai* and *Kagaku kōgyō nenkan*, various issues. Average annual U.S. ethylene prices are from statistics in *Synthetic Organic Chemicals*, U.S. International Trade Commission, various years.

the petrochemical industry never quite got the full amount; but in the late 1980s firms more than made up for it. Nevertheless, although firms negotiating the price might deviate, they always expressed the price in terms of the formula. In the early years, buyers were given a discount because supply-demand conditions favored them.[91] In 1986–90, sellers were given a premium over the formula because the capacity-cutting cartel had successfully gotten rid of excess domestic capacity and international markets for petrochemicals were tight. But, although the formula was modified to express supply and demand, it nevertheless did moderate prices and kept them close to costs. In 1989, manufacturers were successfully negotiating large premiums over the cost-based price but were chafing at the constraints of the cost-based formula and calling for the whole postsales pricing system to be overturned.[92] Even in 1988–89, however, when prices were 28 and 29 percent over the theoretical price, they were at historic Japanese lows relative to U.S. prices, which can be considered a general indicator of international prices. Thus, the industry took advantage of an international scarcity to modify the for-

[91] *Kagaku kōgyō nenkan*, 1988, p. 203.
[92] *Nihon keizai shinbun*, 11 May 1989.

Table 5–7. Import and export prices and ratios in the Japanese ethylene market, 1980–1992
(prices in yen/kg)

	Import price	Export price	Domestic price	Domestic price/import price	Domestic price/export price	Import penetration (%)	Exports/ production (%)
1980	153	159	181	1.18	1.14	0.13	0.32
1981	—	144	174	—	1.20	0	0.44
1982	—	124	166	—	1.35	0	0.43
1983	—	122	145	—	1.19	0	0.24
1984	127	108	139	1.09	1.29	0.52	0.07
1985	123	105	130	1.06	1.24	0.03	0.39
1986	—	56	90	—	1.61	0	1.88
1987	61	59	88	1.44	1.49	0.72	3.03
1988	92	67	88	0.96	1.32	0.62	3.18
1989	92	83	96	1.05	1.16	0.77	3.04
1990	97	91	108	1.11	1.19	2.32	1.88
1991	105	78	107	1.02	1.37	1.45	2.86
1992	52	41	N/A	N/A	N/A	0.25	1.50

Source: Kagaku keizai, Kagaku kōgyō nenkan, various issues; Sekiyu Kagaku Kōgyō Kyōkai (Japan Petrochemical Industry Association), *Sekiyu kagaku kōgyō 30 nen no ayumi* (Thirty years of progress in the petrochemical industry) (Tokyo: Sekiyu Kagaku Kōgyō Kyōkai , 1989); Ibid., *Sekiyu kagaku kōgyō no genjō* (The current situation in the petrochemical industry) (Tokyo: Sekiyu Kagaku Kōgyō Kyōkai, 1993).
Note: Domestic ethylene price is from *Kagaku keizai* and *Kagaku kōgyō nenkan.* Import and export prices are calculated by dividing the total sales value of each commodity by the sales volume.

mula in its favor. At the same time it was constrained by the cost formula and so did not take maximum advantage of its price position. Similarly, in 1984, when domestic ethylene prices were at their lowest levels relative to costs since the first oil shock, the domestic price was especially high by international standards. In short, although the cost-based pricing formula has not been followed to the letter, it has buffered both sellers and buyers from sharper price swings in international markets.

Japanese petrochemical makers have been willing to sell ethylene overseas considerably below domestic prices (see table 5–7). While domestic prices are based on costs, export prices are tied to U.S. long-term contract prices. Thus, even though makers show discipline in the home market and do not undercut each others' prices, they are willing to do so overseas. The *Nihon keizai shinbun* has called cheap sales overseas a strategy for supporting domestic prices.[93]

Table 5–7 also shows that Japan's import prices of ethylene correlate better with the domestic price than does the theoretical price. One might conclude, therefore, that the formula is a sham and that Japan's buyers and sellers of ethylene merely make their transactions at the going international rate. This notion runs counter, however, to our current

[93] Ibid., 2 November 1991.

understanding of the market in Japan. Because it has been difficult to transport ethylene, trade has been limited and imports until 1990 never accounted for even 1 percent of Japan's markets. The Nomura Institute did a comparative study of factors explaining prices in the United States and Japan and found that cost outweighed domestic supply and demand in Japan while supply and demand were much more important in the United States. Out of four chemicals examined, the study considered import prices irrelevant for ethylene because import levels are so low (see table 5–8). A 1983 *Kagaku keizai* article noted that because of the difficulty of transport, there is no international price for ethylene.[94] The Nomura study found that the improvement in capacity use as a result of the 1983 cartel was partly responsible for raising domestic prices.

Japan's users have certainly noted that Japanese ethylene prices are high by international standards. In 1985 PVC makers complained that Japanese prices were in the 140 yen range, while German prices were in the 90 yen range and American prices were in the 80 yen range.[95] As table 5–6 shows, Japanese ethylene prices averaged about 50 percent over U.S. prices in the 1980s.

Ethylene prices have been successfully tied to raw material prices. But even more important is the use of ethylene prices for cost-based pricing of derivatives, which account for the great majority of ethylene-producers' sales. Japanese derivative prices have indeed been stable compared to both costs and international prices. They have also remained high compared to export and import prices without drawing in crushing volumes of imports. Japan exports and imports large amounts of ethylene-based petrochemicals. Its exports are dominated by plastics, such as low- and high-density polyethylene and polystyrene, though it also exports important quantities of styrene monomer, vinyl chloride monomer, and ethylene. Imports are concentrated more heavily in basic standardized commodities such as styrene monomer, ethylene dichloride, ethylene glycol, and ethylene. The monomers (styrene monomer, vinyl chloride monomer, ethylene dichloride, and ethylene) are standardized commodities and, except for ethylene, readily transportable. Nevertheless, table 5–9 shows that Japanese prices for these goods averaged 60 percent higher than import prices from 1982–92. Prices were also 47 percent higher than those for the major standardardized, readily transportable derivatives Japan exported (see table 5–10).

The *Chemical Industry Annual* confirmed the chemical industry's systematic sale of exports below domestic prices when it remarked in 1988

[94] *Kagaku keizai*, September 1983, p. 58.
[95] *Nihon keizai shinbun*, 27 February 1985.

Table 5-8. Correlation of ethylene cost and supply-demand changes with changes in commodity prices

	Cost	Domestic supply and demand	Correlation coefficient
Japan	0.435	0.239	0.958
U.S.	0.419	4.102	0.638

Source: Kagaku keizai 36 (August 1989): 15. Study originally done by Nomura Research Institute.

Table 5-9. Ratio of domestic to import price

	Vinyl chloride monomer	Ethylene dichloride	Ethylene glycol	Styrene monomer	Acrylonitrile	Yearly average
1980	N/A	1.35	1.25	1.35	N/A	
1981	N/A	N/A	1.59	1.41	N/A	
1982	1.37	1.68	1.69	1.31	1.24	1.48
1983	1.28	1.60	1.97	1.25	1.50	1.58
1984	1.18	1.13	1.78	1.26	1.26	1.36
1985	1.34	1.41	1.87	1.46	1.35	1.49
1986	1.50	1.75	2.22	1.85	1.81	1.83
1987	1.04	1.72	2.05	1.22	1.74	1.55
1988	0.77	1.65	1.77	1.12	1.61	1.39
1989	0.99	1.50	1.45	1.35	1.61	1.38
1990	1.31	2.27	2.69	1.39	1.97	1.93
1991	1.44	2.25	2.45	1.83	1.82	1.96
1992	1.49	2.11	3.29	2.05	1.83	2.15
Average (1982-92)	1.25	1.73	2.11	1.46	1.61	1.64

Source: Kagaku keizai, various issues; Kagaku kōgyō nenkan, 1990; MITI, Kagaku kōgyō tōkeihyō Yearbook of chemical industry statistics) (Tokyo: MITI), various issues; Sekiyu Kagaku Kōgyō Kyōkai Japan Petrochemical Industry Association), Sekiyu kagaku kōgyō 30 nen no ayumi (Thirty years of progress in the petrochemical industry) (Tokyo: Sekiyu Kagaku Kōgyō Kyōkai, 1989).

Notes: To give a representative view of prices of standardized commodities, this table includes all the derivatives of ethylene and propylene that are produced in quantities of more than 500,000 tons and are standardized and easily transportable (see figure 5-2). Because ethylene glycol, a derivative of ethylene oxide, is more commonly transported long distances than ethylene oxide itself, ethylene glycol is substituted. Similarly, because ethylene dichloride is commonly sold in place of its derivative, vinyl chloride monomer, it is included as well.

that Japanese prices fell so low (because of their cost basis) that "export prices were even higher than domestic prices, something the industry had never experienced before."[96] Imports have taken important shares of some of the markets for standardized goods, although Japan exports

[96] Kagaku kōgyō nenkan (Chemical industry annual), p. 248.

Table 5-10. Ratio of domestic to export price

	Vinyl chloride monomer	Ethylene glycol	Acrylonitrile	Styrene monomer	Yearly average
1980	N/A	1.36	1.50	1.11	
1981	N/A	1.58	1.45	1.13	
1982	1.10	1.39	1.32	1.32	1.28
1983	1.17	1.74	1.48	1.05	1.36
1984	0.82	1.64	1.33	1.26	1.26
1985	0.94	1.59	1.40	1.38	1.33
1986	1.59	2.33	1.98	2.14	2.01
1987	1.10	2.19	1.72	1.02	1.51
1988	0.80	1.21	1.66	0.86	1.13
1989	1.36	1.31	1.71	1.49	1.47
1990	1.49	2.71	2.01	1.18	1.85
1991	1.87	2.47	2.00	1.96	2.07
1992	1.81	3.24	1.94	2.15	2.28
Average (1982–92)	1.28	1.98	1.69	1.44	1.60

Prices are calculated by dividing the total sales value of each commodity in a year by the total value.

N/A = not available.

Source: Kagaku keizai, various issues; *Kagaku kōgyō nenkan,* 1990; *Kagaku kōgyō tōkeihyō,* various issues; Sekiyu kagaku kōgyō kyōkai (Japan Petrochemical Industry Association), *Sekiyu kagaku kōgyō 30 nen no ayumi* (Thirty years of progress in the petrochemical industry) (Tokyo: Sekiyu Kagaku Kōgyō Kyōkai, 1989).

Note: This table includes the same products as the import table, but ethylene dichloride is excluded because Japan did not export it until 1988.

some of these same materials. Nevertheless, the bulk of the market has been retained by domestic makers despite a huge price disparity.

Partly, of course, buyers pay higher prices because they are locked into relationships with firms with which they are connected by pipeline. But not all companies are physically committed in this way. For instance, about half the polystyrene is made from styrene monomer transported by truck or ship rather than directly by pipeline. Half the PVC, which is made from vinyl chloride monomer or ethylene dichloride, is also manufactured outside the petrochemical complexes. And while pipeline transport within a petrochemical complex presents cost advantages, as little as a 15 percent price differential can offset these advantages.[97] Thus, the margin of cost differentials that exists between import and domestic prices reflects not only the physical limits of petrochemical complex-based plants but also ongoing choices to honor long-term commitments.

Itami Hiroyuki confirmed that Japan's prices for petrochemical goods have been high by international standards when he compared Japanese

[97] Interview, official of Kagaku Keizai Kenkyū Jo, 1988.

Table 5–11. Japanese chemical prices compared to U.S. and West German prices

	All products	Inorganic chemicals	Petrochemicals	Ethylene-based petrochemicals
Japanese chemicals that were cheaper than U.S. chemicals				
1972–73	7 (29)	1 (2)	6 (27)	2 (13)
1978	1 (20)	1 (9)	0 (11)	0 (7)
1980	3 (26)	3 (10)	0 (19)	0 (7)
1982	5 (20)	2 (4)	3 (16)	0 (7)
1984	3 (22)	2 (9)	1 (13)	0 (6)
1988	2 (18)	0 (9)	2 (9)	2 (5)
Japanese chemicals that were cheaper than West German chemicals				
1972–73	19 (29)	1 (2)	18 (27)	7 (13)
1978	7 (20)	1 (9)	6 (12)	3 (7)
1980	5 (23)	3 (10)	2 (13)	0 (7)

Source: Itami Hiroyuki, Nihon no kagaku sangyō, naze sekai ni tachiokureta no ka (Japan's chemical industry: Why is it behind the rest of the world?) (Tokyo: NTT Shuppan, 1990), p. 92. Originally compiled from Kagaku kōgyō nenkan, Kagaku kōgyō handobukku, European Chemical News, and Chemical Marketing Report.
Note: Figures in parentheses represent total number of goods surveyed.

Table 5–12. Japanese styrene monomer market, 1983

Used in-house	343,296	29%
Sales to keiretsu affiliates	576,010	49%
Not keiretsu tied (approximate):		
Buyers committed to buying domestic	75,000	6%
Open to buying imports if cheaper	175,000	15%
Total domestic demand	1,169,306	100%

Source: Kagaku keizai 30 (August 1984): 42; Kagaku kōgyō tōkeihyō, 1984, p. 77.

prices with U.S. and West German prices (see table 5–11). Very few Japanese petrochemicals were price competitive with U.S. goods even before the first oil shocks, and after the shocks they were even less so. Even in 1988, when naphtha prices were lower in Japan than they had been since 1973 and Japanese petrochemical prices were at an all-time low compared to international prices (see table 5–8), only two of nine products surveyed were cost-competitive. A comparison with West Germany shows Japan somewhat stronger than Germany before the first oil shock and weaker after the second one. The survey indicates that the lack of international competitiveness held also for Japan's inorganic chemical sector.

The styrene monomer market is a specific example of a market that has been buffered from import prices. Here, keiretsu ties play an important role in reinforcing the commitment to cost-based pricing. As table 5–12 shows, of the 71 percent of styrene monomer that producers sold to other companies rather than processed in-house, 49 percent went to keiretsu affiliates. In assessing the danger of large amounts of imports, the August 1984 *Kagaku keizai* said that this affiliate half of the styrene monomer market was safe. Non-keiretsu linked firms would need about 250,000 tons, but of these the journal concluded another seventy to eighty thousand tons of demand were unlikely to go to imports because of concerns about quality and stable supplies and problems with negotiating prices from a foreign source. Moreover, although Saudi styrene monomer was price competitive, the local supplier, Shell, was not working aggressively to enter the market but was pricing its imports at Japanese levels. The article also noted that domestic manufacturers tried to keep their less loyal customers by pricing styrene monomer at just five yen above the import price. *Kagaku keizai* concluded that imports were unlikely to go much beyond two hundred thousand tons, and in fact the prediction proved correct. As we can see in table 5–13, styrene monomer imports peaked in 1986 at 14 percent of the market, or 220,000 tons, and then declined. The article warned styrene monomer makers that, although the volume of imports might be limited, manufacturers needed to "stand firm together" to keep imports from eroding domestic prices.[98] That is, long-term ties provide considerable immunity to imports, but coordinated action is necessary to keep prices high enough to maintain industry health.

Remarkably, not only has the styrene monomer market resisted imports but domestic prices, like ethylene prices, have been substantially cost-based and have withstood downward pressure from cheap international prices. As table 5–13 shows, domestic producers have kept a comfortable price margin above imports. In addition, domestic prices have been high compared to export prices, reflecting weak competition in domestic markets compared to international markets. Consistent overseas sales at lower prices indicate a consensus not to upset the domestic market by unloading excess supplies cheaply.

We can see that cost-based pricing has been observed in this market by looking at the margin between the domestic styrene monomer price and the domestic cost of the ethylene that goes into it. Table 5–14 subtracts the Japanese naphtha cost from import, export, and domestic prices. Because imported styrene monomer from Saudi Arabia and North America is based on ethane, is it sometimes even cheaper than raw-material ethylene in Japan. Moreover, Japan's export prices are at times lower than the price of the ethylene. It might seem odd that Japanese exporters sell at less than the cost of their materials, but we must

<hr />

[98] *Kagaku keizai*, August 1984, p. 42.

The Petrochemical Sector   157

able 5-13. Imports and exports in the Japanese styrene monomer market (prices in yen/kg)

	Import price	Domestic price	Export price	Import penetration (%)	Exports/ production (%)	Domestic price/ import price	Domestic price/ export price
980	186	251	226	10.6	0.2	1.35	1.11
981	173	243	215	13.3	0.5	1.41	1.13
982	157	206	157	6.7	1.9	1.31	1.32
983	155	193	184	9.3	0.2	1.25	1.05
984	155	196	156	8.5	0.4	1.26	1.26
985	129	188	136	12.0	0.7	1.46	1.38
986	75	139	65	13.9	2.7	1.85	2.14
987	114	139	136	11.8	3.3	1.22	1.02
988	137	154	178	11.5	2.4	1.12	0.86
989	115	155	104	9.7	5.6	1.35	1.49
990	112	156	132	7.7	5.9	1.39	1.18
991	86	156	80	9.0	7.8	1.83	1.96
992	63	130	60	7.3	11.2	2.05	2.15
verages						1.36	1.28

Source: Kagaku keizai, various issues; *Kagaku kōgyō nenkan,* 1990; *Kagaku kōgyō tōkeihyō,* various ssues; Sekiyu Kagaku Kōgyō Kyōkai (Japan Petrochemical Industry Association), *Sekiyu kagaku kōgyō) nen no ayumi* (Thirty years of progress in the petrochemical industry) (Tokyo: Sekiyu Kagaku Kōgyō yōkai, 1989).

Table 5-14. Price stability in the Japanese styrene monomer market (includes adjusted ethylene price)

	Domestic	Import	Export
1980	49	-17	23
1981	48	-22	20
1982	20	-29	-30
1983	30	-8	21
1984	41	-0	1
1985	42	-17	-10
1986	38	-26	-36
1987	41	16	38
1988	55	38	80
1989	47	7	-3
1990	35	-9	11
1991	36	-34	-40
Standard deviations			
1984-91	6	22	37
1980-91	9	20	33

Source: Kagaku keizai, various issues; *Kagaku kōgyō nenkan,* 1990; *Kagaku kōgyō tōkeihyō,* various issues; Sekiyu Kagaku Kōgyō Kyōkai (Japan Petrochemical Industry Association), *Sekiyu kagaku kōgyō 30 nen no ayumi* (Thirty years of progress in the petrochemical industry) (Tokyo: Sekiyu Kagaku kōgyō kyōkai, 1989).

remember that the same petrochemical companies also make the ethylene. Thus, part of their ethylene price represents their own fixed costs for production. Table 5–14 highlights the stability of Japanese domestic prices relative to Japanese costs. Japanese styrene monomer prices have been clearly cost-based, especially since the October 1983 formula for cost-based pricing. Since 1984, the first full year of the new agreement, prices have varied from a low of thirty-five yen above the cost of ethylene to a high of fifty-five yen. International prices have moved much more erratically, from thirty-four yen below ethylene to thirty-eight yen above for imports, and from minus forty to eighty for exports. (The standard deviation[99] was only six yen for the domestic price versus twenty-two yen for imports and thirty-seven for exports.)

The styrene monomer market has been particularly stable, but markets for most other major derivatives show a similar pattern. As Table 5–15 shows, both export and import prices for all but one of the major derivatives of ethylene and propylene varied more than domestic prices relative to costs. Thus, cost-based pricing gave Japanese petrochemical producers a more predictable environment than the supply- and demand–oriented international market would have.

The Nomura study found that certain Japanese derivative prices were more strongly influenced by costs than those of the United States (see table 5–16). For example, cost factors were somewhat more important than supply and demand for explaining low-density polyethylene prices in Japan, but supply and demand was much more important than cost in the United States. The same was true for styrene monomer, except that import and export prices had even more effect than costs on prices. For ethylene glycol, only international prices appeared to affect domestic prices, in contrast to the United States where both domestic costs and supply-demand factors correlated with price changes. This fits the common understanding in the Japanese industry that ethylene glycol prices are tied to international prices. But while the study merely looked at the timing of changes and found that domestic ethylene glycol prices move parallel to international prices, it did not consider the fact that basic domestic price levels are much higher than international levels. As we saw in table 5–8, ethylene glycol prices averaged 85 percent higher than import prices between 1984 and 1990, while styrene monomer prices were 33 percent higher. In addition, these prices were 63 and 38 percent higher, respectively, than export prices.

Interviews with officials in both the chemical companies selling derivatives and the downstream industries that buy them suggest that Japanese derivative prices are high and stable because they are based on cost

---

[99] The standard deviation is the average distance of value from the mean value.

Table 5–15. Variation of Japanese petrochemical prices minus costs, 1984–90

	Domestic price − materials cost		Import price − materials cost		Export price − materials cost		Import standard deviation/ domestic standard deviation	Export standard deviation/ domestic standard deviation
	Mean	S.D.	Mean	S.D.	Mean	S.D.		
Ethylene derivatives								
Vinyl chloride monomer	31	6	20	22	25	25	3.67	4.17
Ethylene dichloride	−1	13	−25	11	—	—	0.85	—
Styrene monomer	43	6	1	20	12	35	3.33	5.83
HDPE	87	15	77	43	29	18	2.87	1.20
LDPE	88	9	21	15	37	13	1.67	1.44
Propylene derivatives								
Polypropylene	123	11	74	22	82	18	2.00	1.64
Acrylonitrile	83	14	14	19	9	17	1.36	1.21

Source: Kagaku keizai, Kagaku kōgyō tōkei nenpō, various issues; *Kagaku kōgyō nenkan,* 1991; Sekiyu Kagaku Kōgyō Kyōkai (Japan Petrochemical Industry Association), *Sekiyu kagaku kōgyō 30 nen no ayumi* (Thirty years of progress in the petrochemical industry) (Tokyo: Sekiyu kagaku kōgyō kyōkai, 1989).
Note: This table covers all of the derivatives of ethylene and propylene produced in volumes of over 100,000. Ethylene dichloride exports have been negligible.

Table 5–16. Correlation of cost and supply-demand changes with changes in commodity prices

		Cost	Domestic supply and demand	International supply and demand	Correlation coefficient
Low-density polyethylene	Japan	0.213	0.162	0.015	0.821
	United States	0.45	3.306		0.696
Styrene monomer	Japan	0.508	0.356	0.76	0.982
	United States	−0.065	3.215		0.856
Ethylene glycol	Japan	−0.034	−0.036	0.471	0.922
	United States	0.913	1.262		0.976

Source: Kagaku keizai (August 1989): 15. Study originally done by Nomura Research Institute.
Note: Formula: $\ln$ (commodity price) $= a_0 + a_1 \times \ln$ (material price) $+ a_2 \times \ln$ (capacity use rate) $+ a_3 \times \ln$ (import price). Because the U.S. price is the standard for international prices, the effect of international prices on U.S. prices was not calculated.

formulas. Derivative makers pay these prices for security of supply, stable prices, and the advantages of an insurance-based relationship.

As we saw, PVC makers negotiate the main indicator price for ethylene because they are its largest direct purchasers; and their willingness to pay cost-based prices is key to the stability of the industry-wide price system. We also saw that PVC makers are able to pass on their costs because of cartels in the construction industry and MITI's informal organization of the PVC pipe industry into joint-sales companies. An executive with the PVC subsidiary of a major petrochemical corporation said that PVC makers use a cost-based formula in negotiating prices with their buyers, although they have to give buyers a discount when there is an oversupply of PVC. At these times, "the principle [of cost-based pricing] remains, but the power relationship is more important [in determining prices] . . ." He added, "Most customers do not really care that much about the petrochemical companies' situation, but most do follow costs. They watch the ethylene prices negotiated by the champion negotiators."[100] Thus, from the PVC executive's point of view, buyers do not act out of love for their suppliers. But they do expect manufacturers to cover their costs, and they base their estimate of those costs on the prices negotiated by the "champion negotiators" of the PVC industry. The executive I spoke to also emphasized that the insurance component of the relational contract is an important motive. When one company helps another on price, it expects the other company to reciprocate in the future. He called this kind of relational contracting *kashi-kari*, or "borrowing and lending," and said it is reserved for times of extreme duress, such as when one of the companies is losing money. He noted that there is one check on skewing prices: tax officials look to see if prices are out of whack. He added, however, that because price adjustments are usually carried out throughout the industry, no one firm is likely to stand out.[101]

PVC producers, like the other derivative producers, also command high domestic prices. PVC is not a standardized good; thus, overall price statistics comparing Japanese and international prices are not necessarily meaningful. Nevertheless, the domestic price for even the cheapest grade of PVC ("straight" PVC) was 168 yen in 1990 compared to 113 yen for all PVC imports and 130 yen for all Japanese exports (still, imports take only 0.3 percent of the domestic market and exports account for only 0.5 percent of total production).[102]

Much of Japan's PVC is used to make construction materials for domestic consumption and does not have to compete in overseas markets. By contrast, many of Japan's petrochemicals are sold directly or indirectly in the international market. As we have seen, most of the 10 percent or more of petrochemical production that is sold directly overseas is successfully marketed by selling it more cheaply than at home.

[100] Interview, PVC manufacturer, 1992.
[101] Interview, 1992. Chemicals buyers also use the term *kashi-kari* to refer to relational contracting. Interview, electronics executive, 1994.
[102] *Kagaku kōgyō nenkan*, 1991; *Kagaku keizai*, Special Issue, August 1991.

Another 30 percent are exported indirectly as raw material for goods such as cars and electronics, and one might imagine that bearing the cost of high-priced domestic petrochemicals would be difficult for firms that compete in international markets.[103] Nevertheless, Japan's export industries also base their pricing schemes on the formula established by petrochemical trade association officials.

The auto industry has used the industry-wide formula as its basis for pricing petrochemical components. The industry has found that long-term relations based on trust encourage suppliers to invest in better technology. Rather than use a completely open bidding system, firms break down a supplier's costs and compare them with that supplier's costs for previous years and the costs of one or two other suppliers. Price adjustments are made on a semi-annual basis. Smitka writes that, while suppliers have been pressed to improve productivity, changes in materials costs are passed on in a straightforward way.[104]

The auto industry has been able to absorb high domestic materials costs and is keenly interested in maintaining domestic suppliers for the sake of product quality. Cost-based pricing in the auto industry can be illustrated by the case of one of Japan's largest auto manufacturers. The company spreads purchases of its principal chemical materials among five domestic chemical companies to maintain competition and avoid depending on a single supplier. At the same time it acknowledges the need to limit competition and allows the industry as a whole to set the formula that establishes the price of ethylene. The two chemicals buyers for the car firm, whom I quoted earlier, confirmed that the new ethylene price formula established in 1983 was applied to the pricing of auto parts as well and has remained unchanged since then.[105] As we saw, the buyers made clear that the trade association established the price formula for ethylene and that all petrochemicals makers observe this rule rigorously. The buyers simply accept the ethylene price established by the industry association. But while the auto firm accepts the ethylene price as given, it does pressure the petrochemical manufacturers on resin prices and gives them an incentive to improve productivity at this stage of manufacture. Thus, it encourages competition, but only within limits.

Chemical pricing in the auto industry shows how industry-wide rules on feedstock prices can help solve the dilemma of interindustry relational contracting for finely differentiated goods. Industry negotiations over ethylene pricing are often difficult and drawn out, but they are facilitated by ethylene's being a completely standardized good for which the indus-

[103] Interview, official, Kagaku Keizai Kenkyū Jo, 1988.
[104] Michael Smitka, *Competitive Ties: Subcontracts in the Japanese Automotive Industries* (New York: Columbia University Press, 1991), p. 140.
[105] Interview, 1992.

try can agree on a single price. Industry-wide pricing is more difficult for finely differentiated products. Auto companies encourage their suppliers to develop chemicals to exacting and often unique specifications, which makes it difficult to compare their market value precisely with other products or to establish industry-wide prices. The auto industry has solved this problem by establishing industry-wide prices for feedstocks so that at least on this component of the price auto firms can be confident they are not paying more than their competitors. Auto firms also use price leadership to make sure prices are not out of line with those of their competitors. Twice a year, for example, Toyota negotiates prices with plastics makers; and this price leadership is followed by the other auto firms.[106]

The electronics industry also honors cost-based pricing for its purchases of petrochemicals, although it pushes its suppliers harder on prices than do the car companies. Principally, auto firms allow more cost-based pricing because they are more technically demanding than the electronics firms. This also means that the institutional framework of petrochemical price negotiation is different. Whereas petrochemical companies negotiate directly with car companies, joint-sales companies represent their firms in hardball negotiations with electronics firms.[107]

Nevertheless, electronics companies are still willing to pay a high premium for domestic goods. Domestic polypropylene prices in recent years have run from a third to half again as high as the price of imports.[108] A reporter specializing in chemical prices for a major Japanese newspaper confirmed that this price disparity is real and does not merely represent quality differences. According to the reporter, 90 percent of imported polypropylene is standard-grade and completely identical to standard-grade domestic polypropylene. The reporter noted that in February 1992 the domestic price for standard-grade propylene was at 150 yen/kilo versus 90 yen/kilo for imports.[109] Despite this disparity, imports never accounted for more than 3.1 percent of domestic market share in 1982–92. Electronics makers certainly do express cost-consciousness. To counter the effects of the rise in the yen, some switched to cheaper grades of domestic-made materials. For example, video-cassette makers switched from engineering plastics to polystyrene. But electronics makers have not substituted cheap imported materials for domestic goods. The

---

[106] Interview, official, Kagaku Keizai Kenkyū Jo, 1992.

[107] Interview, journalist specializing in chemicals prices for one of Japan's major newspapers, 1992.

[108] Because polypropylene is not a completely standardized product, it was not included with the earlier price comparisons of domestic and foreign petrochemicals that are standardized and easily transportable. *Kagaku Keizai*, various issues.

[109] Interview, journalist specializing in petrochemical prices for a large Japanese newspaper, 1992.

reporter said that the reason is security of supply and reliability of delivery. Electronics makers generally have a long-term relationship with a single petrochemical supplier, although not usually because of keiretsu ties. Thus, electronics firms buy domestic materials from a single supplier as a strategy to maximize their own security and efficiency.

The detergent industry is another example of an industry that engages in cost-based pricing and is unwilling to switch to imports. One official from a large soap manufacturer explained that his company knows the supplier's production costs and adds a reasonable profit to them in negotiating its three-month contracts. As do electronics firms, the company prefers to stick to a single regular supplier but often uses a secondary supplier for safety's sake. The company prefers domestic suppliers because of security of supply. If the price of the regular supplier or overall domestic prices is high, the company might buy "10 percent imports" but "would not go from 0 percent to 100 percent imports."[110] The soap manufacturer is able to disregard international competition in part because materials account for only 20–30 percent of production costs of products such as detergent. The lack of direct competition from imports is also an important factor. Although Procter and Gamble sells in Japan, it also manufactures there. Unlike Japanese firms, it sells through Japanese wholesalers rather than directly to retailers; so it does not put pressure on domestic soap makers.

We noted that the domestic price of ethylene glycol goes up and down with international prices but that the domestic price is much higher than international prices. Imports have had a major impact on the ethylene glycol market, taking 40 percent of the market in 1988 and 27–29 percent from 1989 to 1992.[111] The polyester industry, which accounts for somewhat more that half of domestic demand for ethylene glycol, is responsible for bringing in 80 percent of the imports. But polyester makers are said to be unwilling to buy more than 40 percent of their supplies from abroad because of concerns with security of supply.[112] Thus, even in a sector where imports have taken a large share of the market and prices are linked to international ones, buyers pay domestic makers high prices to cover their high domestic costs.

An FTC finding that plastic-wrap firms colluded in setting prices provides insights into informal price governance in the petrochemical industry as well as into FTC and user attitudes toward such governance. In 1991 the commission accused eight makers of the plastic film used to wrap food in grocery stores of fixing prices. The FTC found that the firms

---

[110] Interview, 1988.
[111] Sekiyu Kagaku Kōgyō Kyōkai, *Sekiyu kagaku kōgyō no genjō* (Current conditions in the petrochemical industry) (Tokyo: Sekiyu Kagaku Kōgyō Kyōkai, 1993).
[112] Interview, official, Kagaku Keizai Kenkyū Jo, 1988.

decided to raise the price by 10 percent in August and again in September 1990 at the height of speculation over oil prices during the Gulf War. The case showed that enforcement mechanisms (which, as we saw, have been used by the cement industry) are not unknown in the plastics industry. The FTC found that the eight companies established a "special body comprising middle-ranking executives to monitor any violations of the cartel."[113] They planned to reward local branches of the industry for closely observing the cartel.

This was the first criminal antitrust complaint in seventeen years and appeared to indicate a strict new enforcement of the Antimonopoly Law. Comments by FTC spokespersons, however, suggest that the new enforcement did not represent a major change in commission policy. First, a spokesperson said that the action was an attempt to "offset, even a little," foreign complaints about weak Antimonopoly Law enforcement.[114] Thus, the ruling was in part a response to U.S. pressure rather than a deep-rooted transformation of approaches to enforcement. The FTC also made clear that the film industry was being punished not for colluding to set prices but for breaking their implicit relational contracts and taking excess advantage of their market power. The FTC complained that, although the companies had used higher labor and materials prices to justify their price increases, the fact that they tried to raise prices twice in two months suggested they were trying to profit at the expense of the consumer. Of course, price fixing always hurts the consumer, but what is significant is that the FTC said that the cartel was illegitimate because it raised prices above levels justified by cost increases. Thus, the FTC implicitly signaled its support for continued collusion to set prices based on costs.

The supermarkets that bought the plastic wrap also made clear that they were not opposed to a price cartel but to pushing up prices faster than costs. The supermarkets successfully resisted what they considered exorbitant increases, but they did allow the price increase justified by cost increases. According to one supermarket executive, "we know exactly the production costs of the makers and thus accepted the range of that price hike."[115] Thus, the 1992 ruling against the plastic industry reveals both the informal practices of this downstream branch of the chemical industry and continued FTC and user tolerance for collusion on cost-based price increases.

The *Asahi nenkan* has likened the pricing mechanism for ethylene to the feudal policy of closing the country to foreigners (*sakoku*), calling it

---

[113] Interview, official, Kagaku Keizai Kenkyū Jo, 1988.
[114] *Asian Wall Street Journal*, 7 November 1991.
[115] *Nikkei Weekly*, 16 November 1991.

"cost-based pricing with no relation to international market conditions."[116] We have seen that ethylene pricing is based on a long-standing system of price governance. It is the linchpin of a broader system of cost-based pricing for petrochemical derivatives and has been deemed essential for maintaining relational contracts.

Relational contracting is important and genuine in the Japanese petrochemical industry. Many upstream firms are joined by pipeline, giving them a good reason to stay committed to their partners. Downstream buyers such as auto firms are interested in providing a secure outlet for their suppliers because they want them to invest in expensive, dedicated technologies. In this sense the petrochemical industry has a technological hook that strengthens buyers' loyalty. Other buyers are interested in convenience and security of supply and in the mutual insurance relationship they can obtain from long-time domestic suppliers. Some have keiretsu ties that commit them to particular suppliers.

While prices are supposed to be fair under relational contracts, neither buyers nor sellers believe that dyadic relational contracts alone can keep prices high enough to ensure the survival of the domestic petrochemical industry. Sellers have long lamented what they call excess domestic competition that drives down prices. Therefore, both MITI and the trade association have created governance mechanisms to supplement and strengthen relational contracts.

Throughout the history of the industry, MITI has provided leadership in formulating and implementing policy to help boost prices by limiting competition. It used administrative guidance to establish cartels in the early growth phase of the industry and limit production in the aftermath of the first oil shock. After the second oil shock MITI pushed industry to reduce competition aggressively. Although industry refused to follow MITI's advice to engage in the kind of mergers that helped American industry become more efficient, it did go along with plans for capacity-cutting cartels and joint-sales firms. MITI pressure and intermediation among member firms continued during the implementation of these policies.

MITI's participation in creating cartels has been both official and unofficial. The early depression cartels were authorized by exemptions under the Antimonopoly Law, while the capacity-cutting cartels of 1983–87 and the joint-sales companies were based on the SDIL. In contrast, the early investment cartels and the production cartel of the mid-1970s were grounded more vaguely in MITI's right to use administrative guidance. Similarly, MITI's role in the late 1980s, in both extending the SDIL capacity cartel informally and organizing a joint-sales

[116] *Asahi shinbun,* 7 May 1988.

company for the PVC pipe industry, does not have a clear legal base and violates the spirit of Japan's agreements with the United States to open markets and make policies more transparent.

Thus, MITI has acted as a leader and a pusher to help industry agree on policies that reduce competition. When industry is opposed to MITI policies, such as mergers in the early 1980s, it does not go along. More commonly, MITI's role has been to solve the problem of individual firms that avoid the risk of leading cartels for fear of being required to make disproportionate sacrifices.

Industry has not simply been passive in the formation of cartels. To understand the true scope of policy, one must look beyond state-sponsored policy to informal policy in the hands of the trade association. The association has shown considerable initiative in supporting relational contracting throughout the industry by establishing rules governing prices for chemical feedstocks. We saw that pricing based on relational contracts is carried out on a postsales basis and that it depends on negotiation of feedstock prices by "champion negotiators"—a process that sometimes seems based on industry consensus. Prices are based on a formula developed through public discussion among trade association leaders and technocratic analysis. This formula piggybacked on price formulas developed officially under the Petroleum Industry Law. According to chemicals buyers in the auto industry, it was endorsed by the industry officials who drew up the capacity-cutting cartels and is observed universally among petrochemical companies.

Can industry-wide governance mechanisms truly be considered the result of interindustry relational contracting, or is this simply the petrochemical industry's way of getting high prices from unfortunate users? It is true that the initiative for industry-wide cost-based pricing came from upstream petrochemical firms and that buyers and sellers both negotiate hard to get advantageous prices. During negotiations, whichever party is weaker at the moment makes claims about fairness while the stronger argues that old-fashioned, indulgent pricing arrangements encourage inefficiency and must be rooted out in favor of tough, internationally recognized, supply-and-demand pricing. Nevertheless, despite the bickering, downstream buyers indicate support for arrangements among petrochemicals suppliers to keep prices at levels that cover their costs. Even the FTC appears to support sellers' collusion as long as they do not get greedy and try to push up prices faster than costs.

Industry-wide pricing gives buyers a mechanism to share sacrifice to achieve a common good. Each individual buyer would be reluctant to pay a higher price than its competitors simply to ensure the survival of a domestic supplying industry. But if the downstream firm is confident that all its competitors are also paying high prices, it need not fear that the high price will threaten its survival. The system has been effective at keeping prices high compared to both import and export prices. This price discrepancy shows that domestic buyers are so committed to domestic suppliers that they will pay them a considerable premium and that petrochemical suppliers are disciplined enough not to undercut their rivals in the home market. Japanese prices are also stable compared to prices in the international market. Although domestic prices are affected by supply and demand, cost-based pricing buffers them from market pressures.

Relational contracting supports suppliers and buyers who work closely to create or improve products. In auto parts, for example, working closely together has enabled auto firms to get parts suppliers to achieve high levels of quality and innovation. But relational contracting can also fail to push suppliers to cut costs, and Japanese petrochemical companies have not been pressured to make the tough scrap-and-build changes that American and European companies made in the 1980s. While official and unofficial price-support policies have succeeded at preventing bankruptcies, they have left an industry of small firms unable to achieve the economies of scale necessary to compete internationally.

What are the implications of this policy for Japan's foreign trade? Petrochemicals is a classic example of a market in which, by ordinary price criteria, Japan should be running large deficits. Even for goods that are completely standardized and readily transportable, where imports often sell for half the Japanese price, Japan is surprisingly resistant to imports. One might argue that this is because of a natural immunity to imports that results from private firms' independently honoring long-term commitments to domestic suppliers. In fact, however such private commitments have not sufficed to maintain prices. Instead, they have been kept up (and many firms have been kept in business) as a result of government and trade association arrangements to standardize cost-based pricing and thus reinforce dyadic relational contracts. Policies such as the establishment of joint-sales companies have been a defense against the erosion of domestic prices by cheap imports. MITI and the petrochemical firms feared that, without such defenses, cheap imports would exacerbate competition among domestic manufacturers. Thus, even if buyers wanted to stick with domestic suppliers, prices might drop so low that domestic suppliers would fail. Had this happened, opportunities might have opened up for petrochemical imports from countries with bigger firms, better economies of scale, and cheaper natural-gas-based feedstocks. It is also possible that bankruptcies might have forced takeovers in Japan that would have created the gigantic chemical firms that have been so successful in Germany and the United States. Whatever the outcome, it is clear that the price-maintenance schemes have helped support a high price-market where imports have limited access and that produces large volumes of cheap sales to overseas markets.

CHAPTER SIX

The Steel Industry

Because of the strength of price leadership in the steel industry, its market-governing mechanisms are simpler than cement's or petrochemicals'; and in recent years MITI's hand on it has been lighter. Nevertheless, the steel industry also fits the pattern of a market governed by a producers' cartel supported by interindustry relational contracts with buyers and enforced by sanctions against firms that try to buy from outside the cartel.

The price structure also fits the pattern of cost-based prices that are quite independent of international price movements. As in cement and petrochemicals, Japanese domestic steel prices are high compared both to export and import prices. A distinctive feature of the Japanese steel market is that approximately half the total sales, or about two-thirds of sales by the large blast-furnace steel makers, are at "big-buyer" prices. These are the sales between the steel industry and their long-term customers. Set oligopolistically, they are very high compared to Japan's export, import, and domestic market, or "dealer," price (see figure 6–1). As figure 6–2 shows, Japan cut its exports significantly due to its own uncompetitive costs; and imports have made some inroads. Nevertheless, the country remains a net exporter of steel despite high domestic costs, as it is of cement and petrochemicals.

Steel, known as the "rice of industry" in Japan, has long been considered a key industry by MITI. With the ministry's support, the steel industry grew rapidly and by the 1970s became the world's most efficient producer.[1] As in other heavy industries, however, demand dropped in the early 1980s because the economy began growing more slowly and industries learned to use materials more efficiently. Not only did the

---

[1] Ira C. Magaziner and Thomas M. Hout, *Japanese Industrial Policy*, Policy Papers in International Affairs, Institute of International Studies (Berkeley, Calif.: University of California Press, 1981).

Figure 6–1. Ratio of big-buyer steel price to export, import, and dealer prices for steel plate

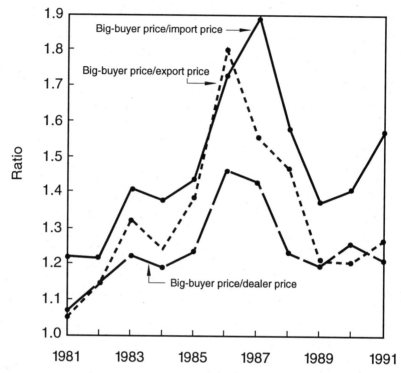

Source: Export prices from statistics compiled by Nihon Tekkō Yushutsu Kumiai (Japan Steel Export Association), based on the *Ōkura shō tsūkan tōkei* (Finance Ministry trade statistics). Import prices are calculated from Japan Tariff Association, *Japan Exports and Imports, Commodity by Country.* The source for big-buyer prices and dealer prices is Paine-Webber, *World Steel Intelligence,* 3 August 1992. The original sources cited are *World Steel Dynamics* for big-buyer prices and *Japan Metal Bulletin* for Japanese dealer prices. My appreciation to Mark Elder for directing me to the Paine-Webber materials and to Paine-Webber for permitting me to use them. Dealer prices for 1992–93 are end-of-the-month prices from *Tonya jōhō* (Wholesale reports).

Notes: From 1980 to 1987 the import price is calculated for category 73.13-231, sheets and plates, of iron or steel, rolled, not less than 6 mm in thickness. In 1988 the categories change, and from there on the import price is based on category 7208.42-000, flat-rolled products of iron or non-alloy steel, of a width of 600 mm or more, hot-rolled, not clad, plated, or coated, not in coils, not further worked than hot-rolled, having a yield point of less than 355 MPa, of a thickness exceeding 10 mm, n.e.s.

World Steel Intelligence lists a random pattern of three or four monthly big-buyer and dealer prices per year, which I averaged to produce annual prices.

Figure 6–2. Japan's international steel trade

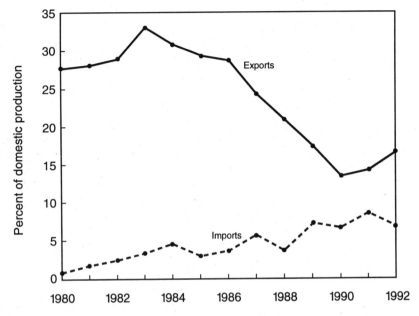

Source: MITI, *Tekkō yōran* (Steel abstract), various editions.

industry face stagnant domestic demand, it lost competitive advantage to developing nations such as South Korea, Taiwan, South Africa, and Brazil.

World Steel Dynamics estimated that in December 1991 Japan's production costs ranked with Germany's as the highest in the world. It estimated that South Korea, Taiwan, and the U.S. had a 7 to 9 percent cost advantage over Japan, while the United Kingdom, with efficient plants, low labor costs, cheap materials, and little outstanding debt, was the low-cost leader (see table 6–1). Japanese sources estimated the cost differential between Japan and its competitors as much greater, with South Korea producing steel at 72 percent of Japan's cost in 1987 and 63 percent by 1994 and China even more competitive at 60 percent of Japan's costs in 1994 (see table 6–2).

The steel industry is dominated by five blast-furnace makers who produced 68 percent of Japan's crude steel in 1992. They produced steel from iron ore through a continuous casting process, while electric furnace minimills produced 32 percent of Japan's steel by melting down scrap.[2] Blast-furnace companies make a number of products that

[2] Tekkō Shinbun Sha (Steel Newspaper Company), *Tekkō nenkan* (Steel annual) (Tokyo: Tekkō Shinbun Sha, 1993).

Table 6–1. International cost to produce cold-rolled sheet, December 1991 (dollars per metric ton shipped)

	U.S.	Japan	Germany	United Kingdom	South Korea	Taiwan	Brazil
Operating rate	80%	85%	90%	90%	100%	100%	90%
Person hours per ton	5.4	5.5	5.6	5.6	7	7	13
Wages per hour	28	26	32	21	9	11	7
Labor costs	151	143	179	118	62	77	91
Material cost	326	335	330	315	335	352	350
Operating cost	477	478	509	433	397	429	441
Financial cost	35	87	60	24	130	87	100
Pretax cost	512	565	569	457	527	516	541
Ratio to Japanese cost	0.91	1.00	1.01	0.81	0.93	0.91	0.96

Source: Paine-Webber, *World Steel Intelligence,* 3 August 1992, p. 25.

Table 6–2. Japanese estimates of East Asian steel costs (1987 production costs for hot-rolled coils)

	Japan	South Korea
Raw materials and fuel	30	30
Labor	13	6
Depreciation	17	16
Other plant expenses	19	17
Overhead	13	1
Interest	8	2
Total cost	100	72

1994 steel production costs

	Japan	Korea (Pohan Steel)	China (China Steel Corporation)
$ per ton	587	370	353
Cost ratio	100	63	60

Source: Nikkei bijinesu, 2 March 1987; *Nihon keizai shinbun,* 10 May 1994.
Note: 1987 exchange rates: $1 = 150 yen = 870 won. 1994 exchange rates: $1 = 125 yen = 783 won = 25.75 yuan.

minimills cannot produce and thus are somewhat buffered against competition from them, although recently electric-furnace producers have been encroaching on their territory by beginning production of items such as H-bar steel. The blast-furnace producers are the oligopolists of the market. They sell most of their steel to long-standing customers at long-term contract prices, although they sell some steel on the domestic spot market at dealer or market prices. Electric-furnace producers sell most of their steel at dealer prices.

This segmented market structure has its roots in the designated price system (*tatene sei*) established in 1925, under which Yawata Steel's prices served as a guideline for the industry as a whole.[3] During the war, prices were controlled by the industry control association, but in 1950 the industry reestablished the designated price system. Under this system Yawata consulted with Fuji Steel and Nippon Kokan to set prices, and Kawasaki Steel, Sumitomo Metals and Kobe Steel followed. The designated price coexisted with a sales price, at which electric-furnace minimills sold their steel, and a market price for steel sold through the black market. The designated price was cost-based rather than simply an attempt to get the highest possible short-term price. The system collapsed in the economic slump following the Korean War boom but was reestablished in 1955. It was hard to maintain, however, in part because its cost-based prices were below the very high market prices of the 1955–57 boom. The system fell apart again during the slowdown of 1957. MITI engaged in heavy-handed cartel leadership in the late 1950s and early 1960s to support prices through the open-sales system and, as it did with petrochemicals, used investment cartels to help firms build plants with maximally efficient economies of scale without producing ruinous competition.[4] After a period of increased price competition in the 1960s, MITI backed the merger of the two largest steel companies, Fuji and Yawata, to form the Nippon Steel Corporation in 1970. This created the basis for strong price leadership, which has been important for maintaining the sharp segmentation of the steel market into a high-priced, long-term contract market and a spot market.[5]

The long-term contract market in Japan is distinct from those in the West because it does not involve individual companies that gamble by locking in a price for a specific period but reflects permanent buyer commitments to domestic producers and their acceptance of cost-based prices. It is similar to the petrochemical market, but the mechanism by which prices are determined is more straightforward due to the greater strength of the steel-industry price cartel.

[3] Seiichirō Yonekura, *The Japanese Iron and Steel Industry, 1850–1990* (New York: St. Martin's Press, 1994), pp. 129–30.

[4] O'Brien, Patricia A., "Industry Structure as a Competitive Advantage: The History of Japan's Post-War Steel Industry," *Business History* 34 (January 1992): 128–59. See also Yonekura, *The Japanese Iron and Steel Industry*, pp. 226–32.

[5] Ichikawa Hirokatsu, "Kokusaiteki kankyō henka to sentan sangyōka he no michi" (Change in the international environment and the path to advanced industrialization), in Kitada Yoshiharu, ed., *Bōeki masatsu to keizai seisaku* (Trade friction and economic policy) (Tokyo: Ōtsuki, 1983), p. 117.

Figure 6–3. Pricetrack history, steel plate

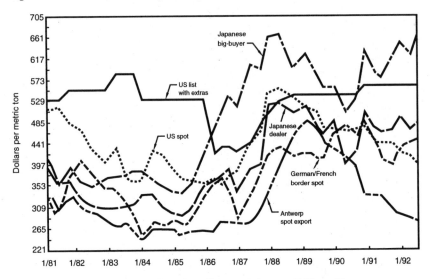

Source: Paine-Webber, *World Steel Intelligence*, 3 August 1992, p. 67.
Note: U.S. spot price is the average of the four regional spot prices.

As in petrochemicals, cost-based prices have been very high. Japanese big-buyer prices soared above international prices in the late 1980s (see figure 6–3). They are unique internationally because they are set oligopolistically and, since 1985, have been extremely high. According to the list-price line in figure 6–3, U.S. producers also enjoyed high prices in the early 1980s and from 1988 on. Although in the 1970s the list price was actually observed by large American steel firms, discounting to compete with cheap imports has rendered it meaningless since 1981.[6] Actual U.S. prices hover around a very narrow band at a much lower level (see table 6–3). For instance, while the U.S. list price for cold-rolled sheet was $703, Paine-Webber lists the real price at $491, with most prices ranging from a high of 2.8 percent over this price for steel from Tier I (highest quality) producers to a discount of 1.2 percent for Tier II (lower quality) contract imports or a discount of 5.2 percent for spot imports. In addition, American steel mills tend to sell about 8 percent of their steel as secondary grade that does not meet the desired specifications. This steel is significantly discounted, from 20 to 50 percent. There is also a volatile market price for distress spot steel from places such as ailing Eastern European mills.[7]

---

[6] Telephone interview with American steel analyst, 1995.
[7] Paine-Webber, *World Steel Intelligence*, 5 April 1991, pp. 17–18.

Table 6–3. U.S. steel prices (as of March 1991)

Price	Hot-Rolled Band	Cold-Rolled Sheet
U.S. list price	$579	$703
U.S. real price	342	491
One-year contract price	355	505
Spot price		
Normal three-month	342	491
"Distress" spot	325	440
Tier I producer price	342	491
Tier II producer price	332	476
Class I product price	355	505
Class II product price	342	491
Primary steel price	342	491
Secondary steel price	242	380
Regular price	342	491
"Special deal" price	312	440
Import spot (Tier I)	410	485
Import spot (Tier II)	390	465
Import contract (Tier I)	420	495
Import contract (Tier II)	410	485
USA regional prices:		
East	347	502
South	331	485
Midwest	347	485
West	380	485

Source: Paine-Webber, *World Steel Intelligence,* 5 April 1991.

Note: Import prices include transport and tariff costs.

The Japanese big-buyer price does reflect the approximate price for at least two-thirds of blast-furnace makers' sales, or at least half of the total Japanese steel market.[8] This can be verified by comparing the big-buyer price with the price that can be calculated from the securities report of Nippon Steel (see figure 6–4).[9] Nippon Steel's actual sales price for steel plate averaged 5 percent above the listed big-buyer price from 1981–84, reflecting the fact that the price was originally intended to give a discount to big buyers. Once the yen rose in 1985 and Japanese steel lost its international competitiveness, firms began giving discounts to buyers who were in particularly difficult straits, such as shipbuilders. This explains why Nippon Steel's actual prices for steel plate fell to 3 percent below the listed big-buyer price in 1985–91. The closeness of Nippon

[8] Ibid., p. 23. Confirmed as approximately correct in interview with retired steel-company executive, 1994.

[9] Interview, Tokyo, 1994.

Figure 6–4. How accurate is the big-buyer price?

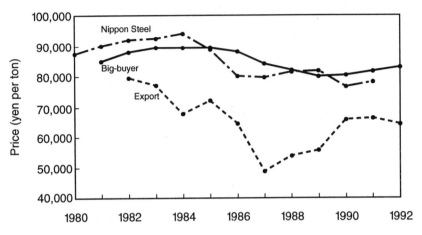

Source: Nippon Steel Corporation securities reports, various years; Nihon Tekkō Yushutsu Kumiai (Japan Steel Export Association) statistics, based on the *Ōkura shō tsūkan tōkei* (Finance ministry trade statistics); *World Steel Intelligence,* August 3, 1992.
Note: The average actual domestic price of steel plate for Nippon Steel Corporation, Japan's largest steel company, was calculated from Section 3.5.2 of the company's securities reports. The calculation was done by multiplying the average actual export price for steel plate by the volume of Nippon Steel's exports (Nippon Steel lists its total plate sales and the percentage of these that are exports), subtracting this amount from the total sales value, and then dividing the remaining value by the volume of domestic sales. See note to figure 6–1 for an explanation of the big-buyer price.

Steel's average price and the official big-buyer price suggests that more than two-thirds of steel makers' sales may be at the big-buyer price. The deviations between Nippon Steel prices and the big-buyer price were slight compared to the wide gap between the domestic big-buyer price and Japan's export quote, which averaged 16 percent below the big-buyer price from 1981–84 and 28 percent below from 1985–91. The export quote also appears to be a fairly reliable guide to actual prices because it hovered close to actual average export prices (see figure 6–5).

As we saw in figure 6–1, the big-buyer price was also much higher than either the dealer or import price: 31 percent above the import price for steel plate from 1981–84 and 57 percent above the import price from 1985–91. By 1991 it was still 58 percent above the import price. The big-buyer price was 15 percent above the domestic dealer price from 1981–84 and 29 percent above from 1985–91. By 1991 it was 22 percent higher than the dealer price. The comparison between the big-buyer and import price may exaggerate the difference because the import price is for only the most common grade of steel plate and does not include the delivery charges included in the big-buyer prices. Nevertheless, even if the gap were fully justified by quality or delivery charges in the early 1980s,

Figure 6–5. How accurate is the export quote?

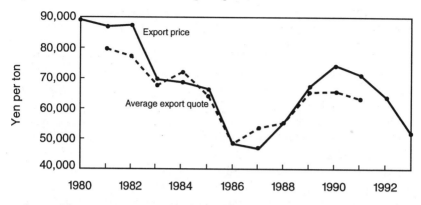

Source: The export quote price is from *World Steel Intelligence*, 3 August 1992, which lists the *Japan Metal Bulletin* as its source. Actual export prices from statistics compiled by Nihon Tekkō Yushutsu Kumiai (Japan Steel Export Association), based on the *Ōkura shō tsūkan tōkei* (Finance ministry trade statistics).

Note: Export quotes are free on board (that is, they don't include overseas transport costs or tariffs) in Japan for non-U.S. destinations.

the increase since 1985 shows that big buyers tolerated a large increase in the price of domestic steel relative to domestic market prices or import prices. Moreover, newspaper reports confirm that there were, in fact, large real-price differentials between imported and big-buyer steel prices.[10]

Steel makers were able to keep their prices so high in part because of the industry's strong price cartel. It is universally said that the blast-furnace sector is very cohesive: firms do not compete over prices and speak with a single voice to the bureaucracy, banks, and other firms.[11] This cohesion helps the industry maintain its high prices. Japanese steel firm's strong discipline keeps them from undercutting one another in the domestic market while they sell cheaply overseas, and the power this cohesion gives them with their buyers helps keep them from cutting prices in the face of cheap imports.

As did the other basic materials industries, the steel industry supported domestic prices through joint capacity cuts. Because of U.S. criticism of its use of cartels, Japan replaced the SDIL with the SCFL in 1987. With this change firms now consulted with MITI to develop individual restructuring plans instead of forming industry-wide cartels. In anticipation of the new policy, seven blast-furnace makers announced plans in late 1986

[10] *Nikkei sangyō shinbun*, 6 April 1987; *Nihon keizai shinbun*, 22 April 1994.

[11] Interviews, retired steel executive, shipbuilder, and electronics maker, Tokyo, 1994; Itami Hiroyuki, *Nihon no kagaku sangyō, naze sekai ni tachiokureta no ka* (Japan's chemical industry: Why is it behind the rest of the world?) (Tokyo: NTT Shuppan, 1991).

and early 1987 to shut down eight of Japan's thirty-four blast furnaces to take advantage of tax breaks under the new law.[12] Although MITI and the firms said the restructuring plans were individual, the seven firms made their cuts based on a general consensus that the industry should cut total capacity to ninety million tons. Some firms were less cooperative, however, and used ninety-five million tons as a goal.[13] Total cuts amounted to 12.85 million tons of capacity.[14] Itami Hiroyuki argues that steel companies, unlike petrochemical companies, were able to make cuts without MITI guidance because of the industry cohesion under the leadership of powerful large firms.[15] Steel firms cut capacity and reduced the work force during the 1980s from 429,000 to 338,000.[16]

As in the cement industry, MITI does not ignore the informal steel cartel but monitors it to prevent price gouging and withholding of production. For instance, when steel makers held back production of H-steel and bar steel in 1987 to force prices up, MITI asked them to increase production.[17] As in cement, MITI permits the cartel with the understanding it must contribute to the provision of adequate domestic supplies at what MITI considers reasonable prices.

A rough guide to which industries are most loyal to long-term purchases at big-buyer prices can be obtained by comparing the distribution of direct orders for steel with its end use. Direct sales are commonly at big-buyer prices, while indirect sales through wholesalers are typically at market prices. Construction, which accounts for half of Japan's steel demand, buys only about half its steel directly. Manufacturing, which accounts for something under half of demand, appears to buy about 80 percent of its steel on a big-buyer basis[18] (see table 6–4). These figures are rough indication that the manufacturing sector is especially loyal to blast-furnace producers and construction firms also buy a large portion of steel at big-buyer prices.

Big-buyer sales take place directly between steel maker and user, with trading companies as intermediaries. Prices do not float but are negotiated on an industry-to-industry basis once a year, or less often if

[12] *The Economist*, 29 August 1987, p. 59; Tsūsanshō Seisaku Kyoku (MITI Policy Bureau), *Kōzō Tenkan Enkatsuka Hō no kaisetsu* (Commentary on the Structural Conversion Facilitation Law) (Tokyo: MITI, 1987), pp. 32–33.

[13] Interview, retired steel executive, Tokyo, 1994.

[14] MITI, *Sangyō Kōzō Tenkan Enkatsuka Rinji Sochi Hō no shikō jōkyō ni tsuite* (On the current state of implementation of the Structural Conversion Facilitation Law). Unpublished document, October 1993.

[15] Itami, *Nihon no kagaku sangyō*, p. 99.

[16] MITI, *Kōgyō tōkei hyō sangyō hen* (Census of manufactures, report by industries), 1980, 1992.

[17] *Japan Economic Almanac*, 1988, p. 183.

[18] A retired steel-company executive confirmed that this was a reasonable way of getting a rough grasp of which industries bought at big-buyer prices. Interview, Tokyo, 1994.

Table 6–4. Summary statistics for the 1991 price survey

Product group	Number of products surveyed	Japanese prices as a % of U.S.	Number of products priced higher in Japan	% of Products priced higher in Japan
All	112	137.1	75	67.0
Elect. & Optical	30	103.3	11	36.7
Auto Parts	10	208.6	9	90.0
Liquor	10	167.1	10	100.0
Autos	7	104.5	4	57.1
Capital	20	117.0	11	55.0
Misc. Cons.	23	159.6	20	87.0
Food	12	146.6	10	83.3

Country of manufacture	Number of products surveyed	Number of products priced higher in Japan	Japanese prices as a % of U.S.
Total	112	75	137.1
Japan	40	12	98.6
US	34	31	170.3
Third	20	19	165.9
Mix	17	13	130.7

Source: U.S.-Japan Price Survey, 1991: Fact Sheet. U.S. Commerce Department and MITI, 1991.

markets are relatively stable. Japan's basic steel price is negotiated between the two price leaders, Nippon Steel and Toyota. Although steel companies are careful not to be too quick to copy the Nippon Steel price for fear of being accused of joint price increases by the FTC, they do in fact follow Nippon Steel's lead.[19] Steel companies are disciplined enough in their cartel to all charge exactly same price.[20] The blast-furnace makers do make as much as a third of their sales at market prices but not normally to big buyers.[21]

During its heyday, the shipbuilding industry was steel's price-setting leader, but autos have now taken over this role. Negotiations over steel prices, like those over petrochemical prices, appear to be organized on an interindustry basis, relational contracting principles of cost-based pricing, and appeals to honor obligations to long-term partners. Thus, in 1986 when Japanese steel prices rose relative to foreign steel because of the rising yen, automakers and other large users appealed to the industry

[19] Ibid.

[20] Interview, shipbuilding executive, Tokyo, 1994. *Japan Economic Almanac*, 1992, p. 142.

[21] Interview, retired steel executive, Tokyo, 1994.

to lower prices because costs for inputs such as coal and iron ore had dropped.[22] When the steel industry was intransigent, automakers, who then accounted for 23 percent of domestic demand, threatened to switch to cheaper imports. The industry responded by arguing that car makers were morally obligated to stick by their domestic suppliers. Inayama Yoshirō, chairman of the Keidanren and former chairman of Nippon Steel, claimed it would be unfair if the auto industry switched to imports because the steel plants had been "built with the blood of the Japanese people."[23] The auto industry did not make good on its threat but was still able to pressure the steel industry into more serious negotiations.

Materials buyers for one of Japan's largest auto companies confirmed that the pricing pattern for auto purchases of steel basically follows the pattern of industry-wide cost-based pricing that petrochemicals uses.[24] Once the auto industry establishes the base price, other user industries follow their lead, with minor adjustments that depend on specific goods they use.[25] Although steel makers' costs are the basic determinant of the price, the financial situation of the users is also taken into account. Thus, the hard-pressed shipbuilding industry receives discounts on its steel. Negotiations to determine the amount of this discount are carried out on an industry-to-industry basis. When I asked a shipbuilder about price leadership, he corrected me and explained that Mitsubishi Heavy Industry and Nippon Steel acted as "representatives" of the two industries in negotiating the price of steel.[26] This is an important difference of meaning. Whereas the term *price leadership* suggests impersonal and independent action by the most powerful firms, *representation* suggests that firms understand their responsibility as governing agents of the industry as a whole.

Despite the large price differential between Japanese and foreign prices, imported ordinary-grade steel rose to a peak of only 9 percent of the domestic market in 1991 and dropped back to 7 percent in 1992 (see figure 6–2). Japan continued to export 17 percent of its production in 1992, making it a net exporter of 10 percent of its production. Obviously, Japanese steel companies were willing to sell exports below domestic prices as long as they would cover their marginal costs. But why would Japanese users continue to pay high prices for Japanese steel?

In the case of cement, Japanese construction companies, because of their own strong cartels, can afford to pay high prices for the sake of

[22] *Japan Economic Almanac*, 1988, p. 183.
[23] *Business Week*, 12 May 1986.
[24] Interview, 1992.
[25] Interview, electronics executive, 1994.
[26] Interview, 1994.

security of supply (although, in fact, many construction companies use market-price or imported steel). But it is hard to think of an industry harder pressed than shipbuilding to cut costs. It is dependent on exports for 60 percent of its sales and competes with South Korea, whose costs are as much as 25 percent below Japan's. The price differential between Korean and Japanese steel was roughly unchanged from 1987 to 1994, with Japanese shipbuilders paying 40 percent more than their South Korean competitors. In 1994 the cost of Japanese steel alone put Japanese shipbuilders at an eight-million-dollar cost disadvantage per oil tanker.[27]

Interviews with steel users make clear that they pay high prices for Japanese steel and resist switching to imports because they are committed to relational contracts with particular firms and also choose to honor a larger interindustry relational contract. Prices are supported by the steel-industry cartel, but they are also supported by buyers' willingness to pay what it costs to keep the domestic industry going.

Most steel users do not rely on a single long-term dyadic relationship for their steel supplies but buy their steel from several stable sources, although these are often weighted in favor of a producer in their own keiretsu. When steel users talk about their obligations to steel producers, they talk about the industry as a whole. Thus, it would be a gross oversimplification to say that users stick to their suppliers because of keiretsu ties or because they are in some sense subsidiaries of their suppliers.

It does not appear that the price gap between domestic and international prices is due to quality differences between Japanese and foreign steel. Fine gradations of quality are not important for the ordinary-grade steel used in construction, which accounts for half of all Japanese steel demand.[28] One Japanese scholar who is very familiar with the shipbuilding industry was vehement in saying that quality was decisive for explaining Japanese shipbuilders' purchases of expensive domestic steel. He argued that it was only in 1993 and 94 that import steel prices had genuinely become attractive to shipbuilders given the lower quality, lack of fine size gradations, and less convenient delivery of foreign steel.[29] Nevertheless, 75 percent of the steel that shipbuilders use is thick plate, a basically standardized commodity. Two shipbuilders' I interviewed said there was no quality problem with ordinary grade South Korean steel. One pointed out that the steel from South Korea's Pohang plant was essentially the same as Japanese steel because it was made with

[27] *World Steel Intelligence*, 5 April 1991, p. 223; *Nihon keizai shinbun*, 6 August 1994; *Nikkei sangyō shinbun*, 6 April 1987.
[28] Interview, retired steel executive, 1994.
[29] Conversation, 1994.

equipment supplied by Mitsubishi Heavy Industries.[30] It is true that Japanese steel makers produce steel plate in some four hundred different sizes for their various customers, and shipbuilders' value this. By 1994, however, the shipbuilders were begging the steel companies to standardize these sizes but to give them some price relief in return. Although the large number of sizes was supposed to simplify shipbuilding, some argued that fewer sizes would actually increase shipbuilders' efficiency and save more money in building costs than steel companies would save by standardizing sizes.[31] If this is true, it suggests that the proliferation of sizes in the steel market has acted more as a barrier to imports than as a genuine contribution to production efficiency.

Auto manufacturers have a greater reason to prefer Japanese steel because 40 percent of their steel is surface treated, a product category in which Japanese quality is said to be superior. But the other 60 percent is hot- and cold-rolled steel plate, which most people in the auto industry say South Korea produces perfectly adequately. In 1994 car makers were examining whether they had exaggerated their needs for high-quality steel and were asking steel makers to shift to cheaper grades.[32]

I asked one shipbuilder why his firm didn't buy cheaper South Korean steel given the competitive pressures from Korean shipbuilding companies. Although he acknowledged that imports were of sufficient quality to provide most of the ordinary-quality steel the industry needed, he said that it was important to have a domestic industry for the sake of security of supply. He went on to say, "People often say, 'Steel is the state' or 'Steel is the rice of industry.' It's true. If steel gets weak all of industry will get weak. If we switch to imported steel, the country will stop developing."[33] The shipbuilder also acknowledged that his industry benefits specifically from having a domestic steel industry that has provided good-quality steel and convenient delivery. In return for these long years of service, he said, his firm owed a great moral debt (*onkei*) to the steel industry.

Electronics has also complained about international competition and, along with transportation equipment (chiefly autos), was in the forefront of the move to shift production overseas to lower costs. By 1992, 10 percent of its activities were overseas along with 17.5 percent of those of transportation machinery.[34] An electronics maker argued that indi-

[30] Interviews, two executives of shipbuilding companies (one retired), 1994.
[31] *Nihon keizai shinbun*, 6 August 1994.
[32] Ibid., 21 April 1994.
[33] Interview, shipbuilding executive, 1994.
[34] MITI, Sangyō Seisaku Kyoku, Kokusai Kigyō Ka (Industrial Policy Bureau, International Firm Section), *Dai 5 kai kaigai jigyō katsudō kihon chōsa no gaiyō* (Summary of the fifth basic survey of overseas business activities), April 1994, p. 20.

vidual companies should buy domestic steel in order to preserve key industrial link in the domestic economy. Although companies might conceivably buy as much as 10 percent foreign steel, "it's hard to imagine buying 30–50 percent of our steel from overseas. Buying our supplies overseas would be a last stage. If we and other big companies buy our steel overseas, then the steel companies would go out of business and we would lose our customers. Our company would have to leave Japan too. And then we wouldn't be able to use Japanese trading practices anymore."[35] This buyer clearly considers his relational contract to be with the Japanese steel industry as a whole, not with particular firms.

Users also said it would be a mistake to choose supply sources based on price. The shipbuilder just cited said, "Japanese steel is number one in the world. Its only problem is price. There's no reason to destroy the industry."[36] And the electronics maker said that, even if market prices for steel are lower in the short term, over the long term the big-buyer's price is a better deal because it buys security of supply.[37]

Users also avoid imports because they fear retaliation from steel makers. Threats of industry-wide boycotts are strongly suggested by a *Nikkei sangyō shinbun* article on Mitsubishi Heavy Industries' (MHI) first purchases of imported steel from Pohang Steel in South Korea. Based on an interview with an official of the Materials Division of MHI, the article reports that the company had wanted to buy Korean sheet steel for some time because Japanese steel, at eighty thousand yen per ton, cost 60 percent more. Although MHI was concerned that South Korean steel might be somewhat inferior to Japanese steel and delivery less convenient, the quality of the Pohang steel was "quite sufficient" for all but the most exacting uses. The article reports, however, that "Mitsubishi Heavy Industries has been unable to [buy South Korean steel] because it has been concerned with the fact that [Japanese] steel manufacturers were both its suppliers and among its principal customers."[38] That is, MHI feared that buying South Korean steel would endanger both its sales of steel-making machinery and its supplies of steel from the Japanese industry. It is crucial to note that MHI was not simply concerned with a relational contract with a specific individual firm but was afraid that it might be shut out of dealings with the *entire* steel industry.

The article quoted a Nippon Steel official as saying, "There is no mistake that [MHI] is importing steel in Nagasaki. . . . What we'd like to tell them is, 'Fine. In return we will not supply you with any of the high

[35] Interview, 1994.
[36] Ibid.
[37] Interview, 1994.
[38] *Nikkei sangyō shinbun*, 6 April 1987.

quality steel that Korea can't produce.' "[39] Thus, Japan's largest steel manufacturer thinks of its sales relationships as a broad, all-encompassing commitment rather than simply an agreement to buy specific products. It considers a customer's decision to switch to another buyer for one product a betrayal that should be retaliated against by withholding other products the manufacturer alone can provide. MHI, one of Japan's largest manufacturing firms, also seems to think in terms of interindustry relational contracts that are enforceable with refusals to deal.

Much as Nippon Steel would have liked to use a refusal-to-deal threat to keep MHI from buying South Korean steel, it demurred because it feared that making MHI's imports an issue might lead other buyers to push harder for price cuts and possibly desert domestic suppliers altogether in favor of imports. Therefore, the company officially treated MHI's imports as a matter of little importance, both because the purchase was small in volume and because Pohang asked MHI to buy the steel in exchange for Pohang's purchase of steel-making machinery.[40]

Mitsubishi never increased the percentage of imports over 10 percent, and Japan's other shipbuilders' have remained completely loyal to the domestic industry. In interviews, two shipbuilders and a retired steel executive confirmed that the threat of retaliation was an important factor deterring shipbuilder plans to buy imports. In describing the relationship between steel and shipbuilding companies, no one used strong terms such as *retaliation*, but rather spoke of mutual obligation and power on the part of steel companies to make sure that shipbuilders don't abandon them. This power is also used to make sure that buyers don't try to play off domestic steel companies against one another to get lower prices.

For most of the major shipbuilders (for example, Mitsubishi Heavy Industries, Ishikawajima Harima, and Sumitomo Heavy Industries), shipbuilding is only a small part of their larger operations in industrial machine production. Shipbuilders fear steel companies may retaliate by cutting off purchases of new manufacturing equipment or telling the shipping companies that handle their raw-materials imports and steel exports to stop buying ships from particular firms. As one shipbuilder put it, "the shipbuilding industry can't do much about getting the steel industry to lower its prices. If we increase purchases from one steel company to try to get lower prices, then the steel company whose purchases were cut wouldn't have its shipping company buy ships from our firm."[41] A retired steel executive also acknowledged the industry's power to oblige shipbuilders to reject imports and added that steel companies had similar power over construction companies, whose

---

[39] Ibid.
[40] Ibid.
[41] Interview, shipbuilding executive, Tokyo, 1994.

services they used when they built new production facilities. He noted, however, that the industry's recent stagnation had weakened its ability to coerce.[42]

The threat of retaliation also appears to affect the small intermediary shearing and coil-center firms that cut and process steel as well as the large trading firms that buy and sell steel. The *Nihon keizai shinbun* reported that "it is common knowledge that the domestic steel makers use tacit pressure to keep out imports and support the price structure. The . . . shearing and coil center firms haven't spoken openly about using imported steel because of fear of reaction from the blast steel makers. The big trading firms haven't handled imports openly."[43] The article doesn't specify what retaliatory measures steel firms threaten, although presumably they involve withholding supplies or business.

Fear of retaliation dissuades users from buying not only imports, but also steel made by domestic outsiders to the blast furnace steel cartel. These outsiders are the mini-mill producers that make steel from scrap rather than from iron ore. The largest of these, Tokyo Steel Manufacturing, finds that construction firms are reluctant to buy its reinforcing bars, even though they are 50 percent cheaper than those of the blast furnace steel firms. In part this is because the government is unwilling to authorize steel purchases from outsiders to the steel cartel for public works projects, and partly because construction firms fear retaliation from the blast furnace steel companies. Iketani Masanari, the president of Tokyo Steel, said in 1994 that, "To sell your products, you have to find some person at each company who is not afraid of retaliation." He laughed at the suggestion that the FTC ought to prevent steel makers' bullying. "Where are they? The Fair Trade Commission is just a small fish. The steelmakers are the big fish."[44]

An electronics maker said that his company's fear of steel firms' reaction to imports was much less in 1994 than it had been twenty years ago. Although his firm was reluctant to buy any imported steel itself, it did arrange for some of its subcontractors to buy imported steel. Instead of protesting, steel companies now accept small subcontractors' buying imports. While this man's large electronics firm does not actually buy any imported steel directly, he thought it could if it gave domestic steel makers advance warning and a chance to match import prices. He said that the threat of buying imports can persuade steel makers to provide discounts on the portion of steel the user might have bought from overseas. In this way, although users buy the vast majority of their steel

[42] Interview, retired steel executive, Tokyo, 1994.
[43] *Nihon keizai shinbun*, 10 May 1994.
[44] James Sterngold, "Elusive Price Cuts Intrigue Japan," *New York Times*, 9 November 1994, pp. C1, C11.

at standard big-buyer prices, they may get discounts on the 5 percent or so they say they are tempted to buy from abroad.[45]

Another explanation for loyalty to Japanese steel producers is that, even if ordinary steel can be bought in South Korea, the best specialty steel is made in Japan. It is considered important to support the steel industry as a whole to safeguard this high-tech production. When the Japanese economy was booming in the late 1980s, car companies asked steel companies to invest in new plants to produce surface-treated steel and worked directly with them on research and development. Because the economy went into recession in the early 1990s, some of the new plants were never started up. Car companies began reconsidering whether they had exaggerated the need for quality and considered substituting ordinary-grade steel for some of the 40 percent they used that was surface treated. But the steel companies demanded that the car companies not buy imports. In part, this agreement was sealed by a personal relationship between the president of Toyota, Toyoda Tatsurō, and the president of New Japan Steel, Imai Kei, who went to high school together. In addition, the steel companies claimed that the R & D costs of producing the new surface-treated steel were not fully reflected in its sales price and that they had expected all along that the car companies would refrain from buying imports in exchange for the steel companies' development of the new steel.[46]

Buyers are *able* to pay the high prices for expensive domestic steel in part because of the weakness of domestic price competition for downstream goods. As I noted in Chapter 1, electronics firms still benefit from the lack of a large network of discount stores. A 1991 survey found that the lowest available price (typically at discount stores) for electronics and optical goods was 3.3 percent higher in Japan than in the U.S. (see table 6–4). While discount prices in the two countries are similar, however, restrictions in Japan on building discount stores have limited consumer access to discount sales. Although the Large Store Law has been relaxed somewhat, it still impedes the growth of the Wal-Mart-style mass retailer that has produced very cheap prices in the U.S. In mid-1994 Japan was widely proclaimed to be in the midst of a retail revolution. But an executive at a large electronics maker told me that discount sales were still only 10 percent of total sales. He said, There is not much discount selling yet in Japan. Japanese consumers can't buy at cheap prices like in the U.S. In the U.S. you have to sell at cheap prices." Thus, he believes that there is little price competition in the Japanese electronics market compared to the U.S. market.[47]

[45] Interview, Tokyo, 1994.
[46] *Nihon keizai sangyō shinbun*, 21 April 1994.
[47] Years after the yen's sharp rise in 1986, weak price competition among domestic

In the U.S.-Japan price survey, electronics, along with autos, was the sector in which Japanese prices were closest to U.S. prices. As the report itself points out, its survey method does not reveal actual *average* prices, which are probably lower in the U.S. because of greater freedom to open discount stores. Even if electronics manufacturers feel Japan lacks a truly price-competitive market, however, the protection of manufacturers from price competition in other markets, such as auto parts and capital goods, is even more generous (see table 6–4). The electronics maker who said there was little discount pricing of electronics goods in Japan pointed out that the cohesion of the electronics and electrical-appliance industries was weak compared to that of the powerful heavy electric machinery industry. The three firms in this industry—Hitachi, Mitsubishi, and Toshiba—have oligopolistic power and speak with their customers, the electric-power companies, as a group.[48] In 1994 MITI admitted that it had been protecting this industry from imports with its performance standards and that, because of U.S. pressure, it would gradually lift its restrictions by the year 2000.[49] Thus, in this case, downstream industry enjoyed oligopolistic power in domestic price negotiations and informal trade protection by MITI and was under no pressure to switch to cheap imported steel supplies.

Although the shipbuilding industry relies on exports for 60 percent of its sales, the insulation of the domestic market from imports appears to help it pay the high price of domestic steel. After the shipbuilder cited previously told me his industry could not buy imported steel because it would be bad for the country as a whole, I asked him why his firm did not just abandon the Japanese steel industry, buy South Korean steel, let the other Japanese shipbuilders worry about supporting the steel industry, and undercut them on price? His answer was straightforward: "If Japanese companies wanted cheaper ships, they could already buy them from South Korea." It is true that although Korean ships are much cheaper than Japanese ships and Korea commands 35 percent of the world market, the country has not sold a single ship to Japan in recent years.[50]

Another reason buyers can afford the price of expensive domestic steel is that for most manufactured goods it constitutes a small fraction of the

electronics makers enables them to maintain high prices at home while selling products more cheaply abroad, prompting many Japanese to continue to go overseas to buy Japanese products. Naoko Yoshida, "Makers Fail to Explain Price Differences in Electronic Prices," *Tokyo Business Today* 61 (January/February 1993): 60.

[48] Interview, electronics firm executive, 1994.

[49] *Nihon keizai shinbun*, 8 August 1994.

[50] Nihon Kanzei Kyōkai (Japan Tariff Association), *Nihon bōeki geppyō* (Japan Trade Monthly), December issues, 1990–93.

end value of the product. Materials costs form the bulk of the end-product value for major manufacturing industries, ranging from 60 percent for electrical and industrial machinery to 76 percent for autos.[51] Most of this, however, is expenditure for fabricated goods from subcontractors. As we saw in table 1–2, the cost of industrial basic materials ranges from 10 to 15 percent of total production costs for the machine manufacturing sectors, while the cost of steel ranges from around 2 percent of costs for precision instruments and electrical machinery to 5 percent for transportation machinery and 9 percent for general machinery. Shipbuilding is unusual in that steel accounts for an estimated 25 percent of total costs. Thus, even though from 1985 to 1991 manufacturers could have saved 22 percent by buying steel plate at the dealer price, 28 percent if they bought at the Japanese export price, or 36 percent if they bought the most common grade of imported plate, these sums represented relatively small fractions of manufacturers' total costs.

This study has revealed that the steel industry shares the cement and petrochemical industry's price and trade patterns. Japanese blast-furnace steel makers do not compete with one another in the domestic market. They keep domestic prices to their long-term buyers uniformly high while discounting exports and a portion of their domestic sales. Despite much cheaper imports, most of their customers have stayed loyal to expensive Japanese steel. Although exports declined and imports increased through the 1980s, in 1992 Japan continued to export a net 10 percent of its steel.

I looked at Japan's export industries to see why they were willing to continue to buy expensive Japanese steel. Interviews with buyers reveal a strong nationalist commitment to an interindustry relational contract with the entire domestic steel industry. The burden of this commitment is alleviated somewhat by the fact that steel purchases represent a relatively small part of total costs, although even the shipbuilding industry is amazingly loyal. Downstream users are able to bear the burden of expensive steel because they are not yet fully exposed to import competition in the home market and in many industries most firms buy expensive Japanese steel.

If we compare steel to the ill-fated domestic aluminum industry, it appears that steel's key advantage is that it has a technological hook with which to maintain customer loyalty. Not only can steel makers hold onto customers for their high-grade steel, but they use this high-grade hook to keep their customers for standard-grade steel as well. In cases such as the

---

[51] MITI, *Kōgyō tōkei hyō: Sangyō hen* (Census of manufactures, by industry) (Tokyo: MITI, 1990).

auto industry, the fact that the steel industry produces surface-treated steel gives buyers a strong reason to buy domestic ordinary-grade steel and make sure the industry remains healthy. Toward the harder pressed shipbuilding industry threats to refuse to sell supplies of high-grade steel or buy ships or machines serve to enforce the interindustry relational contract.

My steel study has not matched the other cases in this book because it has treated the governing institutions of the industry as a black box. In part, this is because the power of the steel oligarchy has meant it has not had to rely on complicated informal mechanisms or state help in governing its markets: governance in this industry is the simplest and the least transparent. In addition, a thorough study of the informal governance of the industry was beyond the scope of this book. Further research might reveal equally interesting governing mechanisms to those of cement and petrochemicals.

Where Does Informal Governance Work?

This book has looked at the most important sectors of Japan's non-energy basic materials industries, in depth at petrochemicals, aluminum refining, and cement, and more briefly at a fourth, steel. It has explored the roles of the state and private firms in guiding Japan's economy and the orientation of the Japanese state toward structural change in the economy. Debate whether the state or the market guides Japan's economy often overlooks the importance of trade associations. Trade associations contribute to Japan's economic stability, providing both official and unofficial private-interest governance that supports or enforces relational contracts. Such cartel-like activities are not typically imposed unilaterally but carried out as part of an interindustry relational contract with downstream industrial users.

This chapter reviews formal and informal policies toward all of Japan's major declining industries. Table 7–1 provides a rough overview of these industries. The check marks should not be regarded as authoritative; they are based on impressionistic assessment.

The broad pattern that emerges shows strong conditions for private-interest market governance in the industrial basic materials industries and, except for aluminum, success in protecting the domestic market with such governance. In the processed and consumer materials sector, conditions for such governance appear weaker and implementation less successful. There is some evidence that both paper and metal products have been closed to imports, although I have no evidence of industry governance. Shipbuilding also seems to enjoy a closed domestic market, but its dependence on exports means it has still suffered dramatic sales losses. Most of the nonmachine consumer goods industries are not concentrated and are unable to run successful cartels or use informal industry coordination to block imports. Coal mining and agriculture are also

Table 7–1. Factors for effective long-term informal protection through private-interest governance

	Necessary factor: Concentrated industrial structure	One of these two factors necessary		Outcomes		
		Hi-tech hook	Downstream cartel or import protection	Successful long-term informal protection	Formal government protection	Import-induced structural adjustment, 1980–92
Industrial basic materials						
Chemicals						
Petrochemicals	×	×		×		
Fertilizers	×		×	×		
Soda ash	×		×	×		
Petroleum and coal products						
Gasoline	×			×		
Kiln products						
Cement	×		×	×		
Glass	×		×	×		
Iron and steel						
Blast-furnace steel	×	×		×		
Electric-furnace steel						
Nonferrous metals						
Aluminum ingots	×					×
Processed and consumer materials						
Lumber and wood products					×	×
Pulp, paper, paper products	×			?		
Metal products				?		
Machines						
Shipbuilding				?		Export drop
Nonmachine consumer goods						
Food processing (including tobacco)						N/A
Textiles (not including clothing)						
Clothing						×
Furniture						×
Leather products						N/A
Coal mining					×	×
Agriculture					×	×

in this situation but have enjoyed official government subsidies and import protection. Nevertheless, most of the coal industry has shut down.

For an industry to use successfully private-interest governance based on interindustry relational contracting, it must enjoy certain key factors. First, it must be concentrated. Second, it must either have a technological hook to command buyer loyalty or buyers must be protected from competition by a domestic price cartel or import restraints.[1]

Aluminum is by far the best case for those who argue that Japan is oriented toward Schumpeterian transformation and more willing than other countries to move to new industries. It is the one industry that could not successfully organize a cartel to cover high domestic production costs. Japan shut down the world's second largest (and highest cost) aluminum refining industry—providing it only relatively small transitional government subsidies.

Domestic users had only weak incentives to pay a premium for domestic aluminum ingots. Refined aluminum was completely standardized and easily transported, and aluminum refiners produced no technologically advanced products that hooked buyer loyalty. The intermediary firms that rolled aluminum were unable to convince buyers to cover the 60 percent of their costs constituted by aluminum ingots and were under great pressure to switch to imports. From 1980–92 domestic buyers did pay an average premium of 13 percent for domestic aluminum, but this was not enough to cover Japan's high energy costs.

As we saw in Chapter 1, nonferrous metals was the one major industrial category in which Japan ran a trade deficit and in which net imports and production grew at least slightly from 1980 to 1992. But even when Japan shut down this domestic industry to make way for imports, state and industry did not simply move with the market. Rather, MITI informally pressured buyers to resist imports, although the ministry had only modest and short-lived success. MITI also bargained with banks to provide the interest rate assistance "owed" to aluminum companies under their implicit relational contracts. The state intervened in the market by providing major funding to establish Japanese-owned aluminum-refining capacity overseas. Although MITI said its subsidies would encourage domestic firms to get out of aluminum refining, in fact the ministry informally rewarded firms for investing overseas and holding onto some domestic capacity until Japanese-owned plants overseas came on line to replace it. Aluminum's unique status meant that it was the one industry that lobbied the Diet for large-scale special subsidies. In this case, political parties and the Keidanren decided on the compromise between MITI's subsidy proposals and MOF's opposition to them.

Cement most clearly fits the model of informal private-interest governance supported by an interindustry relational contract and the state. The construction industry accepts the cement industry's high prices and use of refusals to deal to make sure construction firms do not buy imports in

---

[1] The reader interested in exploring further the political question of how and why downstream industry absorbs the cost of expensive inputs should look for work by Mark Elder, a Harvard Ph.D. candidate currently writing a dissertation on this issue.

exchange for the cement industry's pressing the ready-mix concrete industry not to withhold supplies to raise prices. The Cement Association meets monthly with the construction and ready-mix concrete trade associations to enforce this interindustry relational contract. Although 29 percent of the construction industry's costs consist of basic materials purchases, it has been able to afford expensive cement because of its own strong cartels. Thus, the cement case shows that an interindustry relational contract can produce very strong private-interest governance.

MITI can play a powerful role in supporting industry cartels. In the 1970s, well before the SDIL cartel began in 1983, MITI actively helped the cement industry organize the weak ready-mix concrete trade associations to support cement prices. As it did in aluminum and petrochemicals, MITI initiated and led the formation of the depression cartels. And, as in aluminum, the government clarified its support for private import restrictions when it added its own nontariff barriers to industry's. Richard Samuels points out that it is often difficult to see any evidence of state autonomy when the state is supporting industry interests.[2] Nevertheless, MITI showed that it was more interested in maintaining domestic production than boosting industry profits when it opposed the Cement Association's proposal to broker cement imports to take advantage of the high prices created by domestic market controls.

Diet members have been unusually influential in the cement industry because half of the cement sold is used in government projects. LDP Diet members have arranged exchanges of high-priced government contracts for construction projects and cement for political contributions from construction and cement companies. But MITI has made all the basic policy toward the industry, and MITI and the Construction Ministry have served as intermediaries between the cement and construction industries to work out compromises and guarantees connected with the cartels.

In the aluminum case, interindustry relational contracting worked hardly at all. In cement it worked very well. Petrochemicals, however, presents a more complex picture. Because the auto and electronics companies that buy petrochemicals are vulnerable to foreign competition, they negotiate harder over prices than do the construction companies that buy cement. The fact that petrochemicals, unlike cement, are highly differentiated products also prevents complete price standardization. At the same time, this product differentiation gives petrochemical buyers more interest in relational contracting than aluminum buyers had. The petrochemical industry shows how state policy and industry governance

---

[2] Richard J. Samuels, *The Business of the Japanese State* (Ithaca, N.Y.: Cornell University Press, 1987).

can support individual companies in complex price negotiations to keep prices above costs and firms in business. As in cement, interfirm relational contracts have not been strong enough to stand on their own. Petrochemical firms have feared that unfettered market competition would push prices below the industry's internationally uncompetitive costs. Even in this industry, where many firms are literally tied into sales with pipelines and firms make long-term commitments to develop sophisticated chemicals for customers, industry-wide price governance is considered necessary to back up interfirm relational contracts. As in cement, MITI led the way in creating official capacity-cutting cartels and joint-sales companies, but trade associations also implemented an industry-wide price formula to control competition.

Interindustry relational contracting standardizes prices so that individual buyers can be confident they will not be disadvantaged relative to their competitors. Because of the impossibility of standardizing prices for the large number of petrochemical derivatives, the trade association has created a standard price formula for domestically produced feedstocks (ethylene and propylene), the stage at which Japan's international competitive disadvantage is most pronounced. This formula serves as the basis for postsales negotiation of specific prices throughout the petrochemical market. Because there is this floor for Japan's petrochemicals, domestic companies are not pushed below costs and out of business.

As in cement and aluminum, MITI's main role was to push the petrochemical industry to form official cartels, but it has also used administrative guidance to try to restrain competition. Because the petrochemical industry neither depended on large government subsidies or inflated prices for government projects, Diet members have had little to do with industry policy.

The steel industry shares the cement and petrochemical industries' pattern of continued trade surpluses despite domestic prices that are much higher than import or export prices. Because the industry is more concentrated then cement or petrochemicals, it has been able to maintain high prices with simple price leadership rather than any public cartel actions. For the same reason, MITI has not needed to play a strong role recently in organizing cartels, although it did in the 1950s and 60s. My case study did not look closely at how the steel industry manages the market, but my interviews with buyers did find that they are strongly committed to their interindustry relational contract with steel and that they fear steel companies will enforce their relational contact with refusals to deal.

Thus, informal market governance by trade associations, supported by interindustry relational contracts and the state, holds in cement and petrochemicals and appears to hold in steel as well (but with less complicated institutional arrangements because of the industry's strength of oligopolistic pricing). It did not work in aluminum, which had no technological hook to secure relational contracts with buyers. If we look at a few other subsectors of the industrial basic materials sector, we see further evidence of informal market governance with state backing.

From a cursory review of these industries, I find that the pattern does apply to most of this sector. Glass, the other large volume component (in addition to cement) of the kiln industries sector, appears to be organized in many respects like the cement industry. It is much more concentrated than cement, with only three companies holding steady market shares since 1970. Asahi Glass has roughly half the market, Nippon Sheet Glass about 30 percent, and Central Glass about 20 percent.[3] Like cement, there has been no foreign investment in this market, in contrast with both the European and U.S. markets where shares have changed rapidly and foreign firms have been major players. For example, foreign affiliated companies sell 38 percent of flat glass sold in the U.S., with 21 percent coming from Japanese-affiliated companies.[4] Companies from the United Kingdom, France, the U.S., Taiwan, and South Korea have all attempted unsuccessfully to enter the Japanese glass market despite the fact that their products are much cheaper than Japanese glass.[5]

The downstream firms that deal with glass refuse to handle foreign glass because of their ties to domestic makers, much as truckers, stevedores, and construction firms refuse to handle foreign cement. Yasue Takafusa, president of a local construction firm in Nagano Prefecture, notes: "Even if you bring in American glass, the glaziers are all in the [domestic] makers' keiretsu and won't put it in for you."[6] According to the FTC, the three Japanese glass companies use oligopolistic behavior to control distribution networks and pricing and harass distributors that handle imports. It has also reported cases where "retail stores were pressured by manufacturers or distributors to curtail their business with imported goods."[7] Thus, the industry appears to follow cement's pattern. Although the January 1992 "Tokyo Declaration" by President George Bush and Prime Minister Miyazawa Kiichi contained an "Action Plan" in which the Japanese government recognized that the flat-glass market was

---

[3] Dokusen Bunseki Kenkyū Kai (Research Group for the Analysis of Monopoly), *Nihon no dokusen kigyō* (Japan's monopoly firms), vol. 3 (Tokyo: Shin Nihon Shuppansha, 1974), p. 210; Office of the U.S. Trade Representative, *1994 National Trade Estimate Report on Foreign Trade Barriers* (Washington, D.C.: Government Printing Office, 1994), pp. 173–74, hereafter cited as USTR and date.

[4] USTR, 1994, pp. 173–74.

[5] Ibid.

[6] Uchida Michio and Ōzaki Akiko, "Jūtaku kenchiku hi wa gowari yasuku dekiru" (Construction costs could be 50 percent cheaper), *Shūkan tōyō keizai*, 4 September 1993, p. 7.

[7] Ibid.

closed and promised to increase market access for foreign firms, foreign imports decreased from 5.1 percent of the Japanese market in 1992 to 3.5 percent in 1993.[8] In September 1994 the Japanese government again promised the U.S. government to open its glass market.

In covering petrochemicals I covered the vast majority of the chemical industry. The only portions of the industry not derived from petrochemicals are inorganic chemicals, which account for 13 percent of total basic chemicals, and (in part) fertilizers, which make up 4 percent of basic chemicals.[9] Let us briefly consider these sectors.

The soda ash industry demonstrates one example of market governance to discourage imports in an uncompetitive segment of the inorganic chemicals sector. Japanese companies produce synthetic soda ash that is not competitive with natural soda ash from Wyoming. In response to complaints from U.S. firms, the FTC investigated the industry in 1983 and warned the four major Japanese soda ash producers to stop their cartel activities. In addition to raising prices, the producers reportedly pressured users and distributors to limit their purchases of American soda ash, although the FTC did not investigate these tactics. In a separate market the U.S. reported that the Japan Soda Industry Association was also pressuring users of caustic soda not to buy imports.[10] The 1983 warning against the soda ash industry had little effect, and the FTC warned it again in 1987. As of 1994, the U.S. still complains that restrictive industry practices limit access to the Japanese market.[11] One reason that the industry is able to hold on to its domestic customers is because soda ash is primarily used to make glass. As we have seen, glass makers have done well at keeping prices high and the market closed.

The fertilizer industry presents another case of strong informal market governance. A concentrated industry, it was designated as depressed under the SDIL. It sells to farmers, a well-protected sector that acts, in a classic interindustry relational contract, as a monopsonist that avoids low-priced goods. Seventy percent of fertilizer purchases go through Zennō, the National Federation of Agricultural Cooperative Associations, enabling the industry to engage in a powerful relational contract.[12] Gotō Akira writes that, although there are no formal restrictions, Zennō's monopoly on buying fertilizer effectively shuts the market to imports.[13]

[8] Ibid. For a discussion of U.S. pressure on Japan to open its markets during the Bush and Clinton administrations see Leonard J. Schoppa, *Gaiatsu: What American Pressure on Japan Can and Cannot Do* (forthcoming).
[9] Yamamoto Katsumi, *Kagaku gyōkai* (The chemical industry) (Tokyo: Kyōiku Sha, 1991), p. 77.
[10] U.S.-Japan Trade Study Group, *Progress Report: 1984* (Tokyo: U.S. Japan Trade Study Group, 1984), p. 69.
[11] USTR, 1994, p. 181.
[12] Yamamoto, *Kagaku gyōkai*, p. 106.
[13] Gotō Akira, "Kōzō chōsei to shijō kikō" (Structural adjustment and the market mechanism), *Kōsei torihiki*, 441 (July 1987): 40–46.

The Japanese press has reported that MITI and the Ministry of Agriculture, Forestry, and Fisheries have backed up this relational contract by pressing Zennō to limit its purchases of imported fertilizer.[14] The government ministries are supported by the Fertilizer Price Stabilization Law, which was created ostensibly to ensure stable supplies of domestic fertilizer at reasonable prices but in fact has produced much higher prices than the rest of the world's.

As I noted in Chapter 1, this book deals with only four of the five industrial basic materials sectors, the other being petroleum and coal products. In a certain sense, this sector may not fully belong to the category because a large part of its production is gasoline sold directly to consumers. In a thorough treatment of the energy sector, Richard Samuels argues that MITI intervention in the oil market has been pervasive, but constrained. State power has been most important in closing the market to imports and supporting the domestic price cartel. Although electric utility and petrochemical industry pressure forced the state to open the market to naphtha imports, the state has successfully used informal means to close the gasoline market to imports. When a renegade independent gasoline retailer, Lion's Oil, attempted to bring in a gasoline tanker from Singapore in 1985, MITI blocked the sale by pressuring banks to cut off financing. In 1986 MITI promised European and Americans it would liberalize its gasoline market to take in some of the output from new Middle Eastern refineries. But it permitted only domestic oil refineries, which had been adamantly opposed to liberalization, to import refined petroleum products.[15] Not surprisingly, Japan's net trade deficit in coal and petroleum products was unchanged from 1980 to 1992, at a constant 7 percent of domestic production (sectoral trade balances in this chapter are drawn from table 1–1, on p. 10).[16]

As in the other basic materials industries, MITI organized cartels to support prices, including a capacity-cutting cartel supported by government subsidies under the 1986 Temporary Measures Law for Specified Petroleum Product Imports.[17] MITI also micromanaged the market with administrative guidance to restrict the number of gas stations.[18] Because gasoline refiners sell more or less directly to consumers and have no important quality advantage over foreign gasoline, they probably could not maintain their price cartel without strong informal MITI protection to support them.

MITI has continued to use its licensing authority to tie retail gasoline

[14] US-Japan Trade Study Group, *Progress Report 1984*, p. 68.
[15] Samuels, *Business of the Japanese State*, p. 224.
[16] See table 1–1.
[17] *Japan Law Letter*, 12 November 1985; Samuels, *Business of the Japanese State*, p. 224.
[18] *Japan Law Letter*, 12 November 1985.

stations to high-cost domestic refiners. Japanese domestic prices are the highest in the industrialized world. Although much of this price is due to environmentally responsible high taxes, about 20 yen of the 120 yen price is due to the domestic price cartel and import restrictions. In May 1994 Kanō Katsutoshi, a rice retailer, rebelled against MITI's market restrictions by opening a gasoline station without registering with the ministry and selling gasoline at one hundred yen per liter, twenty yen below the average price. MITI complained that he had not shown where he would buy stable supplies of gasoline and threatened fines and legal action. At the same time, the Petroleum Council, connected to MITI, recommended in June 1994 that import restrictions be abolished in 1996 and restrictions on building gasoline stations relaxed.[19] As of this writing, it is too early to say whether these reforms will occur or open the market. Thus, the gasoline market fits the pattern of MITI organized capacity cartels, an MITI-organized distribution cartel, MITI restrictions of imports, and high Japanese prices. I do not know what, if any, informal role the trade association may play in administering the market.

My study of the nonferrous metals and steel sectors focused on the production of refined aluminum ingots and ordinary-grade steel. Edward Lincoln has looked more broadly at Japan's international trade in metals, which straddles nonferrous metals, steel, and metal products. He found that, although Japan switched to imported aluminum ingots, its metals imports overall are skewed toward the least processed forms of metal. It has not imported significant quantities of worked metals. In 1985 67 percent of Japan's copper imports were ores and concentrates, 31 percent were unwrought metal, and 2 percent were worked copper. This contrasted with the U.S., West Germany, and France, which all imported ten times as much worked copper. Lincoln pointed out that this pattern also held for aluminum, where imports of milled aluminum accounted for only 2.2 percent of domestic consumption in 1985. Similarly, only 9 percent of Japan's steel imports were in the form of worked steel. As we saw in Chapter 1, the country's net trade in metal products and nonferrous metals (which includes worked nonferrous metals) changed only slightly from 1980 to 1992, suggesting that Lincoln's finding probably still holds. I have found no information about industry governance in downstream metal processing industries. Japan's unique unreceptiveness to imports suggests the need for further research.

Japan also imports little paper, although it imports a significant amount of the raw materials used in paper production. The country imported only 3.7 percent of its paper and paperboard in 1990, compared with nearly 15 percent in the U.S. and 31 percent in the European

---

[19] *Nikkei Weekly*, 27 June 1994.

Community. Foreign firms have a hard time convincing paper distributors, which have long-term relationships and capital ties to domestic manufacturers, to buy from alternative sources.[20] As in petrochemicals, long-term relations are so strong that prices are commonly left undecided until after delivery. In addition, paper and paperboard each had SDIL cartels to cut capacity. I have seen no evidence of informal market governance in this sector.

The U.S. has complained that Japan has protected the wood-products industry with high tariffs, subsidies, and discriminatory product standards and building codes. In the 1990 U.S.-Japan Wood Products Agreement, Japan agreed to reduce these barriers. As of 1994, however, the U.S. complained that subsidies still protected the Japanese market. Japan's net trade deficit in lumber and wood products expanded from 4.3 to 9.1 percent of domestic production, while employment in the sector dropped from 252,000 to 237,000.[21] The U.S. government did not complain of any informal restraints on trade.

Let us briefly consider some of Japan's other declining industries. Next to aluminum refining, shipbuilding is the industry that has had to make the deepest proportional cuts. It received large subsidized loans from the Japan Development Bank and the Export-Import Bank, and was subsidized when shipbuilders received special rights to import sugar into Japan's protected sugar market.[22] By the 1970s the industry was making more than half the world's ships. The biggest area of success was oil tankers, which accounted for 22.7 million tons in 1975, two-thirds of Japan's total ship tonnage. The contraction of the oil market as a result of the OPEC price hike in 1973–74 destroyed this demand, pushing the number down to one-quarter of the total by 1978, or 4.9 million tons.[23]

Shipbuilding firms were fairly quick to cut back their work forces but slow to cut capacity. As MITI did with basic materials, the Ministry of Transportation (MOT) took the initiative to retire excess capacity. Under article 7 of the Shipbuilding Law, MOT used administrative guidance to cut production hours and volume, calibrated to require deeper cutbacks from larger builders, beginning in 1977. As it did in the cement industry, the FTC argued that this informal cartel arrangement violated the Antimonopoly Law and pushed the industry to use a stronger official

[20] USTR, 1992, pp. 150–51.

[21] See table 1–1; MITI, *Kōgyō tōkei hyō sangyō hen*, 1980, 1992.

[22] Yonezawa Yoshie, "Zōsengyō" (The shipbuilding industry), in Komiya Ryūtarō, Okuno Masahiro, Suzumura Kōtarō, eds., *Nihon no sangyō seisaku* (Japan's industrial policy) (Tokyo: Tokyo University Press, 1984), pp. 378–80; Douglas Anderson, "Managing Retreat: Disinvestment Policy," in Thomas McCraw, ed., *America versus Japan* (Boston: Harvard Business School Press, 1986), p. 362.

[23] Anderson, "Managing Retreat," p. 362.

cartel—in this case, a depression cartel. This cartel continued MOT's guided production through 1981. There was some complaint from industry that the cutbacks were too favorable to big firms, and that the base level dates should be changed. The Japan Shipowners' Association complained the cartel was putting upward pressure on prices.[24] In addition, MOT organized a capacity-cutting cartel under the DIL, again on a sliding scale, with the deepest cuts (40 percent of capacity) for the seven largest firms down to 15 percent for the smallest twenty-one.[25] These capacity-cutting goals were met.

The challenge to the industry was originally the collapse of the tanker business. In the 1980s, however, the rise of the South Korean shipbuilding industry took away much of its remaining market. Lower-priced South Korean ships cut Japan's global market share from 57 percent in 1984 to 38 percent in 1988. In 1987 the industry implemented a new capacity cartel and cut an additional 20 percent of capacity.[26] These cuts were followed by another surge in orders from 1989 to 1992, but by 1994 the industry was again suffering from its inability to compete with South Korea. The South Korean cost advantage was partly due to much lower labor costs but also to the problem of scale economies that plagues the Japanese chemical industry. In 1994 Japan had twenty-six shipbuilders that could build very large oil tanks—those over two hundred thousand tons. South Korea's four firms that built tankers this size received more orders in 1993 than the twenty-six Japanese companies combined. This lack of scale economies was due to the pattern of capacity cartels that spread cuts fairly evenly, penalizing the largest firms rather than allowing the least efficient firms to be weeded out. Naturally, some firms did leave the industry. Of sixty-one firms in 1977, only thirty-six were left by 1987. There was talk in 1994 of another round of capacity cuts, and the industry expected that MOT would organize it.[27] But pressure to do so was not overwhelming, in part because the diversification of companies into other heavy machine areas meant that poor performance in shipbuilding was no longer devastating for many firms.

The textile industry was the subject of a long series of official cartel policies and subsidies aimed at structurally improving the industry. These cartels, however, were the subject of much cheating.[28] The upstream fiber

---

[24] Yonezawa, "Zōsengyō."

[25] Ibid., pp. 380–84.

[26] *The Economist*, 19 March 1988, p. 68.

[27] Interview, shipbuilding executive, 1994.

[28] Yonezawa Yoshie, "Sen'i sangyō no sangyō chōsei" (Industrial adjustment in the textile industry), in Sekiguchi Sueo, ed., *Nihon no sangyō chōsei* (Industrial adjustment in Japan) (Tokyo: Nihon Keizai Shinbun Sha, 1981), pp. 168–74; Yamazawa Ippei, "Sen'i sangyō" (The textile industry), in Komiya et al., eds., *Nihon no sangyō seisaku*, p. 359; Brian Ike, "The Japanese Textile Industry: Structural Adjustment and Government Policy," *Asian Survey* 20 (May 1980): 532–51.

sector, which has used recession cartels, seems to have effective informal cartels; but this is not true for the downstream weaving sector. MITI used administrative guidance to restrict imports, with little impact.[29] Japanese levels of protection for textiles have been much lower than in the U.S. and European countries, which have used the Multifiber Agreement to protect their markets.

Japan has remained a net exporter in this labor-intensive sector, exporting a net 4.8 percent of production in 1992, down from 10 percent in 1980. Ronald Dore has argued that the strength of Japanese firms in the face of competition from lower-wage countries is in part due to Japanese firms' high rates of investment to produce innovative, higher-quality goods and reduce costs. He also argues that long-term contracts and community-like ties in trade associations inhibit but do not prohibit switches to imports.[30] His argument is persuasive for textiles, although it needs to be supplemented with an explicit account of industry governance to explain market rigidity in concentrated basic materials industries.

In contrast to textiles, the more labor-intensive and lower-wage apparel sector has had bigger losses to imports, dropping from a net trade deficit of 8.1 percent of production to 27.7 percent in 1992. This sector, too, has tried to upgrade itself; but wages fell further behind the manufacturing average during the 1980s, down to 49 percent by 1992.

Coal and agriculture, both labor-intensive and internationally uncompetitive, lie outside the manufacturing sector in the territory of large-scale public subsidies and formal import protection. Like the basic materials industries, coal was developed with state support during the Meiji period. It was expanded to meet wartime demand and built up again after the war to a peak level of employment: 370,000 workers in 1951.[31] Japanese coal became uncompetitive in the 1950s with the increase in hydroelectric plants and imported oil and was largely shut down during the 1960s. Its phase-out fits the pattern of interindustry relational contracting with strong state support, but with the important proviso that buyer industries only promised to buy coal long enough to provide some cushion for a fairly swift decline rather than ensure long-term supplies. Buyer industries such as steel, electric power, and cement negotiated with the coal industry, with the Keidanren serving as intermediary, to agree on the purchase of specific and gradually declining amounts of coal in exchange for reductions in prices. Coal dropped from 31 percent to 8 percent of Japan's primary energy supply from 1961–71, and the

[29] Yamazawa, "Sen'i sangyō," p. 364.

[30] Ronald Dore, *Flexible Rigidities: Industrial Policy and Structural Adjustment in the Japanese Economy 1970–1980* (London: Athlone Press, 1986), pp. 182–94.

[31] Samuels, "Business of the Japanese State," p. 105.

work force dropped from 210,000 to 40,000. By 1989 it was down to 9,000.[32]

Why were Japanese companies unwilling to pay high prices for security of supply? Again, there was no technological hook to make buyers loyal. In the early 1950s even MITI was pointing out that strikes by poorly paid workers meant that the industry, although domestic, was not necessarily a dependable source of supply.[33]

Both miners and coal-mining companies pressured the government to assist industry. Because large numbers of miners worked in remote areas reemployment was difficult. The government intervened to encourage coal-mining companies to scrap inefficient mines and build new, more efficient ones.[34] But the market went ahead of government plans as miners abandoned the mines for industrial jobs in the 1960s. As in aluminum, banks were concerned about holding bad debts for obsolete investments. Government took on banks' outstanding debt so that banks could invest in new mines. Banks, however, mostly took the money and ran.

Agriculture has received heavy government subsidies and protection due to farmers' political power.[35] Import protection raised Japanese rice prices to eight times the U.S. price by 1994, despite heavy government subsidies.[36] These formal policies were supplemented by government and trade association nontariff barriers ranging from attempts to keep out foreign fruit to preventing Japanese cattle from being exported overseas for building stock. Agriculture is extremely unconcentrated, made up of small farmers who cannot directly coordinate cartels. The import market nevertheless was regulated by a government-backed cartel. *Asahi shinbun* reported in 1994 that the Food Agency had long colluded with trading companies to prevent any actual competition over government contracts for grain imports. The agency divides up contracts for rice and grain in advance; and the designated companies meet to negotiate their bidding prices through a system of dangō, just as construction companies have long done.[37]

Japanese basic materials industries have developed governance mechanisms to buffer domestic prices from the effect of imports. Richard Marston shows that this ability to segment domestic prices from international prices is shared by Japanese industries generally; they are much

[32] Samuels, pp. 115–31; Statistics Bureau, Management and Coordination Agency, *Japan Statistical Yearbook* (Tokyo: Statistics Bureau, 1991).

[33] Samuels, p. 113.

[34] Ibid., 115–16.

[35] Kent E. Calder, *Crisis and Compensation: Public Policy and Political Stability in Japan* (Princeton: Princeton University Press, 1988).

[36] *Japan Digest*, 11 April 1994, p. 4.

[37] Ibid., 4 April 1994.

better at this task than U.S. industry is. Marston looked at price indexes for domestic and export goods in both the U.S. and Japan during periods of domestic currency appreciation: 1981–84 for the U.S. and 1985–88 for Japan. Had there been no segmentation between domestic and export markets, the ratio would have stayed the same even when currencies fluctuated. But Marston found that most American industries managed to let these prices drift apart 7–26 percent of the change in exchange rates.[38] This reflected a partial buffering of the American market from international price trends. Japanese industries were much better at segmenting markets, generally letting prices move apart 40–63 percent of the change in exchange rates.[39]

Marston's data suggest that the petrochemical, cement, and steel industries, far from being aberrant cases, share with other Japanese industries the ability to control domestic markets. As we saw earlier, not only does Japanese industry successfully deflect price pressure from imports, imports have not forced structural change except in labor-intensive, low-wage industries and nonferrous metals. Nevertheless, although a large switch to net imports did not force structural change in basic materials, some change did occur. The major change in the distribution of manufacturing production was a drop in the share produced by basic materials from 31.8 percent to 20.3 percent (1980–92), and an increase in that produced by the machine industry, from 32 percent to 43.3 percent (see table 7–2). The magnitude of this shift was in part exaggerated by the drop in energy prices, which lowered the value of industrial basic materials. The change in value added is less dramatic, with industrial basic materials dropping from 26.6 percent to 22.5 percent of the total and machines increasing from 33.3 to 37.7 percent (see table 7–3). Shifts in employment also followed this pattern of moderate change. Total absolute employment figures in the labor-unintensive industrial basic materials industries dropped by 10.9 percent, bringing this sector down to 12.6 percent of the total (see table 7–4). Employment in the core basic materials dropped most sharply, from 2.6 to 1.8 percent of the total. Employment in the machine and other sectors grew fastest, pushing machines up to 39.5 percent of total employment.

[38] For the United States, the outlier to this range was primary metals, for which Marston adduces the price volatility of nonferrous metals. The other outlier was transportation equipment, which Marston says is probably due to changes in auto models shipped to Canada. Richard Marston, "Price Behavior in Japanese and U.S. Manufacturing," in Paul Krugman, ed., *Trade with Japan: Has the Door Opened Wider?* (Chicago: University of Chicago Press, 1991), pp. 121–46.

[39] Nonferrous metals was again an outlier, fitting the highly competitive market I observed in Japanese aluminum. Chemicals was at the other extreme; the industry more than compensated for currency changes with a pricing-to-market elasticity of 1.09 percent. This reflects the strengthening of domestic prices due to the stronger petrochemical cartel during 1984–88.

Table 7–2. Percent of total manufacturing production by sector

	1980	1992
Industrial basic materials	31.8	20.3
Chemicals	8.5	7.3
Petroleum and coal products	7.1	2.6
Cement, glass, and ceramics	3.9	3.3
Iron and steel	8.4	5.0
Nonferrous metals	3.8	2.1
Core industrial basic materials	7.8	4.5
Petrochemicals	3.8	2.6
Cement	0.5	0.2
Blast-furnace steel	3.3	1.6
Primary aluminum	0.3	0.0
Processed and consumer materials	11.7	11.2
Lumber and wood products	2.5	1.4
Pulp, paper, paper products	3.2	2.7
Rubber products	1.2	1.1
Metal products	4.9	6.0
Machines	32.0	43.3
General machinery	8.2	10.2
Electrical machinery	10.4	16.6
Transportation machinery	11.7	15.0
Shipbuilding	0.8	0.2
Precision instruments	1.6	1.5
Nonmachine consumer goods	20.5	20.1
Food processing (including tobacco)	10.5	10.8
Textiles (not including clothing)	3.7	2.3
Clothing	1.4	1.5
Furniture	1.3	1.2
Publishing and printing	3.2	4.0
Leather products	0.5	0.4
Other manufacturing	4.0	5.1
All manufacturing	100.00	100.00

Source: MITI, Kōgyō tōkei hyō, sangyō hen (Census of manufactures, report by industries), 1980, 1992.

Thus, Japanese declining industries did shrink modestly as a proportion of the economy from 1980 to 1992. But, as we saw in Chapter 1, except for nonferrous metals, apparel, lumber, and furniture, this shrinkage was not because of growing sectoral trade deficits. The only major sectors in which trade deficits grew by more than 5 percentage points from were apparel and furniture. (The increase in aluminum ingot imports was largely offset by an improved balance of trade in milled nonferrous metals.) Although there was much hand wringing in Japan over the hollowing out of its basic industries, such hollowing never actually happened. If Japan had not used cartels to support domestic prices and had used the Antimonopoly Law to do away with private

Table 7–3. Total value added by sector, in percent

	1980	1992
Industrial basic materials	26.6	22.5
Chemicals	8.5	9.4
Petroleum and coal products	2.9	2.4
Kiln products	5.0	4.1
Iron and steel	7.7	5.0
Nonferrous metals	2.6	1.6
Core industrial basic materials	7.0	5.4
Petrochemicals	2.5	3.0
Cement	0.5	0.3
Blast-furnace steel	3.8	2.1
Primary aluminum	0.2	0.0
Processed and consumer materials	12.1	11.9
Lumber and wood products	2.2	1.2
Pulp, paper, paper products	2.6	2.6
Rubber products	1.3	1.4
Metal products	5.9	6.7
Machines	33.3	37.7
General machinery	9.4	10.6
Electrical machinery	12.2	15.6
Transportation machinery	9.8	10.0
Shipbuilding	0.6	−0.4
Precision instruments	1.9	1.5
Nonmachine consumer goods	23.7	22.6
Food processing (including tobacco)	10.9	11.7
Textiles (not including clothing)	3.9	2.4
Clothing	1.8	1.7
Furniture	1.6	1.3
Publishing and printing	5.0	5.1
Leather products	0.5	0.4
Other manufacturing	4.3	5.3
All manufacturing	100.0	100.0

Source: MITI, *Kōgyō tōkei hyō, sangyō hen* (Census of manufactures, report by industries), 1980, 1992.

import barriers, cheaper foreign imports would likely have made greater inroads into Japanese markets and produced greater structural change.

To understand the true scope of industrial policy, one must look beyond official state-sponsored policies to unofficial policies initiated and implemented by trade associations. Illegal cartels should not be immediately dismissed as aberrant behavior by outlaw firms; in many cases, they constitute governance tacitly delegated to private interests as an extension of official state policy. First, the trade associations that run cartels do not function primarily as lobbying groups outside the government but are seen as administrative organs that assist government. Trade associ-

Table 7–4. Total employment by sector, in percent

	1980	1992	Percent change, 1980–92
Industrial basic materials	15.3	12.6	−10.9
Chemicals	4.0	3.7	1.4
Petroleum and coal products	0.4	0.3	−22.2
Cement, glass, ceramics	4.9	4.1	−10.2
Iron and steel	4.2	3.0	−22.9
Nonferrous metals	1.8	1.5	−9.2
Core industrial basic materials	2.6	1.8	−24.9
Petrochemicals	1.1	1.0	−2.7
Cement	0.1	0.1	−31.9
Blast-furnace steel	1.4	0.8	−39.2
Primary aluminum	0.1	0.0	−74.9
Processed and consumer materials	15.0	13.8	0.1
Lumber and wood products	3.5	2.1	−34.7
Pulp, paper, paper products	2.7	2.5	0.7
Rubber products	1.5	1.5	12.3
Metal products	7.2	7.6	14.2
Machines	35.1	39.5	23.7
General machinery	10.0	10.8	17.6
Electrical machinery	13.0	17.3	43.6
Transportation machinery	8.6	8.7	9.5
Shipbuilding	0.9	0.4	−49.2
Precision instruments	2.6	2.3	−5.6
Nonmachine consumer goods	30.0	28.4	2.7
Food processing (including tobacco)	10.6	11.2	14.6
Textiles (not including clothing)	6.7	4.4	−28.3
Clothing	4.8	5.1	13.8
Furniture	2.5	2.0	−13.8
Publishing and printing	4.6	5.1	18.9
Leather products	0.8	0.7	−3.0
Other manufacturing	5.5	6.3	24.0
All manufacturing	100.0	100.0	8.4

Source: MITI, *Kōgyō tōkei hyō, sangyō hen* (Census of manufactures, report by industries), 1980, 1992.

ations do not normally acknowledge illegal activities. Nevertheless, in the case of petrochemicals and cement, the industry organizations that produced the official joint-sales companies and capacity-cutting cartels also produced the unofficial policies of refusals to deal and industry-wide price formulas. Second, these unofficial policies are extensions of public policy because they built on official policies and were necessary for achieving public-policy goals. In the case of petrochemicals, the industry-wide price formulas were reestablished in 1983, simultaneous with the beginning of capacity cuts and joint sales. In cement, the implementation of refusals to deal depended on the establishment of strong downstream ready-mix concrete cartels with MITI support in the 1970s. The illegal cartels were also considered necessary to fulfill the official policy goals of maintaining domestic production. In both cement and petrochemicals, MITI and industry saw supporting prices as key to maintaining the health and production of domestic firms. In cement, controlling both foreign and domestic outsiders to the cartel was crucial to keeping prices up. The moves that MITI and the Customs Bureau made to help the industry exclude imports also indicate that informal cement industry import exclusion was an extension of government policy.

The state has supported cartels to preserve domestic materials manufacture not simply because of pressure from powerful political interests but also because of an independent state interest in security of supply. Because MITI's expressed interest in security of supply largely coincides with that of big business, cynics might suspect that the ministry's policy statements are mere window dressing for an agenda pushed by powerful political interests.[40] At times, however, MITI's independent interest in promoting domestic manufacture of basic materials has also been apparent.

In aluminum, cement, and petrochemicals the policy-making process followed this pattern: MITI pushed industry to go along with cartels that individual firms privately believed were necessary but that they could not coordinate on their own. Firms resisted MITI pressure for strong cartel measures that would raise prices over the long term and in some cases increase efficiency. While these cartels served the industries' own interests, the fact that MITI had to push hard to get industry to go along with them shows that the ministry was acting autonomously and not at industries' behest.[41]

Another instance that suggests an autonomous state interest in security of supplies was overseas investment in aluminum. Although aluminum companies took the primary initiative to move to overseas production, the government encouraged the move with large loans. Significantly, however, MITI also used administrative guidance to the same end. It told U.S. trade officials that it distributed tariff rebates on the basis of how much capacity firms had cut but in reality rewarded firms not only for cutting capacity but also for preserving some capacity and investing in Japanese equity plants overseas. It seems unlikely that this subtle ma-

[40] See Eric A. Nordlinger's "Type III State Autonomy," for a discussion of state autonomy in situations where state and societal preferences coincide. *The Autonomy of the Democratic State* (Cambridge: Harvard University Press, 1981), pp. 74–98.

[41] It is logically possible that some other interest group, such as banks, was pressuring MITI to implement the policies; but I have seen no evidence of this. In the case of aluminum, banks' expressed interests seemed to parallel those of the aluminum firms: subsidies in exchange for cuts.

nipulation of MITI resources was the result of industry pressure rather than MITI's own priorities.

The clearest indication of MITI's strategic interest in domestic basic materials production was its disapproval of the Japan Cement Association's plans to import cheap South Korean cement to reap profits from the rigged Japanese cement market. MITI commented that replacing domestic production with imports did not fit its idea of structural adjustment. That is, MITI did not intend to use the SDIL cartels to move firms out of declining industries to make way for cheaper imports. Rather, it designed them to maintain a balanced economic structure by preserving basic materials production.

Thus, it is a mistake to interpret Japan's policies toward its declining basic materials industries as forward looking and efficiency oriented. The policies were intended to shore up inefficient industries, not phase them out. Nevertheless, the policies conformed to market pressures: if markets wouldn't carry an industry such as aluminum, even with the help of cartels, then the capacity-cutting cartels and subsidies offered assistance in shutting down the industry entirely. MITI's *market* philosophy is laissez-faire in the Austrian school's sense of leaving firms free to collude to raise prices and stabilize markets.[42] If firms could use a combination of coercion and persuasion to get buyers to pay high prices, then the SDIL cartels helped them along. If not, they went out of business.

Predictably, prices set by cartels had the disadvantage of failing to encourage efficiency, a problem that MITI and the FTC attempted to remedy. For instance, because firms thought government would eventually reward them for holding on to productive capacity, even uncompetitive firms resisted capacity cuts, although MITI often tried to encourage the least productive firms to make the deepest cuts. Another example of cartel-based inefficiency was the rigid cement market's lack of price signals that would push manufacturers to economize by using the most productive capacity or shipping to nearby customers. MITI tried unsuccessfully to create a shadow market between cement companies that would use realistic prices tied to costs at individual plants. At times, the FTC, MITI, and the Bank of Japan have stepped in to cut cartel restrictions; and buyers always try to keep sellers under some competitive pressure. The cartels prevented ruthless cuts of the least efficient capacity and have left Japan with high-cost plants in cement, steel, shipbuilding, and petrochemicals. Nevertheless, the cartels largely achieved their goal of maintaining a balanced economy with strong basic materials production; they were never intended to promote efficiency.

---

[42] Michèle Schmiegelow and Henrik Schmiegelow, *Strategic Pragmatism: Japanese Lessons in the Use of Economic Theory* (New York: Praeger, 1989).

How can these policies toward major Japanese industries preserve such inefficiency, given the overall success of the Japanese economy? Kozo Yamamura and Ronald Dore both argue that features of the Japanese economy, such as stable relationships between firms, generate considerable efficiencies that outweigh the inefficiencies produced by market rigidities.[43] But the market governance system does not produce all goods efficiently.[44] James Abegglen and George Stalk point out that firms are very efficient at producing goods that require "high volume assembly processes where hundreds, even thousands, of interdependent steps must be coordinated."[45] The system has no particular advantage in simple processing operations, which is the work of the basic materials industries. Japan's strong comparative advantage in steel in the early 1970s derived from farsighted investments in new technologies. In other basic materials industries, high energy costs and rigid cartels have put the country at a disadvantage.

Japan's cartels have created basic materials markets with domestic prices higher than either import or export prices but with few imports. Although all Japanese industries complain about excessive competition, price structures in cement, petrochemicals, and steel show that domestic producers obey cartels and are unwilling to sell as cheaply at home as they do overseas. When they can't find enough buyers at high domestic prices, they unload goods cheaply overseas rather than risk provoking domestic price competition. Scant imports, despite their reasonable prices, sometimes reflect direct collusion by firms to exclude them (for example, in cement). The dearth of petrochemicals imports reflects more complex arrangements. Individual firms are engaged in relational contracts with petrochemical suppliers. Buyers prefer domestic goods and are willing to pay enough to keep suppliers in business, but they also need to keep pressure on suppliers to keep prices down. This competitive pressure has a tendency to push suppliers' prices below costs and ultimately push uncompetitive firms out of business. After the 1979–80 oil shock, MITI recognized that imports combined with domestic over-capacity would put great competitive pressure on companies and drive some out of business. Therefore, it initiated capacity-cutting cartels and joint-sales companies, and industry reinstituted informal industry-wide pricing formulas. The joint-sales companies in particular were conceived

[43] Kozo Yamamura, "Will Japan's Economic Structure Change? Confessions of a Former Optimist," in Kozo Yamamura, ed., *Japan's Economic Structure: Should It Change?* (Seattle: Society for Japanese Studies, 1990), p. 29; Dore, *Flexible Rigidities*.

[44] Herbert Kitschelt, "Industrial Governance Structures, Innovation Strategies, and the Case of Japan: Sectoral or Cross-national Comparative Analysis," *International Organization*, 45, (Autumn 1991):481.

[45] James C. Abegglen and George Stalk, Jr., *Kaisha: The Japanese Corporation* (New York: Basic Books, 1985), p. 61.

as a direct response to the threat of imports. Given the consensus to support domestic suppliers, the strategy was to strengthen domestic suppliers' bargaining power to make sure buyers didn't inadvertently force prices so low as to drive suppliers out of business. Thus, although petrochemicals users choose to pay a large premium for domestic goods, extensive industry-wide cartel arrangements have been necessary to ensure that the premium is large enough to cover costs. Without directly excluding imports, the system has helped high-cost domestic firms survive rather than make way for more efficient producers, either domestic or foreign.

There have been some ambiguous signs of change. The depressed industries laws have been replaced with a weaker substitute, and there has been no recent discussion of reviving official cartels despite a deep recession. In 1991 the Antimonopoly Law was strengthened, and the FTC targeted both the cement industry and a downstream plastics goods industry (plastic wrap) in harsh judgments against illegal cartels. In 1993 a new government promised to weaken the bureaucracy's role in the economy. The new MITI minister, Kumagai Hiroshi, came into office saying that Japanese markets are closed to imports and that large Japanese firms collude fiercely to protect them. He vowed to make Japanese markets more open and transparent.[46] The exposure of corruption in the construction industry also brought the cement industry under some scrutiny.

Nevertheless, as of 1995, no real progress seems to have been made in opening Japan's petrochemical, cement, or steel markets. Recession has shrunk imports and expanded exports of dumped goods. The price structure remains fundamentally unchanged in cement and petrochemicals despite FTC rulings. MITI administrative guidance of at least one informal cartel continued in the downstream PVC pipe industry at least into 1992. And informal governance of the Japanese cement and petrochemical markets is reported to be alive and well. Because Japan's policies include both formal and informal policies, it will be difficult to tell for certain when they are discontinued. The Japanese press is too timid to tell how markets are really governed, and the foreign press lacks the know-how and resources.

The lack of press coverage most likely derives, not only from fears of losing access to business information, but also from beliefs that cartels play some positive role in stabilizing the economy. The depth of this belief and its difference from British or American attitudes about the economy was clarified for me in a 1988 interview with a senior official of a Japanese cement company, before the U.S. antidumping ruling or the

---

[46] *Nihon keizai shinbun*, 12 August 1993, cited in *Daily Japan Digest*, 12 August 1993.

FTC fines against the industry. The official candidly and helpfully described the system of refusals to deal used to prevent construction companies from buying cement from cartel outsiders—who, of course, were all foreign. He then lamented the plight of U.S. cement companies, which had long suffered low prices, and spoke of the Japanese mission of buying American cement plants to bring new hope to the U.S. industry. He praised the openness of the international economy, which was allowing Japanese firms to invest in the U.S. and allowing imports into the Japanese market (albeit in small amounts and in spite of the system he had just described). He ended the interview by saying that he expected that my study, which I had made clear that I planned to publish, would lead to greater U.S.-Japanese understanding. At no point in the interview did he suggest that any of the information he gave me should be kept confidential. Clearly the executive, trained in economics at a top Japanese university, had a very different conception of what constitutes an open market from the dominant free-market ideology of Britain and the U.S. The organization of the domestic cement market, which to an American audience would appear unfair and exclusive, apparently seemed to him a justifiable and commonsense way of making sure that firms don't renege on their commitments.

There continues to be a gap between Japanese and other countries' economic ideas that explains much of the bitterness of the trade conflict between Japan and its trading partners.[47] Such fundamental differences in ideology and in the way in which markets are organized and governed must be recognized and dealt with if economic and political relations are to be cordial and open. More concretely, in order to open its uncompetitive industries to competition with foreign imports, Japan must strengthen and enforce its antimonopoly policies. The conditions necessary for informal trade association-based market protection to work include industry concentration plus either (1) a technological hook, or (2) a downstream industry cartel or downstream import protection. The key to dismantling Japan's system of informal protection lies in tough antimonopoly policy against both upstream and downstream cartels and in doing away with official or unofficial government protection.

[47] Chalmers Johnson, "The Japanese Political Economy: A Crisis in Theory," *Ethics and International Affairs* 2 (1988):79–97.

Index

Abegglen, James, 209
acrylonitrile, 125, 153, 154, 159
agriculture, 190, 191, 201, 202
aluminum industry, 50–79, 191;
bargaining over cuts and subsidies,
62–73; capacity-cutting cartel for,
55–56, 67; change in refining capacity
1973–90, 65; competition from
developing countries, 56; conflict
between refiners and rollers, 67–70;
decline of, 52–62; debt of, 56–57;
deliberation council for, 63–64;
development imports, 58–59; expansion
in 1970s, 54–56; failure to develop
cartel, 16, 50, 192; foreign pressure
against tariff-rebate system, 76–77;
government nurturing of, 53–54,
57–61; investment, 33; Japan not
importing fabricated aluminum, 11,
198; Japan's shutdown of, 1, 9, 12, 15,
21, 47, 50; *keiretsu* and, 51–52, 53–54,
68; lack of technological hook, 50, 192,
195; overcapacity in, 42; peak capacity
of, 64; policy making regarding, 62–76;
political conflict over assistance to,
73–76; price rise of 1974, 67;
profitability of, 66–67; pullback of
capital and labor in, 47; refining
divisions split from parent companies,
76; replaced by Japanese-owned
overseas refining, 52, 57–62, 77, 208;
restructuring of, 77–79, 192; stable
world oligopoly disrupted in 1970s, 56;
stagnant demand in 1970s, 53; tariff-
rebate system for, 59–61, 73–75,
76–77; trade association weakness,
77–78. *See also* Japan Aluminum
Federation; primary aluminum
Antimonopoly Law: amendments of 1953,
31–32; cement industry violations, 48,
116; depression cartel provisions, 32;
establishment of, 29; Fair Trade
Commission enforcement of, 30–31,
48–49; lack of popular support for, 30;
MITI flouting of, 142; plastic wrap
industry violation, 48, 164–65; section
8 on trade associations, 31; spate of
enforcement in 1991, 48, 210;
strengthening in 1973, 37–38;
strengthening in 1991, 25–26, 48, 210;
trade associations and, 22–49; U.S. law
compared to, 30
apparel. *See* clothing
Arase, David, 58
Arisawa Hiromi, 132
Asahi Chemical, 126, 135, 136
Asano Cement, 85–87
Ataka and Company, 43
Atkinson, Michael, 23
atogime (postsale pricing), 142–43
Atsuya Jōji, 25

banks, 19, 44, 72–73
basic materials industries: as capital
intensive, 38; cartels for cutting capacity
in declining, 7–8; decline of production
in, 38–39; MITI definition of, 9, 38;
pullback of capital and labor in, 47;
segmenting domestic from international
markets, 202–3; state interest in
preserving, 19–21; trade associations in,
22; wages in, 38. *See also* industrial
basic materials
blast-furnace steel, 9, 39, 40, 41, 191,
204–6
Bush, George, 195

Calder, Kent, 5
car manufacturing: and petrochemicals,
126, 161–62; relational contracts in, 6;
and steel industry, 179–80, 182;
Toyota, 162, 179, 186

cartels: capacity-cutting, 7, 45, 46–47,
55–56, 66, 67, 91–92, 131–34, 209;
cheating on, 5; depression, 29, 32–36;
early trade associations as, 28; Fair
Trade Commission crackdown of 1973,
35; Fair Trade Commission limits on,
18; formal abolition of, 7; formal and
informal, 17, 19; in heavy industry, 28;
history of, 27–49; industry
concentration required for, 13; as
intermediary between state and market,
2; MITI in formation of, 17, 19, 33–34;
neoclassical economics on, 28–29;
political legitimacy of, 27; recession
cartels, 36; state and, 3, 17–19; tacit
state approval of illegal cartels, 205–7;
U.S. pressure leads to new restrictions
on, 48
Cement Association: cement imports
opposed by, 105, 107–8, 110–11, 114;
in Committee for the Modernization of
the Ready-mix Concrete Industry, 90;
Committee on Special Measures to Deal
with Imports and Exports, 108, 110;
coordination within, 93; Distribution
Committee of, 99; formation of cartel
within MITI guidelines, 91–95; internal
cohesion of, 118; production reducing
cartels formed by, 89; providing setting
for cooperation between joint-sales
groups, 99–101; reduced competition
sought by, 118; staff size, 23; Truckers'
Association and, 106–7
cement industry, 9, 10, 15, 39–41,
80–121, 204–6; Antimonopoly Law
enforcement, 48, 116; capacity-cutting
cartel in, 91–95; cartels in, 13, 206–7;
competition in, 85, 87; concentration in,
85, 87; conditions for informal
governance, 191, 192–93; division into
five joint-sales companies, 94, 95,
97–99, 116; drop in imports, 116; Fair
Trade Commission crackdown on,
115–18; growth of, 87; illegal price
cartel in, 91; inability to form capacity
cartel, 66; Japan as world's largest
exporter, 102–3; Japanese cement prices
1980–92, 117; Japanese domestic
prices, 9, 81, 82; Japanese inability to
produce at competitive prices, 21;
Japanese press support for, 114–15;
Japanese resistance to cement imports,
81, 101–15; Japanese shortage of 1973,
103–5; Japanese trade surplus, 11;
Japan's international cement trade,
80–81; longshoremen refuse to unload
imports, 104, 106, 114; market controls

in, 84; MITI policies to reduce
competition in, 95–99; nontariff
barriers to imports, 119–20; no
progress in opening Japanese market,
210; oil embargo as cause of decline,
89; price decline in, 89; production
costs, 80, 102; profitability of, 87–88;
pullback of capital and labor in, 47;
quality concern about imports, 113–14;
rationalization of transportation in, 96;
ready-mix concrete, 84, 89–91, 100,
116–17, 121; refusal-to-deal agreement
with construction industry, 82, 92,
99–101, 118–19, 192–93; relational
contracts in, 82, 106–7; sanctions by
trade association, 13; security of supply
concern about imports, 114; shadow
market attempted for, 96, 120, 208;
strong cartel in, 83, 86–87, 113; trade
association for, 86; transportation costs,
80, 84; Truckers' Association and,
106–7; vulnerability to competition
from newly industrializing countries,
80. See also Cement Association
Chemical Economics Institute (Kagaku
Keizai Kenkyū Jo), 143–44
chemicals, 2, 9, 10, 11, 15, 22, 39, 40,
41, 191, 196–97, 204–6. See also
petrochemical sector
Chisso Corporation, 44
clothing (apparel), 39–41, 78, 191, 201,
204, 206; change in Japan's net sectoral
trade, 10–12
coal mining, 190–91, 201–2
Coleman, William, 23
competition: excessive, 3, 32–33;
increasing in Japan in the 1960s,
34–35; policies for reducing, 2–3;
protection of downstream users from,
14; reduced by trade associations, 24
construction industry: basic materials cost
as percent of end value, 15; bid-rigging
arrangements (*dango*) for government
procurement, 14, 112; cement industry
cuts opposed by, 94–95; as highly
cartelized, 84; Japanese construction
costs, 85; kickbacks for public works
contracts, 112; labor productivity in,
85; LDP and, 112–13, 120–21; PVC
pipe industry and, 137, 160; refusal-to-
deal agreement with cement industry,
82, 92, 99–101, 118–19, 192–93; steel
prices for, 178, 180–81; using sanctions
to enforce purchase of domestic goods,
13; weak competition in, 84–85
Construction Ministry, 83, 92, 94–95,
193

industrial basic materials (*cont.*)
employment, 206; total value added by
sector, 205. *See also* basic materials
industries; chemicals; core industrial
basic materials; kiln industries;
nonferrous metals; petroleum and coal
products; steel industry
industrial policy, 2–4; aim of, 38; for
declining industries, 7–8; Japanese and
American compared, 20; strategic trade
policy, 3–4
Industries in Depressed Communities Law,
44–45
informal governance: in cement industry,
81–82, 116, 119; conditions for success
of, 190–211; in petrochemical industry,
123, 142, 163–64; private-interest
governance as public policy, 16–19;
private-interest governance by trade
associations, 12–21; and state strategic
goals, 1–21
Ishihara Mitsue, 111
Ishihara Shintarō, 19
Itami Hiroyuki, 128n.11, 154, 178

Japan: *burakumin*, 76; change in sectoral
trade 1980–92, 10; competition from
newly industrializing countries, 39–42;
electricity costs in, 53; factors in
economic success of, 1; lack of discount
stores, 14, 186; market and state in,
2–12; moving out of declining
industries, 2, 7–12; nationalist
orientation in, 14; openness to trade
competition, 1–2; overall trade balance
in manufactured goods, 9; sense of
vulnerability to outside suppliers, 20;
transferring productive capacity
overseas, 1; wages in, 41–42; yen's rise,
42, 61. *See also* basic materials
industries; state, the
Japan Aluminum Federation (JAF):
formation of, 68; negotiating for
assistance to aluminum industry, 64,
73–76; proposed industry law, 73–74;
staff size, 23
Japan Light Metal, 54, 55, 66, 67
Japan Socialist Party (JSP), 30, 75, 78
Johnson, Chalmers, 17
joint-sales companies: in cement industry,
94, 95, 97–99, 116; in petrochemical
sector, 131–38, 148; as response to
threat of imports, 209–10

kaihatsu yunyū (development imports),
58–59
Kanegafuchi Chemical, 136, 147–48

Kanemori Tsutomu, 110
kankoku sōtan (government-recommended
cutbacks), 33
Kanō Katsutoshi, 198
Keidanren (Federation of Economic
Organizations), 22, 73–75
keiretsu: in aluminum industry, 51–52,
53–54, 68; as basis of long-term
business relations, 12; in cement
industry, 89; polyolefin joint-sales
companies and, 134–35; in steel
industry, 181
Kikkawa Takeo, 29
kiln industries, 9, 11, 22, 191, 205. *See
also* cement industry; glass
Kishimoto Yasunobe, 132
Kobayashi Hisaaki, 110
Komatsu Kunio, 70
Krugman, Paul, 3
Kumagai Hiroshi, 210

labor: antitrust law opposed by, 29; basic
materials industries and, 20, 38;
corporatism without, 5; labor
intensiveness by sector, 40; productivity
in construction industry, 85; pullback
from declining sectors, 47; size of work
force in Japanese manufacturing, 39;
wages in Japan, 41–42
Large Store Law, 186
leather products, 39–41, 76, 191, 204–6
Liberal Democratic Party (LDP):
aluminum industry assistance supported
by, 73–76; cement industry influence
with, 83, 113, 193; *dangō* in
construction industry supported by,
112–13, 120–21; industrial policy
supported by, 4; subsidies for domestic
production of strategic materials
supported by, 2
Lincoln, Edward, 11, 198
Lindberg, Leon, 25
lobbying, 26
lumber and wood products, 39–41, 191,
204–6; change in Japan's net sectoral;
trade, 10–12; protection of Japanese
market, 199
Lynn, Leonard, 25

machines, 10, 11, 39–41, 191, 204–6
market, the: cartels and trade associations
as intermediaries between state and, 2;
as determining when and how industries
decline in Japan, 50; extent to which
Japanese state supports market controls,
84; Japanese conception of open
market, 211; market controls in cement